ADVANCE PRAISE FOR *THE SUSTAINABILITY EDGE*

"*The Sustainability Edge* is loaded with real-world examples of sustainability delivering competitive advantage. It examines the responsibilities of individual businesses, employees, suppliers, consumers, government, and NGOs in developing lasting environmental and business solutions. Unlike other sustainability books that are preachy and lack substance, *The Sustainability Edge* gives a roadmap for success."

Robert Abernathy, CEO, Halyard

"If you are convinced that sustainability is a top issue for your organization, you will often be perplexed about what you can do about it. *The Sustainability Edge* synthesizes practical responses to the complex and nuanced challenges of sustainability, helping leaders to fundamentally transform their companies. Read the book even if you are not convinced about the critical importance of sustainability – you will be convinced."

Anurag Behar, Chief Sustainability Officer, Wipro Limited, and CEO, Azim Premji Foundation

"The new frontier in marketing is certainly sustainability. Sheth and Apte have constructed a roadmap to help business leaders gain a competitive edge based on creating sustainable value for all of the firm's stakeholders – not just its shareholders. *The Sustainability Edge* encourages business leaders to integrate business and sustainability strategies, creating value and a better world."

Ralph de la Vega, Vice Chairman, AT&T Inc., and CEO, AT&T Business Solutions and AT&T International

"*The Sustainability Edge* is a must-read for today's business leaders. It shares best practices and practical examples of how leaders can embrace sustainability by working with key stakeholders to grow their business."

Mindy Lubber, President and CEO, CERES

"Businesses have to be financially viable and technologically competitive. That they have to be ecologically sustainable as well is an idea whose time has come. Jagdish Sheth and Suhas Apte have written a seminal book that makes a persuasive case for viewing ecological sustainability as an integral part of corporate strategy and demonstrates vividly that it makes eminent business sense to do so. They discuss numerous examples of companies that have embraced this new thinking to their advantage and to that of their stakeholders. This is a book that CEOs all over the world will find very useful as they reorient their businesses to be anchored in ecological sustainability."

Jairam Ramesh, Member of Parliament
and former Cabinet Minister, India

"Apte and Sheth have produced a compelling framework combining big-picture insights with practical 'how to' guidance. A valuable, inspiring read for business students and seasoned executives alike."

P.J. Simmons, author, and Chair, Corporate Eco Forum

"The expectations of business – from consumers, employees, communities, and other key groups – are growing daily. *The Sustainability Edge* provides business leaders with a roadmap through this complicated world of stakeholder expectations. The guides on this journey, Apte and Sheth, know what they're talking about – they've worked within, and outside, companies for decades, proving that sustainability is the next frontier of competitive business advantage."

Andrew Winston, co-author of *Green to Gold* and author of *The Big Pivot*

the SUSTAINABILITY EDGE

HOW TO DRIVE TOP-LINE GROWTH WITH TRIPLE-BOTTOM-LINE THINKING

SUHAS APTE and JAGDISH N. SHETH

UNIVERSITY OF TORONTO PRESS
Toronto Buffalo London

© University of Toronto Press 2016
Rotman-UTP Publishing
Toronto Buffalo London
www.utppublishing.com
Printed in Canada

ISBN 978-1-4426-5068-8

♾ Printed on acid-free, 100% post-consumer recycled paper
with vegetable-based inks.

Library and Archives Canada Cataloguing in Publication

Apte, Suhas, 1952–, author
The sustainability edge : how to drive top-line growth with triple-bottom-line
thinking/Suhas Apte and Jagdish N. Sheth.

(Business & sustainability series)
Includes bibliographical references and index.
ISBN 978-1-4426-5068-8 (cloth)

1. International business enterprises – Management – Environmental aspects –
Case studies.   2. Industrial management – Environmental aspects –
Case studies.   3. Social responsibility of business – Case studies.   I. Sheth,
Jagdish N., author   II. Title.   III. Series: Business & sustainability series

HD62.4.A68 2016   658.4'08   C2016-904889-6

University of Toronto Press acknowledges the financial assistance to its
publishing program of the Canada Council for the Arts and the Ontario Arts
Council, an agency of the Government of Ontario.

Canada Council   Conseil des Arts
for the Arts   du Canada

ONTARIO ARTS COUNCIL
CONSEIL DES ARTS DE L'ONTARIO
an Ontario government agency
un organisme du gouvernement de l'Ontario

Funded by the   Financé par le
Government   gouvernement
of Canada   du Canada   Canadä

We dedicate this work to our grandchildren – Ryan, Mira, Rehna, Maya, Anaya, and Arya – as ensuring a more sustainable world will be critical for their future and the future of their generation.

Contents

Foreword by Philip Kotler   ix

Foreword by Bob Willard   xi

Preface   xv

Acknowledgments   xvii

1 Introduction   3

2 Motivating Consumers   25

3 Collaborating with Customers   49

4 Inspiring Employees   70

5 Nurturing Suppliers   91

6 Investing in Communities   111

7 Attracting Investors   131

8 Leveraging Media   146

9 Engaging Government   162

10 Partnering with NGOs   178

11 Stakeholder Sustainability Audit (SSA) Tool   203

Notes   219

Index   237

Foreword

PHILIP KOTLER

Sustainability is a word that came into our consciousness over 30 years ago. Many people do not know what it means and as such give it a variety of different meanings. I think of it as covering the practices of individuals, groups, and organizations that are conscious of the impact of their activities on the health of our planet. If timber companies cut down too many trees, it will lead to more greenhouse gases and warm up our planet. If fishing boats overfish, an important food source will grow scarcer. If chemical companies drop toxic chemicals in our rivers, it will hurt the water quality for future generations of citizens.

In the past, business firms mainly focused on making profits. The world seemed rich in resources and consumers appeared to have infinite needs. Management's job was to use up as many natural resources as needed to create a steady stream of products and services to satisfy an ever-growing consumer appetite.

Some people started to voice alarm about our unbridled level of resource use and consumption. Rachel Carson, in her 1962 book *Silent Spring*, documented the harm being done to our rivers and streams. In 1972, the book *Limits to Growth* was published suggesting that unlimited consumption could damage the health of our planet. Increasingly, people began to talk about conservation of our resources and sane consumption.

This new perspective greatly troubled the business community. All companies thrive on More! More! More! How could companies maintain their profitability if more consumers began to think that *less* is *more*?

One company, Unilever, thought hard about this problem. Paul Polman, CEO of Unilever, made the following statement: "Our ambitions are to double our business, but to do that while reducing our environmental impact and footprint … It has to be done via more responsible consumption." Polman was saying in effect that his company could attain good business growth and profitability and yet adhere to sustainability standards. Since then, Unilever has become a leader and an icon in the practice of sustainability.

It took more than Unilever doing creative marketing and brand building to earn high profits. What Unilever and other sustainability practitioners did was to get all of their stakeholders committed and motivated to practice sustainability. And this is why I am so impressed with this new book, *The Sustainability Edge*. It is written precisely to help businesses know what they can do with their stakeholders (consumers, customers, employees, suppliers, and the other five stakeholder groups) to contribute to a healthy planet. Each stakeholder chapter presents excellent material on sustainability and many compelling examples of what that stakeholder group can do.

Business no longer sees sustainability practice as only a cost or an ethical imperative. Businesses are increasingly recognizing that pursuing sustainability makes their company leaner, quicker, and more open to cost savings and growth opportunities. They are recognizing that a company's sustainability record draws kudos from the public and the investment community. Sustainability can be the next competitive advantage. We are receiving more annual reports and emails from companies proudly listing what they have accomplished that year when practicing sustainability.

We may come to a point where increasing numbers of consumers look up companies' sustainability standings before deciding which brand to buy. Consumers, after all, are voters, and they can vote for the companies that care, other things being equal.

There are many interesting books providing guidance on sustainability. I would count *The Sustainability Edge* as one of the most useful and enriching of these books.

Philip Kotler
S.C. Johnson Distinguished Professor of International Marketing,
Kellogg School of Management, Northwestern University

Foreword

BOB WILLARD

The subtitle of this book prompts the question: Is top-line growth a good thing?

Direct that question to investors, and their resounding "yes" will likely be as full of conviction as the "no" that one might receive from concerned environmentalists. The reason for such polarization is not that one respondent cares about society and the environment while the other doesn't; rather, they have different perspectives on what "growth" implies.

Many passionate, principled environmentalists find growth repugnant. In their minds, growth requires the continuous ravaging of virgin natural resources to satisfy the insatiable wants of over-consumers. It is against their core values to suggest that continuously growing company revenues is more sacred than protecting ecosystems. In nature, continuous growth is called cancer; to many environmentalists, corporate growth is nature's cancer. Science says that if the environment goes out of business, human society and companies go out of business, and we are already overshooting the carrying capacity of the planet. In fact, that's why some sustainability advocates consider "sustainable development" to be an oxymoron—development implies growth, and continuous growth is unsustainable on a finite planet.

On the other hand, MBA schools teach that growth is an imperative. "Grow or die" is the undisputed maxim of business leaders. The stock market punishes companies that do not meet "growth expectations." In the corporate mindset, growth is good. It is synonymous with progress and with winning in the game of business. The executive who dies with the biggest top line wins.

The problem is that growth, especially as measured by GDP, has been tightly coupled to biophysical throughput – the amount of raw materials we take out of, and later dump back into, the environment. When we pursue traditional growth, we devour and soil our own nest. Our dominant economic model requires the relentless extraction of raw materials to produce more and more products for more and more consumers who generate more and more waste. But we are running out of nonrenewable materials (e.g., minerals), or at least those available through traditional extraction techniques. And we are over-extracting renewable resources (e.g., fish and trees) to the extent that they can no longer replenish themselves.

So continuous revenue growth appears to be at odds with sustainability principles. That's why many executives are understandably leery that sustainability advocates have a hidden agenda: to compromise company growth. No wonder they are reluctant to embrace strategies that are billed as being more respectful of society and the environment. Executives want to accelerate growth, not hit the brakes. To engage executives, sustainability champions need to show how sustainability strategies are relevant and *support* companies' revenue growth goals. How? They can use triple-bottom-line thinking to show how companies can grow revenues sustainably by using three sustainable top-line growth strategies.

First, businesses can *decouple* revenue growth from depletion of virgin natural resources. They can drastically reduce their materials footprint by using recycled and renewable materials and taking back their products at the end of their useful lives to ensure that they are responsibly disposed of or reused. That is, they can collaborate with customers, communities, and suppliers to create a circular economy. Plus, they can grow revenue by creatively supplementing and replacing their current product revenue with associated *service* revenue streams. They can lease their products instead of selling them and package products with value-add services and financing alternatives.

For example, when I joined IBM Canada in 1967, most of its revenue came from the sale of its computing systems. It was a hardware company. Not today. IBM's 2014 annual report showed that it made 40 percent of its revenue from its outsourcing, optimization, cloud, and maintenance *services*; 20 percent from its consulting, systems integration, and application management *services*; 27 percent from *software*; and 2 percent from its *financing services*. Only 11 percent of its revenue came from sales of its hardware. That is, IBM has dematerialized 89 percent of its revenue stream and decoupled most of its revenue growth from the use of raw materials. IBM evolved this way because it's a smarter business model; it is also better for the environment.

Second, businesses can *produce fewer products*. We need to share a few goods instead of owning many. Customers desire the services that products provide (e.g., transportation versus vehicle ownership). Mind*ful* consumption is supplanting mind*less* consumption. Sustainable consumption is replacing overconsumption. Consumers are more ready for the "shareable economy" in which they rent tools, cars, hotel rooms, and other things that they only use occasionally. When we share things with friends and family, we do it for free. When companies do it for customers, they do it for fee. They open up new ongoing renting and leasing revenue streams that more than compensate for lost revenue from outright product sales.

Third, we need to redefine growth. Growth of what? The "Prosperity without Growth" report by Tim Jackson for the Sustainable Development Commission argues for the growth of *prosperity and human well-being*. It analyzes the complex relationships between traditional growth, environmental crises, and social recessions and proposes a creative route to sustainable, prosperous economic growth that benefits all stakeholders. Peter Victor's book, *Managing without Growth*, also reinforces that an economy can perform well without traditional growth assumptions while improving our quality of life. Patient investors, like pension funds, are starting to take systemic societal and ecosystem well-being factors into consideration when assessing the long-term prospects of a company in which they might invest their capital. They want to ensure that their investment is safe and that the company is fit for the future on a more socially and environmentally stressed planet.

So growth is fine if it is the right kind and it is achieved the right way. How can companies position themselves to capitalize on the right growth opportunities? By practicing true partnership and pre-competitive collaboration with others in their sector to reconfigure their collective supply chains, to strengthen local communities, and to protect security of supply. By educating and incenting customers to vote with their wallets for more environmentally responsible products and services without sacrificing price, quality, or convenience. By engaging employees who share the company's sustainability values and unleashing their creativity and innovation to help the company make the necessary changes to its business model. By doing well by doing good.

This book shows that nine stakeholder groups are ready to embrace responsible product and service offerings, while doing no harm to the silent tenth stakeholder – the environment. Companies can grow *and* be sustainable. Read on to learn how.

Bob Willard
Author and speaker, *The Sustainability Advantage*

Preface

The current generation of business students and emerging leaders inspired us to write this book. Their keen questions and intense interest about our sustainability experiences in the business world were highlights of our lectures at Emory University. It became clear to us that this generation can bring about a major transformation in the business world. We knew that a guide was needed not only for these budding leaders, but also for experienced leaders, especially those sitting at the top of their organizations, who see the change coming but are not sure what to do about it. Enlightened executives can mentor and encourage emerging leaders to achieve unparalleled leaps forward in the business world. We are all in this together.

The terms "sustainability" and "sustainable development" have been around for nearly 30 years, first being introduced in the United Nations World Commission on Environment and Development 1987 Brundtland Commission's report. The report defined sustainable development as "development, which meets the needs of current generations *without compromising the ability of future generations to meet their own needs."*

Although there has been some progress by businesses in terms of embracing the sustainable development concept, realistically a lot needs to be done, with an elevated level of urgency, if we expect businesses to survive and thrive over the coming 20 years and more. The scope and magnitude of challenges that business faces (currently and in the future) are enormous. The world's physical resources are limited and becoming ever costlier, the advantage of scale and automation are declining, new innovations are copied at a faster pace, and societal problems are growing at alarming rates. Incremental change won't address these challenges. What is required is a transformational change in business strategies, practices, and tactics with triple-bottom-line thinking. Today's best companies recognize that doing "good" is more beneficial than doing "less bad" and that, in addition, doing "good" actually creates more measurable financial value for the business. There is a growing recognition that businesses more than ever need to engage and energize all of their stakeholders in order to achieve top-line growth and continue to deliver triple-bottom-line outcomes. Doing so is business's *sole path* to ensuring long-term competitive advantage.

This book provides a virtual *sustainability roadmap* for enlightened business leaders. In it we highlight how best-in-class, progressive companies work with various key stakeholder groups to embrace a triple-bottom-line mindset and achieve sustainable prosperity. The book identifies nine key business stakeholder groups and suggests action plans for today's businesses to improve results by engaging each of these stakeholders in a 360-degree way with triple-bottom-line thinking. A Stakeholder Sustainability Audit tool enables businesses to determine where they can best make improvements that will ultimately provide the competitive advantage they seek.

In recent decades, sustainability has proven itself as both an inspiring and value-generating business strategy. Yet many businesses have been slow and even resistant to change their old ways. That is not only impeding their growth but also reducing their profits and thus leading them on the path to irrelevance. As Benjamin Franklin said during a time when society moved much slower, "When you're finished changing, you're finished." Through the suggestions in this book, we can all embrace the fast-changing landscape of economics and attitudes and see them not as a threat but as the key to lasting prosperity for us and for all who will be impacted by our choices.

Acknowledgments

We are grateful to the wonderful team that worked with us hand in hand to bring together this book. First and foremost, we want to thank Tim McFarland and David Papa for their ongoing feedback and for the significant time they devoted to rewriting and adding to the richness of the manuscript. The pair participated in the stakeholder interviews and helped us synthesize and distill the key messages gleaned from the many sustainability and business experts. Both read and contributed to the many chapter iterations, often asking provocative questions to help us anticipate how a business leader could get the most value from this book. Tim's years of experience as a sustainability professional and David's marketing acumen were of enormous help in making the book's final version both inspirational and impactful. In addition, during the book's genesis, two bright business students, Aarya Budhiraja and Ishan Dey, assisted us by conducting early research on select companies and by setting up our electronic filing system.

We would also like to thank Hugh O'Brian and Dr. Roland Bardy, who read drafts of this book and provided constructive comments, many of which were incorporated, as well as Mona Sinha, Alice Korngold, Howard Sharfstein, Angira Apte, and Peggy Ward, who provided constructive feedback on specific chapters. We would be remiss not to acknowledge Gabe Brambila, Roman Smith, Dharna Dhamija, Manisha Telkar, Lucas Saldhana, Linda Quin, Tim Knight, Raphael Bemporad, Candace Taylor, Tara Wilkie, Fani Koutsovitis,

Kathy Soyka, Jonathan Tozar, and Alexis Williams for providing material for the case studies and furnishing the charts and photos found throughout.

We sincerely want to thank the many colleagues who generously contributed their time, expertise, and valuable insights when participating in the sustainability-focused interviews that brought richness and relevance to these pages. They include Anurag Behar (Wipro), Kersti Strandqvist (SCA), Bill Morrissey (Clorox), Charlene Lake (AT&T), Matt Kistler (Walmart), Jens Dinkle (Siemens), Dr. Mukund Rajan (Tata), Thomas Schaefer (IKEA), Mindy Lubber (Ceres), Megan Cunningham (Magnet Media), Lisa Morden (Kimberly-Clark), Jim Hartzfeld (Interface), and Rolf Skar (Greenpeace). The case studies and other examples used in the book include quotations from the interviews and correspondence between these people and the authors, between June 2014 and March 2016.

We thank Sandra Mackey for her invaluable help in pulling the drafts together and making them ready for submission. She was able to assemble the charts, graphs, and photos to meet the publisher's standards. We also appreciate the administrative support provided by Nicole Smith to Dr. Sheth. We would like to thank Jennifer DiDomenico, acquisitions editor at University of Toronto Press, for her patience and guidance in helping us reach the finish line, to Kimberly Booker and Leah Connor, also with University of Toronto Press, for redrawing charts and graphs to meet the publisher's standards and managing the production process, respectively. And last, to Barbie Halaby, of Monocle Editing, for her copy edits and valuable suggestions.

Additionally, I, Suhas Apte, would like to express my deep appreciation to Dr. Jag Sheth for his encouragement and mentoring throughout my maiden journey as a coauthor.

And finally, thanks to our spouses Megha Apte and Madhu Sheth for their understanding and continued support. Their ongoing encouragement during the last couple of years helped both of us focus on and deliver this manuscript.

THE SUSTAINABILITY EDGE

How to Drive Top-Line Growth
with Triple-Bottom-Line Thinking

1 Introduction

What Tomorrow's Business Leaders Need

Today, businesses around the globe are at a critical crossroad. The scope and magnitude of the challenges they face are unprecedented. The resources that were plentiful in the past and that served as business's growth engine are becoming costlier and scarcer. In addition, supply chains have become more global, less resilient, and pose confounding new reputational risks. The traditional tools in their arsenal are no longer sufficient to provide them the competitive edge required to succeed in today's marketplace. Any new tool they innovate and deploy is copied and adopted by their competition within a short time. Government policies are uncertain. Customers are less trusting than ever before. All of these elements are changing more rapidly than at any time in history.

Many business leaders see that their companies are entering a long, slow path of decline and dissolution. It doesn't have to be that way, which is why we wrote this book. This book provides leaders with a way to address these challenges. It delivers a framework for defining and deploying a roadmap to build a formidable and sustainable competitive advantage. Continuing to pursue strategies and tactics that have been adequate in the past is indeed a dead-end road and will put the viability of any business at stake. What's needed is a complete transformational change in business practices, strategies, and tactics to guarantee lasting competitive advantages. Businesses need help from all those connected to them to weather this transformation. The headwinds fueled by external challenges are so strong that only the businesses that fully engage and energize all of their stakeholders to bring about change will survive and thrive in the emerging world.

Looking Backward: The Journey

From the onset of the Industrial Revolution, and continuing through the first two-thirds of the twentieth century, businesses pervasively outcompeted each other through mass production and automation. As the Western economies began to significantly mature in the later part of the twentieth century, the benefits of scale and automation slowed down and consumers started to become more discerning. The 1980s saw a trend toward achieving a competitive business advantage through total quality management (TQM). As the new millennium dawned, the prevalent source of competitive advantage shifted to customer relationship management (CRM). However, in today's marketplace, all of these strategies have been rapidly equalized among competitors; the traditional sources of competitive advantage are becoming mere table stakes and are thus no longer sufficient.

I (Apte) saw this firsthand as a leader at Kimberly-Clark during the 1980s and 1990s when Kimberly-Clark and Procter & Gamble (P&G) fought many competitive design and marketing battles over their branded baby diapers (Huggies and Pampers, respectively). These battles were waged on performance attributes like leakage, dryness, or fit, as well as through marketing positions that sought to provide emotional differentiation and appeal. But none of these strategies were long-lasting, as each competitor was ultimately able to match or exceed the other's performance or marketing edge. This ultimately leaves price as the choice discriminant, resulting in eroding margins and budget pressures.

External Challenges

In addition to struggling to find effective ways of gaining a competitive advantage, today's businesses are facing enormous external

challenges to sustainment and growth. Most of these challenges ema-
nate from the evolution of policy, markets, investors, and consumer
sentiment. The business landscape is changing more rapidly than
ever before and thus presents significant challenges to today's businesses. The most notable of these challenges include the following:

- The markets in the developed world have reached mature status, as existing product categories are largely fully penetrated,
  including many household product categories such as diapers,
  soaps, shampoos, and appliances. Only businesses able to alter
  their paradigms or fully embrace innovation are still experiencing growth.
- The majority of global business growth is coming from developing
  and emerging markets. These markets are forcing businesses – for
  example, cell phone companies, electricity distribution networks,
  and "smart cities" – to re-examine the established business models
  and spawning the need for transformative thinking across the
  value chain.
- Financial institutions and investors are demanding full disclosure regarding the projected impacts of climate change and
  other social and environmental sustainability issues on business results and operations. Recent examples of such issues
  that have led to business disruption include (1) poor air quality
  in New Delhi, India, and Beijing, China, leading to social unrest,
  (2) recent catastrophic weather events that have caused supply
  disruptions, and (3) political unrest and action, e.g., the Arab
  Spring and China's blocking of Google within its borders.
  Business disruption could have multiple consequences in
  terms of direct losses and challenges to business continuity.
- Governments and nongovernmental organizations (NGOs) are
  demanding that businesses lower their greenhouse gas emissions, as the negative impacts of inaction on human health are
  becoming more and more evident. This phenomenon led to the
  Paris summit in December 2015, when a non-binding treaty
  was approved that set a target of limiting global warming well
  below 2 degrees Celsius by 2100. On April 22, 2016, Earth Day,

175 countries signed the Paris climate accord, for which every signatory country sets its own timeline and targets. These targets could have an impact on all companies operating in these markets. Congratulating the global leadership members and recognizing this historic event, UN secretary-general Ban Ki-moon was quoted in *USA Today* as stating, "Today is a day for our children and grandchildren and all generations to come."[1]

- Sourcing continuity affected by climate change has had a negative impact on many businesses' bottom lines; for example, the floods in Thailand shut down parts supply and idled auto assembly plants all around the globe. Weather-related insurance claims have skyrocketed for insurance companies around the world. Munich Re, a global insurance group, estimates that over $500 billion in weather-related losses have been incurred in the U.S. market alone between 1980 and 2011.[2]

- The planet's resources are finite and therefore under increasing stress as more and more emerging market consumers enter the middle class and subsequently begin to demand access to better and more sustainable products. Pope Francis's letter to Prime Minister David Cameron, chair of G8 meeting in June 2013, sums up well the need for a sustainable global model: "Every economic and political theory or action must set about providing each inhabitant of the planet with the minimum wherewithal to live in dignity and freedom, with the possibility of supporting a family, educating children, praising God and developing one's own human potential. This is the main thing; in the absence of such a vision, all economic activity is meaningless."[3]

- Millennial consumers, equipped with ready access to information through social media, are demanding more business transparency and accountability in areas such as material sourcing, fair labor practices, and product life cycle management. According to a 2015 Nielsen global sustainability survey, 66 percent of global respondents are willing to pay more for sustainable products and services; this increased by 11 percent over the last few years. In an analysis of responses by age segment, millennials stand out compared to other age groups, as almost three out of four respondents are willing to pay extra for sustainable products. Additionally, millennials are willing to check package label details for sustainable data and prefer to work for a sustainable company. The average millennial response for these three questions is two times more favorable than the response from Generation X (ages 35–49) and four times more favorable than that by baby boomers (ages 50–64). This highlights the importance of companies focusing on millennials.[4] Millennials will soon become the majority of workers and consumers.

- There is a growing awareness and a call to action with regard to the global trend of "income inequality." This issue will have an impact on the future growth potential of many businesses and industries, as income inequality effectively deprives companies of prospective customers who are willing to buy but unable to afford the companies' products. For example, in the United States, the richest 1 percent earns 20 percent of the country's income and the wealthiest 160,000 families have as much wealth as the poorest 145 million families.[5]

- According to the 2014 Edelman Trust barometer, companies and CEOs are ranked at the bottom of the list in terms of public trust. Despite the fact that the overall global business trust rating is at 57 percent, over half of the 27 countries surveyed reported lower than a 50 percent trust rating. The low CEO trust rating scores are even more alarming given that CEOs receive ratings below regular employees.[6]

The Key to Lasting Competitive Advantage

All this contributes to the fundamental premise of this book: incremental improvements in business practices will no longer be sufficient to guarantee lasting competitive advantage and long-term business sustainability. Only the businesses that are willing and able to make the required transformative and sustainable changes will stay ahead of the pack and prosper. It is only by adopting a longer-term view that companies will be able to uncover the next great opportunity required to win in today's increasingly complex market.

There are many definitions of the sustainable competitive advantage, but we believe Kevin P. Coyne conveys it best: "Sustainable competitive advantage is the unique position that an organization develops in relation to competitors that allows it to outperform them consistently."[7]

What are these transformational changes required for long-term success? What are the avenues left to a business that wants to develop a self-sustaining strategy? In the complex, interrelated, and challenging world in which we now live, the answer is much simpler than many have believed. The next major competency that businesses will need to pursue and fully integrate to gain a sustainable and consistent competitive advantage will be *sustainability* itself. As our subtitle suggests, businesses that embrace this practice can only effectively drive their top-line growth through bottom-line thinking.

Anurag Behar, chief sustainability officer at Wipro (a large and profitable IT services and consulting firm based in India), reinforced this point in an interview for this book. He stated, "When Newsweek International recognized Wipro as the second most sustainable company in the world, instead of being thrilled and happy, I was in a sense horrified." He continued, "While I knew that we at Wipro were doing a fair bit on Sustainability, and that we were leaders in many ways, I equally knew how much more needed to be done. And, if this was the state of Wipro, the global leader on Sustainability, then one can only imagine what complete transformation businesses across the world need to go through to adequately deal with the multi-dimensional challenges of Sustainability."

Jim Hartzfeld – ex-VP of strategy at Interface, Inc., the world's largest manufacturer of modular carpets – shared a real-life example illustrating the power of transformational changes applied to sustainability. In August 1994, Ray Anderson, the Southern gentleman and intensely competitive industrialist at the head of the company, started a sustainability revolution with just one 20-minute speech delivered to 17 of his employees, a speech he originally didn't want to make. Finally relenting to Jim's repeated prodding, Ray challenged his employees to travel to a mystical place called "Sustainability," which nobody on his team had heard of. To some of the engineers in the room, the word seemed perhaps to be a new name for perpetual motion. Later in the journey, Ray began to share a powerful metaphor. Every chance he got, Ray would say to his team, "I have a mental image of a mountain to climb. This mountain is taller than Everest, infinitely more difficult to scale, and we are only on the lowest slope but we know the way to the top of the mountain. The name of this mountain is Sustainability." Over the years, he shared the vision of "Mission Zero," which was impossible to many and so ambitious for others that most didn't know where to start. He shared the vision with all his employees in sales and in his plants, his customers and suppliers, one man at a time – 3,000 people in total. Initially some of his leaders thought he had gone insane, or as he used to say, "gone round the bend." Eventually, the employees bought into Anderson's vision, internalized it in their own way, and even carried it home and into their communities. Twenty years later, the results are inspiring and the group is on their way to the top of the mountain.[8]

As of 2015, Interface boasted the following business results and sustainability-related accomplishments.[9] Interface

- Delivered consistent low-single-digit compound growth in sales and profits over the last few years despite the impact a strong dollar had on global sales.
- Is recognized as a global leader in modular carpet made with recyclables and bio-based materials with sales outside of the United States surpassing sales within the country.
- Has expanded to non-office commercial markets, emerging markets, and direct-to-consumer channels to reduce the impact of a maturing office market.
- Established FLOR modular carpet brand for consumers via online, catalog, and in-store offerings.
- Continued to make progress on their "Mission Zero," further establishing their sustainability leadership position:
  - The greenhouse gas (GHG) emissions per unit of production are down 92 percent since 1996.
  - The energy use from renewable sources makes up the majority, with 84 percent of the total energy consumed.

- Recycled and bio-based material composes 50 percent of their total raw materials used.
- The water intake per unit of production is down 87 percent since 1996.
- The waste to landfill was reduced by 26 million pounds since 1996.

Rather than simply the exploitation of leading-edge energy or recycling technologies, Interface's success was built mostly on Anderson's ability to inspire and align his people around an audacious vision that "took people's breath away," turning carpet making into work that mattered to his engineers, designers, salespeople, accountants, and even forklift drivers. Jim refers to this as "the HumanTech that drives the GreenTech." From that "one-mind-at-a-time" human connection, technologies were developed, customers were engaged, new products emerged, and an industry was changed.

"Sustainability" is now common parlance in the business world, used to mean operating with an understanding that we live in a connected, resource-constrained world – doing business in a way that does not damage the environment in which it operates and that improves the social and economic fabric of the community in which it operates. This flavor of the word "sustainability" is so common that many business people no longer think about its much simpler original meaning – long-lasting and self-sustaining. Are not "long-lasting and self-sustaining" the very qualities a business looks for in its strategy? Business leaders today turn over every stone, do week-long retreats, and hire expert consultants to formulate the competitive strategy so that their company can achieve long-term success. But they have forgotten to look in the most obvious place – the connection between the simple definition of "sustainable" and the new more complicated one of "sustainability."

This connection, this simple idea of a long-lasting and self-sustaining strategy, has given rise to all the frameworks and suggestions we make for strategic success. The only path remaining in today's market to achieve long-term success is to fully embrace sustainability – the practices that put a business in harmony with its whole ecosystem and environment – with all of its stakeholders in a 360-degree arch of reciprocated engagement and shared success. This is what customers demand, what investors seek, and what savvy leaders realize is the key to leaving a legacy we can be proud of after all our years of hard corporate work.

Advocating and delivering triple-bottom-line outcomes (profit, people, and planet) to the company's many stakeholders will ensure that the company retains its competitive advantage for years to come. The data that supports our conclusion have gone from fringe activity several years ago to a mountain of evidence in today's market.

Sustainability Contributes to Business Value

A number of studies and reports support the contention that sustainability can contribute to the value of a business.

In the January 11, 2016, *Wall Street Journal*, John Streur, president and chief executive of Calvert Investments, Inc., one of the original sustainable-investing firms, wrote, "We can look at 2015 and say this was a transformative year for this investment discipline. We've really turned the corner."[10] The chart in Figure 1.1 from Morning Star, a leading provider of independent investment research of competitive returns, supports John's statement, as the long-term returns of "sustainable" mutual funds outpaced ones that are not.

Most U.S. investors desire to see statistically significant evidence that climate change is linked to business performance. The *S&P 500 Climate Change 2014* report unequivocally delivers this proof. This analysis completed by the Carbon Disclosure Project (CDP) clearly shows that the S&P 500 member companies leading the way in climate change management with higher CDP scores, by and large, deliver superior results versus the ones which are rated laggards, in terms of both profitability (18 percent higher) and stability (50 percent lower volatility). These leaders also utilize the higher profitability to increase dividends to shareholders (21 percent stronger than their lower-scoring peers). The superior profitability, sustainability credentials, and growing dividends make these top-tier companies more attractive to equity investors.[11]

Figure 1.1. Competitive returns: Performance of sustainable (or SRI) mutual funds vs. traditional funds

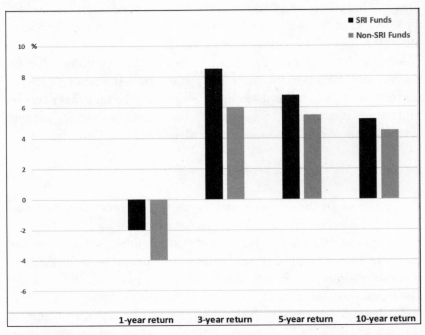

© 2015 Morning Star, Inc.

In a 2012 *Sustainable Investing* report, the Deutsche Bank Advisors found corporate social responsibility (CSR) and environmental, social, and governance (ESG) are becoming synonymous. Among 89 percent of the studies examined, the companies with a high rating for ESG factors outperformed the market. Furthermore, as the market recognizes that these companies have a lower risk profile, they are rewarded financially with lower cost of capital in terms of debt and equity, at least over the medium to long term.[12]

CSRHub, a leading sustainability analysis firm, has done research with leading organizations globally and shows proof of the impact of sustainability on brand strength and other key performance measures, such as reputation risk, digital communications strength, and cost of credit. According to Cynthia Figge, cofounder and COO of CSRHub, strong sustainability performance is having an increasing impact on operating performance across many domains that drive corporate value. Four specific studies she shared with us prove the point.

- CSRHub matched their ratings of 15,000 companies worldwide with each of the three leading brand agencies – Brand Finance in the United Kingdom and, in the United States, Interbrand and Reputation Institute – and found the overall correlation between sustainability and brand reputation was 22 percent.
- CSRHub's joint research with RepRisk found a 29 percent correlation between sustainability and reputational risk.
- Research on the correlation between CSR-perceived performance and the strength of digital communications, as measured by Investis IQ, showed digital communications are impacted by 6 of CSRHub's 12 factors, with a correlation of 39 percent.
- Capstone research published by graduate students at Columbia University found that CSRHub's 12-variable model for sustainability explained 9.3 percent of the variance in the cost of debt, or an estimated $343 billion in interest expenses for a group of 1,625 companies. Thus, doing well in sustainability translates into a significant market advantage through brand reputation and decreased cost of capital.

Corporate Knights, a media, research, and financial information products company based in Toronto, Canada, is focused on promoting companies that are sustainable around the globe. Ranking companies based on their sustainability performance is a daunting task, so the group first shortlists all companies using a proprietary four-screen process looking at sustainability disclosure, Piotroski F-Score, business classification, and sustainability sanctions. The shortlisted companies are then assessed via 12 key performance indicators (KPIs), including management of resources (such as energy use, emissions, water use, and waste generated), financial sustainability revenue, EBITDA, the ratio of CEO compensation to the average employee's compensation, employee management practices, fatalities

or lost time, turnover, diversity in leadership, and female represen-
tation on the board and in management. Those receiving the highest
performance are ranked in the annual Corporate Knights Global
100 Index.[13]

Corporate Knights has been tracking the data since 2005. As
Figure 1.2 illustrates, the Global 100 consistently delivered better
total returns than the Morgan Stanley Corporate Indexes (MSCI) All
Country World Index (ACWI), regardless of market conditions. This
is true for the first nine years it was reported, 2005 through 2014.
The year 2015 was the first that the ACWI slightly outperformed the
Global 100. Does this mean the evidence for sustainability as a financial decision is weakened? No. The main reason for this difference in 2015 is that the U.S. dollar grew stronger compared to other
currencies; the Global 100 is only 19 percent U.S. currency businesses,
whereas the MSCI ACWI is 50 percent U.S. currency business. In addition, the Global 100 Index is less volatile, which is increasingly important given the current volatility of the global stock markets (e.g.,
the Shanghai in China, the Dow Jones in the United States). When
we take that into account, the ability of sustainably minded companies to produce returns consistently outperforms non-sustainably-
minded peers.

Accessing these financial wins and achieving lasting sustainable
competitive advantage through sustainability itself requires consistent and persistent efforts on the part of every business and industry,
as the market performance bar is constantly being raised. A business's efforts will need to go far beyond simply changing to more
energy-efficient light bulbs and recycling office paper. To embrace
sustainability as a competitive advantage, businesses will need to
realize a transformative change in their traditional sustainability
(triple-bottom-line) approaches and practices. They must embed
sustainability into their DNA and corporate culture, and strategically invest in new and innovative processes, practices, and systems.
This entails embracing sustainability itself as an overarching strategy embedded into every business operation and relationship.

This may sound like quite a bit of work and quite a bit of change,
but it's not much different than what was required to implement

Figure 1.2. Corporate Knights' Global 100 Index:
Returns for Global 100 Index vs. MSCI All Country World Index

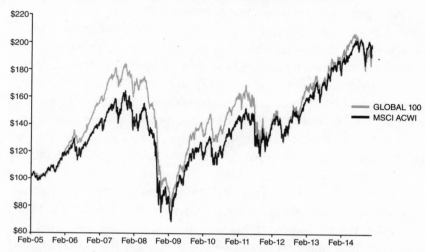

Source: Corporate Knights Inc. and TD Asset Management Inc.

TQM, mass production, and CRM. We believe the new imperative is the *only* sustainable (long-lasting and self-sustaining) way forward. Becoming increasingly sustainable is the only way a business can both create a lasting competitive advantage in the market and preserve its own longevity in the face of evolving global challenges. If businesses want to win now, last into the future, and even leave a positive legacy for future generations, then they need to be sustainability-driven at every level and juncture of their operations.

To bring about this transformational change, businesses must effectively and strategically identify, engage, and energize all of their key stakeholders. No single business can hope to begin to be successful in the midst of the societal and environmental issues challenging the twenty-first century and beyond if they hold a narrow view of their company activities that includes only investors, customers, and employees. No single company or government alone can simply accomplish sustainability. The world is too connected and too interdependent for that. The traditional African proverb, "It will take a village to raise a child," is appropriate here: the village refers to a business and all of its stakeholders, while the child is analogous to a sustainable world.

The transformational concept or philosophy being recommended can be described as *maximizing benefits for all stakeholders as a source of competitive advantage*. This is fundamentally different from the concept of *maximizing business profit by satisfying customers*, which many businesses prescribe to today. Buying into this traditional business philosophy only serves one stakeholder at the expense of all others. Businesses can provide exponentially more value to customers when all stakeholders are engaged; we include several examples throughout this book to illustrate how value is derived by engaging the various stakeholders.

Maximizing benefits for all stakeholders as a source of competitive advantage is also fundamentally different from *maximizing shareholder value*, which has been a dominant business ideology for decades. This outdated premise makes the erroneous assumption that what is good for an investor is good for the business and also ultimately good for the economy and society. There are many false assumptions embedded in this chain of logic that don't take into account how the financial markets or real markets, or humans for that matter, actually work. Few statements could be farther from the truth, and we need only look at the financial data. As outlined in the book *Firms of Endearment: How World-Class Companies Profit from Passion and Purpose* (published in 2003), in a study of 30 firms the authors found that the "shareholder versus stakeholder dichotomy" is false – the most profit-oriented companies were usually not the most profitable, whereas the most highly profitable companies were usually not primarily driven by profit motives. The book defines the term "firms of endearment" as companies that people love doing business with, love partnering with, love working for, love investing in. According to the authors, their book "is about gaining 'share of heart,' not just share of wallet. It's about aligning stakeholders' interests, not just juggling them."[14] This finding is completely counterintuitive to what we learned in business school, which is why so many resist it, but it is also in lockstep alignment with the realities of today's market. Change is happening more quickly in the real world than in most business school classrooms and most boardroom meetings. Today, the best companies are generating *every* form of value that matters: emotional, experiential, social, and financial. And they're doing it for *all* their stakeholders, not because it's "politically correct" but *because it's the only path to long-term competitive advantage.*

To be successful over the long haul, companies must actively market and promote their hard-earned sustainability credentials and actions and engage all of their important stakeholders. High-level stakeholder engagement is how businesses can successfully drive sustainability at every level. This is what stakeholders want, and this creates results.

The Sustainability Edge Roadmap

We've titled this path to success "the Sustainability Edge" based upon the logic that sustainability is a clear, proven path to achieve an advantage over the competition in these trying economic times. There is another meaning to "edge." An edge describes a boundary, a limit to the known world, a frontier of sorts. In this case, we might even call it a precipice or sheer drop-off. Business leaders have the choice to work and thrive at this edge of sustainable engagement, forging a new path forward, or they can ignore the data, the market, and their own inner wisdom at their own peril and fall off the edge as the ground shifts beneath them. Like it or not, the new competitive playing field is emerging right now. To adapt to it and ultimately succeed in this economic landscape, business leaders need to embrace sustainability in a holistic and transformative sense. Leaders need to maintain a balanced, triple-bottom-line approach to sustainability and business while maintaining a constant and consistent focus on engaging and energizing all of their stakeholders in a long-term, focused, and self-sustaining way.

We aim for this book to act as a virtual sustainability roadmap for business leaders. We share examples of how best-in-class, progressive companies work with various key sustainability stakeholder groups to adopt a triple-bottom-line mindset and achieve sustainable prosperity. We break down their methods and offer action plans for today's businesses to engage all stakeholders in a transformative and holistic way.

Each stakeholder interacts with or supports a business in a different way. Unfortunately, most businesses only engage a minority of all the potential players/stakeholders that can help bring them business success. The Sustainability Edge is the ideology and process that can help every business stand on a firmer foundation, reach higher, and travel farther in this uncertain world than traditional business thinking will ever take them.

We have identified and focused on nine key sustainability stakeholder groups, which we have organized into three classifications based on the nature of their impact on businesses. Figure 1.3 illustrates these classifications in a framework.

We have classified consumers, customers, and employees as "direct impact" stakeholders because these stakeholders are already present in almost every business model, and their changing needs have already forced many companies to seek new ways to interact with these groups. Energizing and engaging these stakeholders can have an immediate and significant effect on the company's long-term sustainability and prosperity.

The next classification of stakeholders includes suppliers, investors, and communities, which we have termed "enabler impact" stakeholders. They are enablers because businesses that engage and leverage these stakeholder groups effectively can make their sustainability journey faster and smoother, and thereby see resulting returns sooner.

The last classification – NGOs, governments, and media – we have termed "indirect impact" stakeholders. These groups are not as fundamental to driving profits in typical business models, and so true engagement of these groups is less often pursued in the business world. This is a mistake. While engaging these groups may take more time than direct or enabler impact stakeholders, these groups are no less significant in affecting the long-term prosperity of businesses.

Figure 1.3. Sustainability stakeholders framework

Sustainability Stakeholders Framework

Each chapter in this book is dedicated to one of the aforementioned key stakeholder groups and addresses the following specific questions in each group.

Chapter 2: Motivating Consumers – What do companies need to offer to the choosers and users of their products and services to leverage market forces and become sustainability leaders? What could the users do to help a company make this a better planet?

Chapter 3: Collaborating with Customers – How can businesses best engage their business-to-business relationships with customers, distributors, and key accounts to increase their competitive advantage and play roles in promoting sustainability choices and driving policy changes?

Chapter 4: Inspiring Employees – How can companies use sustainability to engage and energize their employees, and what can employees do to help make the company prosper as a sustainability leader?

Chapter 5: Nurturing Suppliers – How can companies extend their sustainability agenda up their supply chains for deeper financial and sustainable impact? How can suppliers promote innovative sustainable solutions and technologies to help the company grow?

Chapter 6: Investing in Communities – How can companies help their communities prosper, and what can communities do to help the company grow and become more sustainable?

Chapter 7: Attracting Investors – How can companies reduce costs and increase revenue through sustainability efforts and thus improve shareholders' return? How can investors and shareholders ensure that companies manage sustainability-associated risks and focus on long-term sustainable growth?

Chapter 8: Leveraging Media – How can companies leverage the current media interest to evangelize sustainability? How can they influence the various forms of media to promote sustainability behavior?

Chapter 9: Engaging Government – How can companies promote public-private partnerships to gain an advantage and also address societal issues? How can governments develop and implement policies that foster partnerships?

Chapter 10: Partnering with NGOs – How can companies influence markets by engaging NGOs and thought leaders in the development of their sustainability vision and programs? How can NGOs and thought leaders achieve their own goals while supporting a company's sustainability mission and growth?

When a company effectively engages all of its key stakeholders and influences them to embrace sustainability as fundamental to their joint mission, it creates the most productive and longest-lasting version of sustainability, one that is at once financially, environmentally, and socially successful. Such a company has succeeded in creating a culture where sustainability is embedded in its DNA and which in turn becomes the driving force behind its business success. That company has a superior and unique competitive advantage that is extremely difficult to replicate.

Case Study: SCA (Svenska Cellulosa Aktiebolaget)

SCA, a leading global hygiene and forest products company, has one of the most comprehensive and strategic approaches for stakeholder dialogue. They actively engage with all their stakeholders to ensure that the company's business priorities and methods are relevant. Kersti Strandqvist, senior vice president of sustainability at SCA, shared their story: "Back in 2010 when we changed our view from 'Inside Out' to 'Outside In' and put ourselves into the shoes of the stakeholders, our dialogue with the stakeholders became richer and more strategic."

The company has since evolved a two-step process. First, the team pulls together a heat map of what could be the most relevant topics based upon interaction they have with the stakeholders all year-around. The company then sends a biannual web-based survey to a list of targeted stakeholder types. For example, they might send the survey to 1,000 consumers, 50 investors, 15 NGOs, 1,000 employees, 100 business customers, and so on. Each stakeholder is shown 10–12 topics and asked to rank the five most important ones. The survey requires 2 to 10 minutes to complete, depending on the sustainability literacy of the respondent. The senior management team at SCA completes the survey as well. After the results are tabulated and analyzed by the sustainability team at SCA, senior management discusses the results and then uses them to ensure the company is appropriately addressing the hottest issues and that progress is being properly communicated to each stakeholder group. Table 1.1 illustrates the outcome of the two-step process as communicated in their annual Sustainability Report.[15]

Table 1.1. SCA 2015 Sustainability Report

Stakeholder group	Main areas	How we work with the issues/ activities in 2014 (page reference)
Customers	Carbon footprint Ecolabelling Working conditions Fiber sourcing Human rights compliance Customer insight Innovation	Customer surveys (10, 36) People & nature innovations (12, 36) Hygiene solutions (14, 38) Global supplier standard (19, 41) CO_2 targets (22, 45) Sourcing targetsFSC® and PEFCTM certification (26, 46) Life cycle assessments (36) Code of Conduct audits and Business Practice Reviews (39, 40) Human rights assessments (40)
Consumers	Impact of products on nature, for example, carbon footprint, ecolabeling Product safety Consumer insight Innovation	Consumer surveys and focus groups (10, 36) People & nature innovations (12, 36) Hygiene solutions (14, 38) Life cycle assessments (36) Product safety (37) Eco Actions (www.libero.se/Eco-Actions, www.libresse.com, www.tena.com)
Employees	Recruitment and succession planning Training Compensation and benefits Business ethics Health and safety Working conditions	Code of Conduct training (39) Human rights assessments (40) Management system (42) OHSAS 18001 certification (42) Diversity survey (43) Global Performance Management System (43) Global All-Employee Survey (44)
Investors	ESG (environmental, social, governance) integration into business strategy Resource efficiency Risk management	Investor/analyst meetings (35) Conference participation (35) Inclusion in sustainability indexes and funds (35) ESAVE (45) Risk analysis (AR 78)

Stakeholder group	Main areas	How we work with the issues/ activities in 2014 (page reference)
Suppliers	Supplier audits Raw material sourcing	Sourcing targets (26) Global supplier standard (41) Sedex reporting (41) Code of Conduct supplier audits (19, 41)
Stakeholder organizations	Forest management CO_2 emissions Energy utilization Water consumption	Continuous dialogs, such as consultation with reindeer herders (31) Membership in industry initiatives and organizations such as WBCSD, Consumer Goods Forum, FSC, etc. (www.sca.com)
Society	Environmental issues Local issues Community involvement	Public Affairs (31) Ongoing dialog with authorities and local communities (31) Hundreds of community involvement initiatives (45)

SCA's strong business results – realizing 17 percent sales and 31 percent operating profit growth between 2012 and 2014 – supports the contention that their strategic approach to stakeholder engagement is working.

We have taken a page from SCA's book and compiled our own assessment survey so that we could provide business leaders with an effective tool for benchmarking their sustainability-driven competitive activities. Our self-assessment tool, the Stakeholder Sustainability Audit (SSA), allows readers to score any company's progress on its current sustainability advocacy practices. The tool is available via a simple and quick web-based survey. Survey participants receive an overall company rating, as well as a breakdown of their individual stakeholder ratings. We highly recommend that this survey is taken by both internal teams (sustainability staff, line management, operations) and external stakeholders to better understand the gap between internal and external perceptions. That gap must be crossed for real strategic engagement (see chapter 11 for more details on the SSA).

We equate the sustainability journey to playing the game of golf, where the intent is not to always get the best score but rather to pursue continuous improvement and, when one makes a great shot, marvel at how far one has progressed. Therefore, we recommend that all relevant internal and external members repeat the survey regularly (we suggest annually) to evaluate the progress the company has made and identify where opportunities for improvement lie.

Taking the survey can act as a first simple step in the journey we advocate in this book. It is a journey that hopefully leads to more and better business profitability, certainly. But even more importantly, it leads to the moment when a business leader can look back on their career and know that they have done their *best* to ensure prosperity for themselves and those they care about, including their customers, their employees, their children, their grandchildren, and even the entire human race.

2 Motivating Consumers

Make sustainability relevant and personal to the consumer by focusing on "my environment" close-in "in me, on me, and around me" benefits and consumers will join you for the ride.

Bill Morrissey, former chief sustainability officer
of Clorox Corporation

Figure 2.1. Sustainability stakeholders framework: Motivating consumers

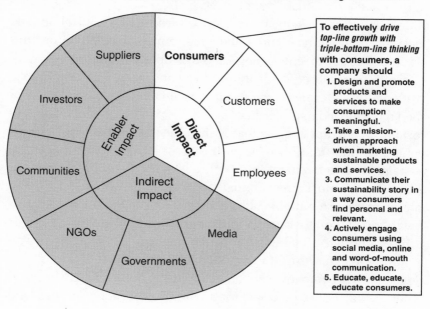

To effectively *drive top-line growth with triple-bottom-line thinking* with consumers, a company should

1. Design and promote products and services to make consumption meaningful.
2. Take a mission-driven approach when marketing sustainable products and services.
3. Communicate their sustainability story in a way consumers find personal and relevant.
4. Actively engage consumers using social media, online and word-of-mouth communication.
5. Educate, educate, educate consumers.

Clorox, predominantly a chemical bleach company, has transformed itself in the last six years in an attempt to address the results of its own strategic consumer mega-trend study, which showed four key drivers of consumer behavior: health and wellness, multicultural market-place, convenience, and environmental sustainability. A small "Eco-office" was created to lead and coordinate sustainability efforts inside the company, and this work has resulted in company acquisitions, new products, and even complete rebranding efforts.

Bill Morrissey, a well-seasoned, 30-year veteran business leader, was chosen to lead Clorox's Eco-office. Bill shared that changing a 100-year-old company was not without trials and tribulations. It was a steep climb, one that required fully engaging both internal and external stakeholders.

In 2008, the company acquired Burt's Bees; a small personal grooming products company built on the foundation of natural products and sustainability. The Burt's Bees employees felt that the devil had come to buy their business; it took months of trust building to eventually win them over and to make them believe that Clorox had a sustainability mindset.

Shortly after the acquisition, Clorox introduced a natural-derived cleaning brand, Greenworks. Bloggers immediately called out this product line as "greenwashing" and attempted to discredit Clorox's efforts. Clorox subsequently forged an alliance with the Sierra Club to overcome the allegations and to gain sustainability credentials. Clorox then repositioned its water filter brand, Brita, on a sustainability platform in an attempt to grow that brand. The transformational journey continues today for Clorox, as the business has set a goal of 50 percent sustainable improvement in its entire product portfolio by the year 2020. Clorox's most recent annual report not only showcases its financial performance but also talks about its journey to attain its hard-fought reputation for outstanding corporate sustainability.

Bill's advice to all other sustainability officers and practitioners attempting a similar transformation is to engage the individual business units of a company early on in the sustainability discussions and to let the key issues percolate for a while. Patience, persistence, and facts will, in the end, garner the right participation, from the right areas of the company, for the right reasons.

Competing for Sustainably Minded Consumers

Consumers' spending their money for a company's goods or services is akin to gaining their purchasing votes. Buyers and users are figuratively voting for products and services, and what those products stand for, when they purchase them. This is well articulated by Ashley Brown, Coca-Cola's group director of digital communications and social media, who stated, "Every day you (consumers) have a choice of what to read and what to drink. Every day is 'Election Day,' and our team will be here – working hard to get your vote."[1]

More and more consumers are using their "votes" to reflect their personal value set and convictions. These value sets may include environmental concerns, desired ethical behavior on the part of companies or governments, respect for workers' rights, societal conditions, animal rights, and any number of other causes they feel connected to. The ease of access to and pervasiveness of social media today allow consumers to learn about and communicate with companies much more readily. The volatility of public opinion about a company, its brands, and its products is greater than at any time in history.

Companies that widely practice sustainable and ethical behaviors and, in turn, effectively communicate and engage consumers in a transparent way can achieve a competitive advantage in the marketplace. Taking it a step further, businesses can provide consumers with products, services, and the education that will help them progress on their journey to more-sustainable consumption.

A Case for Sustainable Consumption

Humanity has largely had an exploitative relationship with our planet; we can, and should, aim to make this a symbiotic one.

Michael Mack, Syngenta International AG

According to some projections, if humanity's consumption rate continues unabated and businesses continue to operate as they have, by the year 2050 we will require 2.3 times the planet's current resources to meet those needs.[2] This means shortages in all forms will abound, and the price of nearly everything will increase. At the time of this writing, 2050 is just over 30 years away. Is that enough time to make the changes we need? If businesses want corporate profits to grow or even maintain, and if we want our children to have the same or better lives than we have had, we need to make the move to symbiosis with the planet now.

Consumers are inarguably a large piece of this symbiotic puzzle. Encouraging and enabling the billions of global consumers to practice and adopt more sustainable behaviors, and to embrace a cradle-to-cradle consumption mindset, is necessary for long-term sustainability and corporate growth.

In the *Journal of the Academy of Marketing Science*, Sheth et al. claim that current business sustainability strategies are largely ill informed. They neither provide adequate focus on consumers' increasing global overconsumption, nor are they sufficiently holistic in their approach. The authors profess that businesses both widely ignore their primary stakeholders, consumers, and are not proactive toward social and economic aspects of sustainability, but rather focus solely on environmental aspects of sustainability. They go on to state that societal consumption drives sustainability outcomes. To fill this void, the authors introduce the concept of "mindful consumption" (MC). MC is based on a consumer mindset of caring for self, for the community, and for nature. This concept mitigates the excesses due to acquisitive, repetitive, and aspirational consumption. Businesses can benefit from encouraging their marketing teams to adopt and engage in a more customer-centric approach to sustainability.[3]

Businesses must work to shift the consumption mindset if they want to be successful for the long term, just like customers are already beginning to shift the business mindset by modifying their consumption patterns based on their values. We may see a future with a change in the definition of *consumerism*, from its current negative societal connotation of social excess, greed, and waste to a more positive definition of responsible growth and a means to gain fair market value for goods and services that enhance consumers' quality of life. This is essential for achieving the sustainability of the planet and its population. More and more smart businesses that subscribe to fostering a positive legacy are taking this position.

Engaging Green Consumers

Based on current consumer data and communication methods, businesses can achieve business objectives while successfully leveraging and engaging consumers to embrace more-sustainable consumption and lifestyles by undertaking five simple activities.

1. Understand Consumers' Evolving Attitudes Toward Sustainable Products and Services

Consumers' engagement in environmentally friendly activity has been plotted and tracked by agencies employing various segmentation models that define a green consumer spectrum.

One such agency that conducts research about green consumerism is Nielsen, a leading global information and measurement company that provides insights and data about what people watch, listen to, and buy. They have classified consumers into various "shades of green," or environmental segments, based on their shopping habits and attitudes. Their model divides consumers into three segments: Dark Greens, Light Greens, and Non-greens.

The *Dark Greens* segment will go out of their way to purchase a sustainable product. They do the required research, and they will pay more for sustainable products and services.

Those in the *Light Greens* segment feel they need to do something about the resource crunch and environmental protection as well as social issues. They may be attracted to sustainable products, but the products have to pass the value test. They won't pay materially more for sustainable products, but all aspects being relatively equal, they will choose sustainability.

Lastly, the *Non-greens* don't really consider social or environmental issues in their purchase decisions. It's not a factor in their decision-making process.

Nielsen's global corporate responsibility report, entitled *Sustainability Imperative – New Insights on Consumer Expectations*, from October 2015 is based on an online survey of 30,000 consumers in 60 countries. The study was designed to assess how sustainability influences purchasing decisions. The report shares that more than two-thirds (66 percent) of global respondents are willing to pay more for sustainable goods and services to stay true to their values, up from 55 percent in 2014 and 50 percent in 2013. This finding holds true for consumers across all regions, income levels, and categories. For example, those earning $20,000 or less per year are actually 5 percent more willing than those with annual incomes greater than $50,000 to pay more for products and services from companies committed to positive social and environmental impact (68 percent versus 63 percent). Interestingly, the findings show that it is generally harder to influence consumers in developed markets to purchase or pay more. Consumers in Latin America, Asia, the Middle East, and Africa are 23–29 percent more willing to pay a premium for sustainable offerings (Figure 2.2).[4]

Consumers in the developing world tend to feel more emotionally and intellectually connected to the planet's ability to cope with the resource needs of humanity. For example, according to National Geographic's 2014 *Greendex* study, the developing economies of India and China, followed by consumers in South Korea, Brazil, and Argentina, have the most sustainably minded consumers. In contrast, consumers in the United States have consistently scored the lowest with regard to environmental concerns since they began conducting the study in 2008.[5]

Figure 2.2. Trends in consumers' willingness to pay more for sustainable products

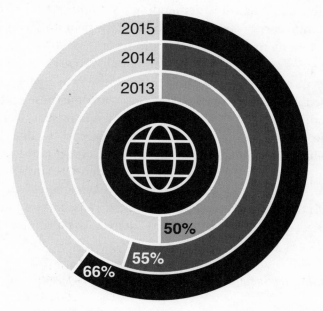

2015
2014
2013

50%
55%
66%

Source: A.C. Nielsen Global Responsibility Report, October 2015

The general consensus is that skepticism still persists when it comes to purchasing products with a sustainability benefit. Many consumers expect a "sustainability sacrifice." Based on previous experience, they expect that sustainable products will entail trade-offs or compromises – i.e., they will cost more than the traditional products, they are of inferior quality, and product designs will not be as appealing or attractive. In addition, consumers express that environmental claims are often untrustworthy and confusing. For instance, Seventh Generation, a major green products manufacturer, adds brown pigment to the absorbent wood-fiber material used in its environmentally positioned disposable baby diapers and training pants in order to reinforce the perception of natural and sustainable sourcing, thus demanding a premium price.[6] These are major mental barriers that have inhibited the penetration and proliferation of many more-sustainable products.

Companies are not currently creating innovative green-positioned products at a rate in proportion to the growth in sustainable consumer sentiment. Smart companies can overcome these market barriers and close this gap, capturing consumers just waiting for someone to provide them the exact quality, cost, availability, and sustainability combination that they crave. Great examples of smart companies catering to sustainability-minded consumers include Chipotle, Whole Foods, and Patagonia. Consumers will happily vote with their dollars, euros, or yen for sustainable companies that provide products or services that make them compromise the least, or ideally not at all.

2. Communicate Sustainability in a Personal and Relevant Way

Another challenge affecting consumers and companies is the nearly constant noise of sustainability messaging. Words like "green," "eco-friendly," and "ethically sourced" have become so ubiquitous as to render them nearly meaningless. There's a reason for these succinct messages – today's issues are complex and interwoven; few labels could fit a full sustainability explanation. There is power in simplicity, but educated consumers aren't simpletons. Marketers need to make sure that their communications capture the complexity of sustainability in order for consumers to believe that a brand or company is being transparent and truthful.

In addition, if businesses really want sustainability to become mainstream, thus garnering a significant market share, they need to lead with and deliver on messages and attributes that consumers do in fact care about – style, price, function, and all the traditional aspects of utility and appeal – and only then let sustainability attributes serve as the figurative "icing" rather than the "cake."

To maximize the impact of sustainability communication, companies need to make sure they are consciously addressing "the what" and "the who" of their products in precise ways.

THE WHAT

Michael Wilde, communications and sustainability manager at Eosta, an international distributor of fresh organic fruits and vegetables whose "trace and tell" system provides transparency to consumers, advises businesses to adopt the "what's in it for me?" approach when communicating with their customers or consumers. Only then will these important stakeholders grasp the concept of how their purchases directly or indirectly have a positive effect on them or on loved ones. In turn, this realization will cause such purchases to become routine.[7] This starts with me and then extends to my family, then to the broader community, followed by the nation, and last, the planet (see Figure 2.3).

For example, GE launched a hybrid water heater with a simple message: "For the first time consumers have near total control over

Figure 2.3. Bullseye chart illustrating sustainability impact

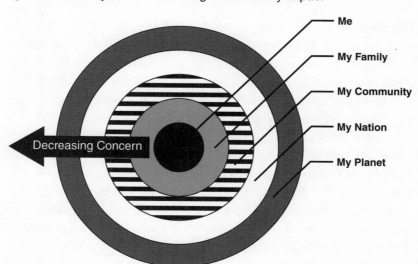

how much energy they use to heat water for the home." These produce over twice as much hot water for each unit of electricity consumed as any other type of electric water heater (storage or tankless).[8] The ability to forgo tradeoffs and actually deliver superior performance or value is a powerful message and resonates well with consumers. There are countless examples of products positioned with green features or benefits that are simply not compelling enough on their own to drive purchase, so they find themselves in retailers' clearance aisles.

Kimberly-Clark (K-C) took a similar approach for their tissue brand Scott Naturals, which resonated well with consumers. They discovered that the brand and its product positioning was most effective when their sustainability-focused messaging conveyed personal, empowering actions that its target consumer base identified with. For example, K-C's Scott Naturals Tube-free bath tissue ads stress the absurdity of the astronomical number of bath tissue tubes discarded every day in American homes and then offers consumers an affordable and innovative alternative product that eliminates the waste-associated guilt and inconvenience.

THE HOW

Whatever companies claim about being green, they will add credibility to these claims when they ensure that the performance of their products and services matches consumer expectations. While this seems obvious, far too many corporations do not interweave their sustainability function with their business processes when designing and producing their end products and services. Sustainability does not work well as an add-on consideration or as a stand-alone business function. It works best when viewed as a business imperative, as a viable means to better meet business objectives and sales growth, and then integrated into business processes.

There is another trap that many sustainably managed companies fall into: only focusing on their positive results rather than presenting a balanced account of their progress on their sustainability journey. Consumers may view the unbalanced reporting and communication approach as an attempt to hide or downplay negative results, or even as a lack of authenticity on the part of the company. Consumers and other stakeholders often assess such communications as the business falsely touting corporate sustainability and responsibility with no real action or data to back it up. Being perceived as authentic and upfront is critical in the digital age; otherwise consumers will ultimately negatively tweet about it.

In the spirit of transparency and authenticity, Patagonia created the *Footprint Chronicles*, in which they share how and where 30 of their products are made, communicating both good and bad sustainability aspects of their value chain. As a result, consumers reward Patagonia with a virtually unwavering belief in Patagonia's commitment to the planet.

This is all about transparency and authenticity. Smart, sustainable companies are finding ways to credibly become more transparent and authentic than their competitors. Through the Sustainability Consortium, Walmart and 20 other large companies are collaborating with global NGOs, academic institutions, and governmental agencies, working together to create what they refer to as a Sustainability Index. If its creators are successful, this index will eventually provide consumers the ability to determine the most sustainable product offering in any product category, on the shelf or online, regardless of what labels and associated manufacturers' advertising claim.

This may mean that smart, sustainability-minded consumers will continue to upgrade their expectations of companies to address environmental and social impacts associated with their products or services, and smart companies will strive to provide products that rise above this bar. For example, GE voluntarily holds all of its Ecomagination-certified products to higher sustainability standards than those offered by its competitors.

THE WHO

The millennial, or Generation Y, demographic (born 1981–2003) is the most opportune place to start when considering where sustainability-related trends are heading. This group of varied individuals are the future decision-makers and influencing agents of the planet.

Sustainability has been embedded in the millennial purchasing agenda from the beginning of their shopping careers. They are extremely discerning consumers. Generation Y is absolutely going to be voting for sustainability with their dollars for decades to come. They're not listening to traditional advertising. They're actively communicating among themselves. They are all cognizant of the world's problems and challenges, and they are a completely different breed from previous generations of consumers.

A defining characteristic of millennials is the way technology shapes their lives. They see social media as a force for change and use it to share experiences and opinions that shape behavior. Millennials also seek to connect digitally with brands to make a difference – or even change the world.

Brands that communicate best with this generation provide an effective digital platform, with the overarching objective of creating incremental or even transformational behavioral change toward a more sustainable future. This digital platform works best with transparency, while the most successful brands also provide inspiring content regarding what that future can be. Companies that do not paint a picture of a better future and a path to achieve it will be outcompeted.

Unilever's Real Beauty campaign, for example, seeks to redefine beauty and improve girls' and women's self-esteem. Their message is that true beauty comes from the inside out, removing the oppressive and damaging stereotypes pervasive in the media and society at large.

3. Educate Consumers on the Product Life Cycle Way of Thinking

Sustainability-focused consumers located in the United States and elsewhere increasingly expect companies supplying sustainable products and services to address their full life cycle impact, which encompasses four basic aspects of production.[9]

- sourcing inputs or materials responsibly (e.g., sustainable agriculture, respecting workers' rights, avoiding conflict minerals);
- making a product (e.g., minimizing the natural/nonrenewable resources consumed, such as the oil or mineral used to manufacture it);

- using a product (e.g., creating a product that requires less water or electricity to use or is designed to last longer);
- disposing of a product or end-of-life considerations (ensuring it is recyclable, compostable, or biodegradable or that manufacturers take the product back, as with large appliances or electronics producers and retailers).

To determine the environmental impact of each activity, companies can conduct or commission life cycle assessments (LCAs) of their products and services and then make these LCAs publicly available. A thorough, well-considered LCA should assess the magnitude and sources of impacts of a product or service across its entire value chain. Surprisingly, often the most significant environmental impacts arise from unexpected sources or activities, for example, in use of the product or in the disposal of the product. Knowledge of the origin of impacts through a product or service's life cycle can lead to innovative new products, services, and processes; big cost savings; and compelling and persuasive consumer messaging.

For example, Kimberly-Clark's LCA for bath tissue uncovered the fact that out of the total water consumed in the manufacture and use of this product, only 30 percent was attributable to the actual paper production, while a surprising 70 percent was attributed to the flushing of toilets with post-consumer use. With this finding in hand, K-C focused more of their water-conservation sustainability strategy at the point at which the biggest impact could be achieved – disposal. They created the consumer Smart Flush campaign in an attempt to encourage and enable consumers to reduce the water consumed during toilet flushing – inserting a specially designed bag into toilet tanks at their homes – thus reducing the water during flushing by one quart each time. This engaged consumers in reducing water use with every flush, saving money and water and better reflecting their values.

Procter & Gamble's LCA for laundry detergents ultimately resulted in the development of successful new products that offered the consumer an option to consume less energy in the laundry process. Their studies indicated that 50 percent of the energy consumed in the laundry process could be attributed to heating the water used in clothes washers. This led to the birth of Tide Coldwater Clean laundry detergent and several similar offerings from other manufacturers that clean effectively in cold water. These new sustainably positioned product offerings are marketed by touting the benefit of saving energy while getting the same performance the consumer expects from their normal detergent.

4. Encourage Consumer Participation in the Proper Disposal of Products

Consumers are voicing concerns about the environmental and social impacts of the post-use disposal of their products and associated packaging. This is an area in which consumers feel they have some control as well as some responsibility. Increasingly, consumers consider the method of disposal at the point of purchase. Sustainable packaging is often one of the earliest forays into sustainability for many businesses, as consumers widely perceive packaging as inevitable waste. This could entail simply minimizing packaging or making packaging compatible with recycling streams.

The disposal part of the product life cycle extends far beyond packaging. Kimberly-Clark recognized that their responsibility doesn't stop at the shelf but extends all the way through to post-consumer use. They invested in a program and technology designed to collect soiled baby diapers and then convert them into usable compost and energy. This collection scheme was first piloted in New Zealand to demonstrate a win-win partnership with governments and business and was subsequently expanded.

Patagonia provides a best-in-class example of closed-loop and mindful consumption. They are assuming responsibility for the resources they consume in the products they manufacture, from resource acquisition to disposal, and demonstrating how the closed-loop consumption model can work. To drive home the company's position, Yuon Chouinard, founder of Patagonia, recently stated, "Think twice before you buy a product from us. Do you really need it or are you just bored and want to buy something? Then we're taking responsibility for our product forever. If it breaks down, we promise to fix it. We're going to come out with little booklets and videos showing people how to repair their Patagonia stuff themselves and when you're finally either tired of the product or you've outgrown it or whatever, we're going to help you get rid of it. We're doing deals with eBay that you can sell it. And we're going to start selling used Patagonia stuff in our stores. And then when the product is finally finished, give it back to us, and we'll make more product from it. So it forces us to make products that don't wear out, but it also forces us to design a product so that it can be recycled."[10]

There can be no question in consumers' minds about where a company stands on sustainability. In addition to this clarity and transparency, the real competitive advantage is building processes that make it easy for consumers to take more-sustainable action. In this way, sustainability goes from something abstract and uncomfortable to something simple and personal – choices that help people feel they can make a real difference. People will likely pay top dollar to attain that feeling.

5. Engage Consumers on Sustainable Consumption
and the Societal Impact of Products and Services

Getting the world's consumers to consume more sustainably is a long-term behavior change issue. The required support and necessary change will come about only after all stakeholders partake in that behavior.

Overconsumption is a difficult problem from every angle. The first challenge is getting enough people, and businesses, to believe that overconsumption is actually happening and is a substantial issue. Statistics about depleted oil reserves, biodiversity, deforestation, or melting ice caps do little to motivate individual consumer or business behavior. These concepts are too abstract and distant to be tangible to most consumers and many businesses. Even arguments that point to the expected rapid increase in energy and water costs, which will erode corporate bottom lines over time, do very little to move most corporate leaders.

This is partly because, in developed countries, consumers and businesses remain relatively sheltered from global trends and resource scarcity in their daily lives. They rarely feel the strain or see any of the real consequences of overconsumption.

Furthermore, in the developed world, there is very little resource scarcity for anyone above the poverty line. They have few experiences that would serve to alter that perception. For generations, the majority of people in the developed world have had access to virtually anything they've needed from a consumer goods perspective.

There is little evidence to suggest that consumption has any correlation with improved health and happiness of individuals or of society as a whole. In the United States, where consumption and consumerism are a way of life, rates of chronic disease including heart disease,[11] cancers,[12] obesity,[13] and autoimmune-related illnesses[14] continue to rise. In fact, the United States is near the bottom of the wealthiest countries in terms of children living in poverty (one in three).[15] It has also been found that American's subjective measures of happiness have slightly declined.[16] In summary, the consumption model is not the equation for a healthy or happy life.

An opportunity exists in the developed world to promote new, more sustainable ways to consume – ways that run counter to the message that consumers as a society have received for the past 60 years. They have been conditioned in the developed world to pursue the accumulation of stuff or possessions, to purchase the biggest and best of what they can afford. Consequently, individual success is often measured by the total of accumulated things. But in reality, things do very little to make them happy or healthy, or to allow them to live lives of which they are proud.

There are major trends taking place within the millennial generation to change this. "Downshifting" is a fairly popular cultural phenomenon, where millennials choose to work less and consume less, all for the benefit of more free time to allow them to live their unencumbered lives as they please.

The most persuasive arguments for less consumption, therefore, still come down to personal convictions and beliefs. What do individuals want their lives to mean, to contribute, and to leave in the world – their legacy? It's going to take many, many people making the right, sustainable personal choices to dramatically alter the current trend of overconsumption.

Fortunately, many people are beginning to ask these questions and challenge the status quo. These people are also consumers. They increasingly seek out businesses that act sustainably and that develop deep relationships to win over consumers' loyalty. They demand more-sustainable consumption, and business leaders can make choices that address their views and recruit these consumers as active members in sustainable business models. These choices not only will begin to address the overconsumption problem but will also provide an opportunity to create a sustainable competitive advantage.

With all the sustainability-focused market data in hand, one might be led to believe that saving the planet is on the absolute top of the list of consumers' priorities, but it's not. According to Gallup (a leading global polling agency), terrorism emerged as the top concern among Americans following the numerous terror attacks in 2015, including San Bernardino, California, and Paris. In 2016, government and the economy have resumed top-ranking positions on Gallup's list of the most important problems.[17] At times, it seems the world is terrified for their personal safety and that of their families. So while there is a growing sustainability pull from consumers, they still have other, bigger concerns. Sustainable consumption will only become mainstream when businesses, governments, and consumers fully support this endgame.

One obvious retort to this idea is the fundamental desire of most businesses: they want their customers to buy more. How can we encourage the concept of less consumption but more revenue?

Less consumption and more revenue are not necessarily opposing objectives and can in fact coexist. Some time ago, the business world was introduced to the concept that if all consumer products were viewed as delivering services, then we (businesses and society) might be able to begin to decouple profits and consumerism from unsustainable consumption. The best example to illustrate this is the incandescent light bulb. If a lighting company is viewed as being in the business of providing light to consumers or companies as a service, rather than selling consumable light bulbs, it would strive to innovatively deliver light in the most resource-efficient and cost-effective way due to competitive pressures and profit. Consider this model versus the current one, which encourages businesses to supply consumers with low-cost, resource-intensive, disposable incandescent light bulbs that are designed to expire, be disposed of in landfills, and be replaced/repurchased to provide continual profits.

Several businesses are making profitable opportunities out of the desire to consume less. Millennials generally don't want to own one of everything; they often want to rent or share certain assets. They believe more in the "sharing culture" than the "ownership culture." This has given a boost to new companies collectively worth billions, like Zipcar, Uber, and Airbnb, all of which find latent value in stranded assets.

Marks & Spencer, as they strive to build sustainability into their own branded products, are making it easier for consumers to reduce the packaging waste associated with their food products by removing 20 percent of packaging and driving their "love food, hate waste" campaign. This is another no-compromise approach that allows M&S to build repeat customers with sustainable goals while continuing to grow.

General Electric is commanding a premium for building smart capabilities into its appliances so that consumers can better control, even remotely, their usage pattern to conserve energy. These smart appliances have embedded data control centers that can support management of household energy use. Nest, owned by Google, is another great example of how consumers can control the home environment by simply managing the thermostat remotely with their iPhone, thus reducing their energy consumption. The tension between more corporate profits and reduced consumption is resolved when a business focuses on making consumption smarter and ensuring that this more intelligent mode of consumption is well communicated to consumers.

Suresh Ariaratnam, a literary agent for Surya Lumen, which covers nonfiction topics from Buddhism to the benefits of financially

valuing the natural environment, writes, "If businesses were to engage with customers not simply as consumers but as citizens, it
would be a meaningful acknowledgment of the existence of something much larger."[18]

Case Study: Brita Products, Clorox

Background

A German entrepreneur invented the Brita water-filtration pitcher in
1970. The Brita filter used a carbon and ion exchange resin to remove
impurities like lead and chlorine from water. Brita Germany did not
have success with penetrating the U.S. market and was looking for
partners to grow the business. Clorox purchased the U.S. distribution
rights for the Brita brand and technology in 1988, as Clorox deemed
the Brita brand presented a growth opportunity and a foray into the
growing bottled water category, while simultaneously addressing
consumer concerns about water quality, especially lead content.

Clorox's initial focus was on educating consumers and promoting
the Brita filter's benefits (i.e., "makes tap water taste great" while
removing impurities like lead and chlorine). The distribution expansion plan and increased marketing investment started to pay
off, as Brita turned profitable by 1993. Consumers associated Brita
filters with providing clear, clean, refreshing water, and that made
them feel they were doing something good for themselves, which
helped reposition the brand.

By focusing on natural imagery and by leveraging associated
emotional benefits, Brita continued its successful ride. U.S. household penetration rose to 18 percent, brand awareness to 70 percent,
and distribution to over 70 percent of target accounts. Brita was well
positioned as a profitable, growing brand in the Clorox arsenal, and
by the late 1990s it averaged a 40 percent year-on-year growth rate.

In June 1999, Brita missed its launch date for a new faucet-mount
water-filtration system and faced aggressive promotion from its ri-
val brand, PUR. Both factors affected sales. Despite its first setback,

in 2000 Clorox purchased sole rights in North America to the Brita brand, which by then had become synonymous with its Brita pitchers, thus ending its 12-year-old licensing-and-distribution agreement with Brita GmbH.

By 2003, the Brita team had reversed the volume decline driven by growth in pour-through systems, thanks to the introduction of Brita "smart" pitchers with electronic filter change indicators. The brand then expanded with innovations like the AquaView faucet-mount filtration system, which lets consumers see what the product is removing and features an electronic indicator light that reminds consumers when it's time to change the filter. Despite the consistent stream of innovations, the middle of that decade was a challenging time for the brand. The growth of the bottled water business, which touted the advantages of convenience and sourcing from the natural mountain springs, had started to impact the business. Brita was no longer the darling brand for the Clorox Company.

In 2007, Clorox announced that although the Brita brand remained quite profitable, its sales had stagnated as consumers who focused on convenience were increasingly buying bottled water rather than filtered tap water. Clorox's chairman and chief executive, Don Knauss, said in an interview, "It has not grown in the last five years, it's been a real challenge and I think it's because it's flying in the face of the convenience. We're going to give another effort against figuring out how to grow it." He said, "I think it's (the Brita brand) going to be a reasonable timeline. In the next one to two years, we've got to figure out what we're going to do with this business if not even before that."[19]

The Turnaround

In 2008, Bill Morrissey's sustainability team and the Brita brand team hunkered down, studied the emerging consumer trends, and decided to reposition the brand to capitalize on sustainability and convenience.

The idea was to encourage consumers to kick their bottled water habit and reduce plastic bottle waste. Brita's new consumer

Figure 2.4. Brita System: Pitcher and Bottle

Source: Clorox Company

proposition urged people to replace bottled water with filtered water, thus reducing packaging and energy use. This concept, which
grew big and became the centerpiece of Brita's advertising later in
2009, started with a request from the City of San Francisco to develop a filtered water bottle that could replace bottled water.

U.S. consumer demand for bottled water from retail outlets such
as grocery and convenience stores and gas stations has reached the
billions of gallons.[20] By and large, environmentally conscious consumers seek products that reduce landfill waste or help the planet in
some way. The Brita filter replaces 300 plastic water bottles. It is estimated that Americans dispose of over two million tons of polyeth-
ylene bottles each year. Reducing that amount by even a small
amount is a step toward social responsibility.[21]

The new concept led Brita to introduce a Brita-branded filtered
water bottle (Figure 2.4), partnering with Nalgene Outdoor Products
and kicking off the "Filter for Good" online public relations program, which urged people to pledge to replace bottled water with
filtered water. Bono, the leader of the blockbuster band U2, contacted Clorox requesting that Brita become the sole source of all of the
water backstage at U2 concerts. The Sundance Film Festival made a

similar request. Clorox was also able, through paid contract, to have NBC's *The Biggest Loser* show substitute all bottled water from its set with Brita Nalgene bottles.[22] These are the opportunities available for branding with a cause.

The Filter for Good campaign was focused on Gen X and Gen Y consumers, who are more attuned to change and sustainable behavior. Filter for Good was started as a PR idea in partnership with Nalgene. The website FilterForGood.com allowed people to get information on where to purchase the products or, more importantly, what they can do to make a difference. Though started as a grassroots idea, the PR campaign gained so much traction that Brita actually altered the broad-scale mass-media message to reflect that as well. The campaign created a demand by appealing to the growing public concern for the environment caused by unnecessary consumption of bottled water. The campaign teaches consumers about bottled water waste, including how much money they can save each year, and encourages them to demonstrate their commitment by switching to reusable bottles and filtered tap water.

At FilterForGood.com, consumers can pledge to switch to reusable water bottles filled with home-filtered water. Brita explains how making the pledge takes only seconds but can have a long-term effect on the earth by helping to reduce the more than 60 million plastic water bottles thrown away every day in the United States.

Brita's in-store message, "Better Water, Less Waste," ties strongly to the online campaign and to the intersection of three key consumer megatrends they are tapping to drive growth: health and wellness, sustainability, and affordability.

In addition, in January 2009, the Brita brand teamed up with Preserve, a leading maker of 100 percent recycled household consumer goods, to collect and recycle Brita pitcher filters. Through Preserve's Gimme 5 programs, Brita pitcher filters can be dropped off at select retail locations or shipped directly to Preserve for recycling. There, the plastic is transformed into new Preserve products like toothbrushes and razors.

The Brita brand continued to innovate and, in 2011, added the Brita On-the-Go bottle (Figure 2.5), which includes a filter inside that helps remove the taste of chlorine. Based on extensive research about "on-the-go" consumers, the bottle allows people to use any drinking fountain or tap water source and still drink filtered Brita water. The Brita On-the-Go bottle is free of BPA (bisphenol A), dishwasher safe, and recyclable.

By combining consumer insights, internal strengths, external capabilities, and expertise, Clorox successfully repositioned the Brita brand at the sweet spot where health and wellness, sustainability, and convenience meet. Building on this success, in fiscal year 2012, the team redesigned the original bottle and launched a new Brita bottle for kids. The kids' bottle is dishwasher safe, BPA-free, and recyclable. Both contain a replaceable activated carbon filter to purify water. It claims to removes chlorine, metals, bad tastes, foul odors, and other contaminants. As concerns about childhood

Figure 2.5. Brita On-the-Go bottle

Source: Clorox Company

obesity grow, the new smaller and more colorful bottles serve to help encourage healthier drinking habits at a young age, while also reinforcing a message of sustainability.

KEY TAKEAWAYS

- Consumers are voting with their dollars for products that align with their personal values.
- Consumers are increasingly willing to pay higher prices for more-sustainable products and services.
- Companies must communicate sustainability in an authentic and transparent way, focusing on consumers' motivations.
- Companies should educate, engage, and encourage consumers on sustainability topics like mindful consumption, life cycle thinking, and proper product disposal.

To effectively *drive the top-line growth with triple-bottom-line thinking* **with consumers, a company should:**
1. Design and promote products and services to make consumption meaningful.
2. Take a mission-driven approach when marketing sustainable products and services.
3. Communicate their sustainability story in a way consumers find personal and relevant.
4. Actively engage consumers using social media, online, and word-of-mouth communication.
5. Educate, educate, educate consumers.

3 Collaborating with Customers

Our goal in everything we do is to create a better, smarter, more connected future because we know that life is better when everyone and everything works together.

Randall Stephenson,
AT&T chairman and CEO[1]

Figure 3.1. Sustainability stakeholders framework:
Collaborating with customers

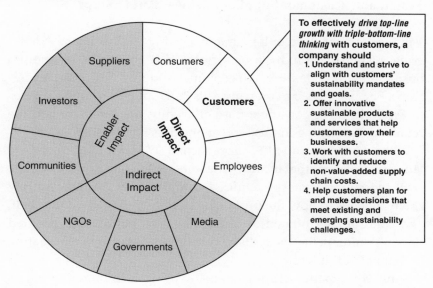

To effectively *drive top-line growth with triple-bottom-line thinking* with customers, a company should
1. Understand and strive to align with customers' sustainability mandates and goals.
2. Offer innovative sustainable products and services that help customers grow their businesses.
3. Work with customers to identify and reduce non-value-added supply chain costs.
4. Help customers plan for and make decisions that meet existing and emerging sustainability challenges.

We define "customers" broadly to include all business-to-business (B2B) relationships, where the businesses obtain or purchase products or services from finished-product manufacturers and service providers (supplier businesses) for internal consumption and/or resale. Typical B2B customers include retailers, distributors, or even other service businesses like consultants, media agencies, and financial firms. They may be both brick-and-mortar (those with a physical location) and Internet-based businesses.

Customers in B2B relationships in virtually every market are under increasing pressure to provide access to more sustainable product and service choices that will better enable them to meet their consumers' needs and expectations and compete in their field. This creates an opportunity for supplier businesses to engage with their customers on a more multidimensional strategic level. By bringing sustainability and its related motivators into the B2B equation, suppliers and companies are able to not only leverage partnerships for competitive advantage but also drive sustainability issues throughout and around their organizations.

Sustainable Customer-Supplier Business Partnerships

Value chains for developing, manufacturing, and ultimately delivering sustainable products or services to a consumer, or another business entity, often involve customer-supplier business partnerships. For example, if a company sells its products through a retailer to access its large consumer base efficiently, the company and the retailer are engaging in this type of business partnership.

When Unilever and P&G approached Walmart about compact laundry detergent that includes the same product in a bottle half the size, the simple concept required complex and dramatic supply chain changes in how the product is stored, presented on the shelf, and conceptually offered to consumers. The partnership resulted not only in reducing the costs to consumers but also in eliminating potential landfill waste.

Similarly, a manufacturing company using distributors to sell its products to other businesses is engaged in this type of partnership.

Brick-and-mortar business partners may include retailers such as Target, Walmart, Costco, Lowes, Tesco, Kingfisher, and IKEA or distributors such as United Natural Foods Inc. (UNFI).

Alternatively, finished-product manufacturing companies or service companies may choose to sell or distribute their products through web-based businesses, which generally enjoy lower operating costs and greater distribution and sales flexibility (e.g., Amazon and Alibaba).

While these business partnerships are not uncommon, sustainability partnership opportunities are often incredibly underused or even completely overlooked by partnering companies. All retailers (especially big-box retailers) and distributors are almost certainly interested in partnerships that ensure the long-term sustainability of their businesses. Such partnerships often result in the growth of sales, profits, reputation, employee satisfaction, and community engagement – all of which are necessary for the achievement of their long-term business goals. Yet each retailer or distributor sees the impact of sustainability on their own business strategy slightly differently and often with a short-term focus.

By studying the sustainability strategy of the customer, a supplier business can recognize the key focal points that they share with the customer and those that are different. This can serve as a strong foundation for a mutually rewarding partnership of sustainability.

Not unlike product value chains, value chains for developing and delivering services to consumers or other business entities often benefit from the development of sustainability-focused partnerships. Service partners may include, for example, the Yellow Pages, which produces both hard-copy and online business directories that support thousands of goods and services providers. As consumers spend more time online, digital services will become more relevant to customers and increase the opportunities to create deep, integrated customer-consumer relationships. As an example, the web-based service provider company Angie's List now claims to have more than two million members and about $220 million in annual revenue.

Relationships that result in the delivery of a service rather than a product often enjoy a deeper level of interaction with consumers or client companies. Despite this difference, many of the opportunities for mutually reinforced sustainability successes between finished-product and service provider partners are similar.

Reputation is of ultimate importance to virtually every business. Every sustainable product or service that a retailer puts on its shelves or that a distributor sells to businesses presents an opportunity for them to enhance their company brand reputation and, in turn, provides an opportunity for a supplier's business brands to build equity as well. This shared elevation of brand equity provides a tremendous opportunity for significant added value for all participants across the value chain.

There are various roles that customers can play in the marketplace and online, as well as within the community at large, to promote sustainable product choices to their consumers. By aligning themselves with sustainable mindsets and gaining an understanding of each partner's role, customers and supplier businesses can advance their individual and collective strategic missions and accomplish their respective sustainability objectives and goals.

In many instances where sustainability initiatives and standards are mandated by governments, effective marketing (orchestrated through partnerships between suppliers and retailers) is the only way to persuade consumers to be mindful of their respective roles in compliance. While this marketing activity may be limited to the retailer's customers, it can also be directed internally toward employees or outwardly toward the community. Collaborative customers and suppliers may even band together to lobby the government for sustainable progress; for instance, lead-free gasoline was brought about through automobile makers working with oil companies, resulting in a ban on lead additives in gasoline by the U.S. EPA in the mid-90s.

There are two basic types of customer-supplier business partnerships that provide strategic opportunities to work together to deliver sustainability-related benefits to consumers and societies and increased value for all parties. These include (1) collaborations with customers to deliver sustainable products and services efficiently and (2) partnerships to enhance and advance the sustainability of an entire industry.

Collaborating with Customers to Deliver
Sustainable Products and Services

There are eight practices that customer businesses almost universally undertake which serve as opportunities for supplier businesses to engage, influence, and collaborate with them to drive sustainability and, in doing so, to build competitive advantage: choice editing, choice promoting, consumer education, environmental footprint reduction, employee engagement, community development, sustainability forums and conferences, and asset optimizing of products and services. The best thing a supplier business can do is to identify and influence areas in which customers and buyers have decided to pursue sustainability. Only then is it possible to effectively support and engage them on these decisions in their business plans.

CHOICE EDITING

Sally Uren, chief executive at the nonprofit Forum for the Future, noted that though retailers choice edit (decide which product offerings are available to their shoppers) on a daily basis, it's not always through the lens of sustainability. This presents an opportunity for a supplier company to help the retailer make sustainably sound strategic editing choices. A supplier company has a better chance of influencing the editing criteria of the categories in which they compete if their products or services align with the customer's sustainability vision and strategies. The supplier company can then better communicate how their products relate to editing decisions and help their partner enhance their image and long-term sales goals.

Smart supplier businesses consider whether their products or services can be positioned in such a way as to deliver an enhanced value proposition while maintaining a lower environmental footprint and/or deliver positive societal impacts. Additionally, if possible, they reinforce this positioning with appropriate credentials or certifications. This can provide the competitive edge a supplier business needs to make or close a transaction and form a long-term partnership that powers success.

One strategic way to promote sustainability with customers is to educate them so that they exclusively carry products that achieve certain environmental or socially focused certifications or credentials. These preferred certifications vary from customer to customer and may include the FSC (Forest Stewardship Council) for wood/ paper, the EPA (Environmental Protection Agency) for energy, the MSC (Marine Stewardship Council) for fish, or at times retailer-defined sustainability criteria. In addition, by meeting these retailers' defined criteria, qualified products or services might command higher margins or price points at the shelf or online.

With a modern globalized trade, most companies participate in annual, or more frequent, business planning exercises, outlining strategies, and activities that often include aspects of sustainability. Smart supplier businesses engage and educate customers about sustainability trends in their category. They often share consumer research or insights that highlight their products, services, sustainability-related benefits, or credentials. These give product or service providers the means to defend why their particular offering will help customers reach their sustainability goals more effectively than those offered by the competition. These steps not only help maintain a supplier business's shelf presence during annual planogram exercises but also potentially increase the number of finished products or services the customer chooses to carry.

For example, Kimberly-Clark developed a bathroom tissue that was FSC certified and featured bamboo as an alternate wood-fiber source; as a result, the product had no difficulty securing additional shelf space at Tesco in the United Kingdom, as Tesco had already embraced FSC certification for all their private-label products as part of their sustainable procurement practices. Such a move further reinforces their image as progressive sustainability leaders.

Companies who produce certified organic, non-GMO, gluten-free, or Fair Trade products have an opportunity to promote these products at Whole Foods Market, which has devised a comprehensive sustainability rating system for fresh produce and flowers in an attempt to encourage responsible production. This system involves quantification by third-party certification bodies. Many supplier businesses might be intimidated by such rigorous standards, but smart suppliers will see this as an opportunity to position themselves as uniquely capable of serving their partners' standards and desired offerings to the end consumer.

CVS Pharmacy recently made a bold move, publicly announcing the elimination of all tobacco products from their shelves. While their decision may hurt sales in the short term, CVS believes they will develop a stronger bond with their consumers by strengthening their corporate position on a healthcare platform. Companies providing products to CVS would be more likely to build sales by pitching how their products could help CVS further reinforce their healthcare platform in their consumers' minds.

Supplier businesses wishing to sell their products through UNFI, the leading independent national distributor of natural, organic, and specialty foods and related products in the United States, whose customers include Whole Foods and Trader Joe's, must first meet stringent sustainability criteria. UNFI extensively vets products and suppliers before agreeing to distribute their products.

Smart, sustainable supplier businesses often do their research and talk to the end consumers regularly to uncover current and emerging concerns and issues. Associating and aligning with like-minded customer partners will in turn help a supplier business promote its own sustainable agenda. Clorox introduced concentrated bleach, which saved customers valuable shelf space and lowered Clorox's environmental footprint for this product. Clorox did its research and educated both customers and consumers about how to properly use the bleach to maximize cost efficiency and environmental advantages.

When the end user of a customer's product or service is a business, there are common selling propositions already in play that can be attached to sustainability outcomes. Common selling propositions are lower cost-in-use for a product and increasing productivity of the end user business; both of these propositions lead to higher profitability and improved sustainability outcomes. A good example of an effective sustainable product and selling proposition in the B2B market is Georgia Pacific's e-Motion paper towel dispensers. By dispensing one sheet at a time, they eliminate wasteful consumption in bathrooms and deliver a more hygienic solution for their customers (distributors).

CISCO Systems offers a host of business productivity tools, including online meetings and videoconferencing systems, which have improved their businesses' client effectiveness as well as efficiency for customers by eliminating costs while simultaneously reducing the environmental impacts associated with travel.

CHOICE PROMOTING

Almost every customer uses promotions to motivate end consumers to purchase their products or services. Customers seeking to promote a sustainably focused image often preferentially promote products that meet their preferred certification standards or those that address their stated sustainability goals. Supplier businesses have an opportunity to garner increased trade and promotional support if the products carry a customer's desired certifications or if the promotional platform enables retailer to achieve their sustainability goals.

To illustrate this point, after IKEA committed to remove incandescent light bulbs from their shelves and website and to encourage their consumers to switch to energy-efficient LED bulbs, they requested assistance from their bulb suppliers. By collaborating with suppliers, IKEA innovated and produced new and more energy-efficient LED bulb offerings at attractive price points that would appeal to consumers. The initiative has benefited IKEA, who has seen rapid consumer acceptance of the new LED bulbs, as well as their suppliers, whose new product innovation's funding, at-scale pricing, and promotion soared with IKEA's backing.[2]

The Honest Company, cofounded by actress Jessica Alba and former CEO of Healthy Child Healthy World Christopher Gavigan, claims to differentiate itself from its competitors by providing non-toxic, eco-friendly, and aesthetically pleasing products that are affordable. Their selection of personal and home care products includes baby diapers, biodegradable wipes, organic skin care, and laundry detergent. In 2015, Target stores publicly shared that they would begin carrying Honest Company products in stores and at Target.com. Target felt that this action would support their goal of offering "better-for-you brands" to their shoppers.[3]

CONSUMER EDUCATION

Educating consumers about sustainable practices is a mammoth task but one that is especially ripe for partnership between customers and supplier businesses. Some sustainability education of the customer by the supplier business may first be necessary, as the supplier business likely has experts on staff on their specific categories of product offerings. When done correctly, successful collaboration can allow both partners to have a more significant impact and enable more effective sustainability strategies. For example, Kimberly-Clark partnered with Costco in a campaign designed to educate consumers about the merits of FSC certification and how it helps protect biodiversity and promote sustainable forestry practices. This campaign had the effect of creating more sustainably minded consumers and resulted in increased sales for K-C's tissue-based products.

The distributor UNFI monitors trends in natural and organic products and analyzes sales in the independent channel to highlight top new items and strong growth categories; UNFI provides future projections and consumer trends that its business partners can use to engage and educate their customers and end users.[4]

ENVIRONMENTAL FOOTPRINT REDUCTION

Customers are not only interested in improving their own environmental footprint but are often equally concerned about their suppliers' environmental footprint. They are also interested in ensuring that the supplier businesses that provide them products or services are held accountable for playing their respective roles in meeting environmental and social standards. Smart supplier businesses actively volunteer information, and even internal experts' time, to help inform the customer committees and sustainability teams responsible for creating policy or standards. This proactive stance ensures that good information is available to decision-makers within the customer's organization. For example, Walmart sets aggressive targets on their own environmental footprint as well as on the footprint embedded in their supply chain. They announced in 2010 their goal to cut 20 million tons of carbon creation from the supply chain by 2015. They recognized that this cannot happen with changes only in their internal operations' footprint; in fact, it will require significant participation by and contributions from supplier companies. Progressive companies – those wishing to be viewed as valued partners – can help Walmart meet their goals by showcasing how their products best align with Walmart's goals as a supplier.[5]

EMPLOYEE ENGAGEMENT

Both sustainability-minded customers and their supplier businesses have recognized that their employees can play a vital role in realizing their respective sustainability and competitive advantage visions. Both supplier businesses and customers can help each other in this endeavor to activate and engage their employees by sharing best practices and learning from each other. For example, Kimberly-Clark developed their Small Steps employee engagement program, which encourages their employees to take small steps like changing light bulbs to energy-efficient bulbs, bicycling or carpooling to work, or reducing the water flow from showers to help conserve valuable resources. They then openly shared the program elements with customers like Walmart. Walmart developed its own employee sustainability program it calls My Sustainability Plan (MSP), which is featured in the case study at the end of this chapter.

COMMUNITY DEVELOPMENT

Customers and their supplier businesses recognize that long-term success requires the prosperity of the communities they operate in and serve. That's why they often sponsor or enact programs that help communities address pressing social, environmental, and economic issues. These may include waste collection and disposal, sustainability education, or even helping local charities reach their goals. Supplier businesses can partner with customers on these programs, further enhancing their own image in the community and creating a symbiotic bond around the common good. For example, in Costa Rica, Kimberly-Clark teamed up with Walmart to collect waste paper in store. Costa Rica doesn't have a well-developed waste-paper collection system, so this effort not only helped address the local issue by encouraging a waste recycling infrastructure but it also provided to K-C inexpensive access to the raw materials critical to their ongoing success.

To promote consumption of more environmentally friendly products by consumers, Tesco Lotus and Unilever Thai Holding initiated a pilot project in Thailand. Unilever fueled green product consumer acceptance by reducing their retail cost and increasing availability at shelf. In an attempt to promote this initiative, Tesco Lotus formulated and launched their "Preventing Global Warming and Let's Go Green" campaign. This campaign was one of many local activities devised by the Tesco Group to reach their goal of halving their 2006 combined baseline carbon emissions by 2020.[6]

SUSTAINABILITY FORUMS AND CONFERENCES

Progressive customers want to be viewed as champions of sustainability and often engage not only suppliers' businesses and their customers/consumers but also like-minded retailers, academic institutions, and NGOs, helping to generate the required scale for their sustainability initiatives. Conferences and events provide opportunities for supplier businesses to showcase their offerings and connect with like-minded customers attempting to expand their sustainable products and services portfolios. For example, the Consumer Goods Forum is a global partnership involving progressive supplier companies and retailers with a goal to develop and promote sustainable practices and policies. By actively participating in the forum, companies are able to engage sustainably focused retailers and also to ensure that policies adopted by them are science-based, fair, and just for all, with the common goal to create a better future for the next generation.

The Sustainability Consortium is composed of retailers and suppliers, academics, governmental organizations, and NGOs that was seed funded by Walmart. The primary aim of the consortium is to define common sustainability standards and measurement tools across all retail product categories. Retailers want to know what companies are achieving on key sustainability metrics, and companies want to know the same from their suppliers. The Sustainability Consortium has developed what it calls category sustainability profiles, or CSPs, which retailers and members are using to develop tools to evaluate performance on key sustainability metrics; Walmart's Sustainability Index is one example.

Practice Greenhealth, the leading membership association for businesses and hospitals engaged in sustainable healthcare, presents the CleanMed Conference each year in collaboration with Health Care Without Harm, a campaign for enacting environmentally responsible healthcare and advocating for environmental health and justice across the globe. This conference is a forum for healthcare supply companies to showcase their sustainable products and services and to advance their healthcare customers' sustainability journeys.

ASSET OPTIMIZING OF ONLINE PRODUCTS AND SERVICES

In the last few years, consumer-focused supplier businesses and customer partnerships have entered a new era by applying online technology. As a result, new businesses regularly form that leverage the Internet to optimize and find value in latent assets and then provide this value to end users. These businesses challenge conventional wisdom and, in some cases, find new value where none existed before. They promote sustainable practices by focusing on sustainable consumption and often blur the boundary between the business provider and the end user. For example, thredUP, a fashion resale website, allows consumers to get value from unused clothes and allows these used clothes to be repurposed.

Uber is a ridesharing service that uses a smartphone application to connect passengers with drivers of vehicles for hire. This has created job opportunities for many and improved vehicle utilization.

Zipcar is the largest car-sharing and car club service. It is an alternative to traditional car rental and car ownership and provides automobile reservations to its members, billable by the hour or day, which eliminates waste and costs. Airbnb began in 2008 when two designers who had space in their own home to share hosted three travelers looking for a place to stay. Now, millions of hosts and travelers create free Airbnb accounts so they can list their space and book unique accommodations anywhere in the world. This has created monetary value for latent housing assets. Kardia by AliveCor is a smartphone application that allows a practicing doctor to administer an ECG (electrocardiogram) to a patient at home or at a remote location. This $300 app is changing the cost of healthcare services in dramatic fashion.

A similar evolution has taken place in which customers or other businesses are the end user, as an app or web portal allows smaller business players to have advantaged access to a market once reserved for only large businesses. This promotes sustainability by eliminating waste and extra costs and promoting social fairness. Alibaba has changed the B2B landscape across the world, especially in China, by allowing access to a large market of potential business customers for small businesses and sustainable providers that would not typically have had access to that customer set. By allowing companies to host their platforms on the cloud, companies like Amazon, IBM, and Microsoft are providing opportunities for small companies to succeed through lower cost and less waste in their IT infrastructure.

Industry Partnerships to Enhance Sustainability

These types of partnerships are most successful when facilitated by a neutral but interested third party, such as a nonprofit, that brings an entire industry together for improved sustainable advantage. Smart businesses seek out the right forums to join and take an active role in shaping the future of their industry. Each of the three "forum-like" organizations described below has delivered tangible tools and a clear roadmap for businesses that seek to enhance their industry for more sustainable success.

- The World Business Council for Sustainable Development (WBCSD) – a Geneva-based, CEO-led organization of forward-thinking companies – galvanizes the global business community to create a sustainable future for business, society, and the environment. Through its members, the WBCSD applies its respected thought leadership and effective advocacy to generate constructive solutions to drive business action on sustainability in the coming decade and beyond. One such tool is the Global Water Tool (GWT), a Microsoft Excel–based software tool designed to encourage sustainable water management practices by highlighting water consumption risks as well as opportunities. By employing this tool, interested companies create a water use map for a given site or watershed using a host of relevant factors including water, sanitation, and population, as well as biodiversity data sets and stress indicators. The GWT tool is capable of running future scenario plans, enabling companies to consider water risks related to their own operations, supply chains, and business plans.[7]
- Forum for the Future (FFTF) is an independent nonprofit working globally with businesses, governments, and other organizations to solve complex sustainability challenges. Their collaborative focus has been on transforming food, revolutionizing energy, and looking to future changes in telecommunication, fashion, finance, and tourism. For example, Tea 2030 is a collaborative initiative involving companies committed to forging a sustainable future for tea. The Tea 2030 partners, which collectively account for the majority of the world tea market, include tea suppliers S&D Coffee and Tea, Starbucks, Unilever, Tata Global Beverages, James Finlay, Ahmad Teas, and Yorkshire Tea, as well as several influential NGOs, such as Ethical Tea Partnership, Fairtrade International, IDH – the Sustainable Trade Initiative, and the Rainforest Alliance. If the Tea 2030 initiative is successful, tea will be regarded as a "hero

crop" by 2030, and the tea sector will provide the consumer commodity in an environmentally and socially responsible way. The partners' ultimate goals are to improve the lives of the people and conditions of the environment where tea is grown. Collectively, they seek to influence and educate customers and end consumers, leading to a sustainable and prosperous global industry.[8]

- The World Wildlife Fund (WWF) maintains a vision of building a future where human needs are met in harmony with nature. They have multiple industry forums in the areas of forestry, food, climate change, fresh water, and oceans. For example, in the forestry industry, WWF uses a multi-pronged approach to ensure that the world's most important forests are protected and properly managed and that these efforts are sustainably financed. They help get large areas of forest designated as protected areas so wildlife can roam free and so natural resources in the areas are not exploited. They created the Global Forest Trade Network (GFTN), where 200 companies and other entities interact to create a market for environmentally responsible forest products. On the consumption side, WWF encourages customers and governments to buy products with the FSC label, which ensures the product was made with material from a responsibly managed forest.[9]

Case Study: AT&T's Industry and Customer Collaboration to Advance Sustainability

BACKGROUND

AT&T Inc. is a 137-year-old company with more than $132 billion in revenues and more than a quarter million global employees. The products and services provided by AT&T include wireless communications, data/broadband and Internet services, video services, local exchange services, long-distance services, telecommunications equipment, managed networking, and wholesale services. The company offers its services and products to consumers, businesses, and other providers of telecommunications services in the United States and across the globe.

As with many other global companies, AT&T's history of sustainability can be viewed as another leg of its journey. After a series of mergers from 2003 to 2007, the company realized it needed to develop a common approach to sustainability. At about the same time, various external stakeholders started asking questions about the company's commitment to sustainability: policymakers were asking for energy and environmental reports, the investment community was proposing shareholder propositions, business customers were voicing their expectations, and the media demanded action. With these needs in mind, AT&T began developing its sustainability roadmap in 2008.

Figure 3.2. AT&T value-chain map

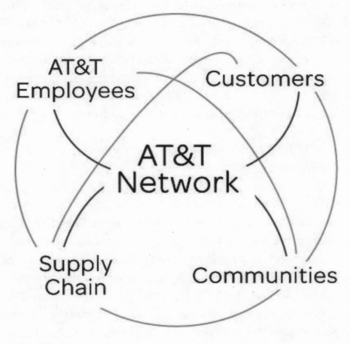

Source: AT&T Company

AT&T developed a "value chain" map showing an interconnected web where employees, customers, the supply chain, and communities are not only part of AT&T's network but are also connected to each other in a variety of ways (Figure 3.2). The map demonstrates how each member of its value chain is linked to others, as well as how and where environmental and social issues affect the value chain.

The company's current focus areas in sustainability include greenhouse gas emissions, human and labor rights, conflict minerals, lead acid batteries, energy efficiency, sustainable packaging, water, recycling, diversity, and ethics.[10]

For example, AT&T is very cognizant of the millions of mobile cellular devices that can be easily discarded when they become obsolete. The company focuses on the devices' entire life cycle – from design to recovery – to maximize sustainability. Gary Duffy, director of marketing at AT&T, stated, "Recycling your phone can be like finding money in the couch cushions! AT&T offers a store credit equal to the value of a phone that can be used on new devices, accessories or to pay a bill. For other, older, devices that may not have value, we will make sure that they are responsibly recycled, rather than have them end up in landfills. The EPA estimates that only 8 percent of cell phones are collected properly – a stat we aim to change."[11]

INDUSTRY COLLABORATION ON STANDARDIZING SUPPLY CHAIN
SUSTAINABILITY MEASUREMENTS

AT&T is working with QuEST Forum to develop a sustainability measurement model focused on sustainability-driven business improvement and profitability. QuEST Forum is a global communications association that is a unique partnership of industry service providers and suppliers dedicated to continuously improving products and services in their industry. The model offers a data-driven process that empowers companies to share and apply best practices. The goal is to provide the industry benchmarking methodology with holistic sustainability measures to drive business improvements and control costs. The model measures environment, resource management, carbon, corporate social responsibility, supply chain, stakeholder engagement, organizational capacity, eco-design, logistics, and circular economy. Companies using the model must demonstrate how they meet each measured criteria. Beyond QuEST and AT&T's immediate target audience of ICT (information and communications technology) companies, these metrics can easily be adopted and used by other industries as well.

INDUSTRY/CUSTOMER COLLABORATION TO ADDRESS AND SOLVE SOCIETAL ISSUES

Like many other countries, the United States' infrastructure is aging, and its water distribution infrastructure is no exception. According to the U.S. EPA, 30 percent of the pipes serving populations of more than 100,000 people are 40 to 80 years old. The United States, according to American Water Works Association, loses about seven billion gallons of water a day because of aging and leaky pipes. The World Bank estimates that water loss costs utilities an estimated $14 billion a year worldwide.[12]

These realities – and the facts that California and other areas in the west are now experiencing water shortages due to drought and the U.S. Government Accountability Office indicates 40 states will have at least one region facing a water shortage in the next decade – all point to the need for more efficient water solutions.

Working together with Mueller Water Products, AT&T is making possible a solution that can help detect leaks in water mains, enabling utilities to repair or replace the pipes before the leak causes significant damage. Acoustic sensors from Mueller Water Products placed along the pipes trigger alarms when they sense sound changes that may indicate leaks. AT&T's LTE network carries the sensor information to computing resources running a water management application.

The companies came together after the federal government issued an invitation for companies to showcase smart city solutions. Initially, the joint solution was a proof of concept for the U.S. Department of Commerce's National Institute of Standards and Technology (NIST) program 2015 Challenge, with related trials in Atlanta, Las Vegas, and

Los Angeles. The trial in Las Vegas, a leak-monitoring project run through Las Vegas Valley Water District, is a water-conservation showcase site for the Global City Teams Challenge. The AT&T and Mueller Water Products partnership is one example of a collaborative effort by project teams, working on innovative applications of IoT (Internet of things) technologies within a smart city/smart community environment (Figure 3.3).

"AT&T has been on the forefront of delivering smart water solutions," says Mobeen Khan, associate vice president of industrial IoT. "Within the U.S., this is a big deal because our water infrastructure is old and when there is an issue – a leak – it takes time to detect and fix that. Return on investment of this technology is fast, he adds, noting that the solution can be offered as a managed service or purchased."[13]

Although the water pipe system in this country is old (most pipes were installed in the 1950s), the cost of ripping out and replacing this infrastructure is tremendous – typically in excess of $1 million per mile.[14] A more tenable solution is to monitor pipes for leakage; technicians can address these problems, which sometimes go undetected for hours or days, as they occur.

Smart water solutions are merely the tip of the iceberg, so to speak, in the effort to apply machine-to-machine technology and the IoT to addressing sustainability issues. AT&T is promoting a collection of IoT solutions including Cargo View, Connected Jukebox, and Smart Bin. In 2015, 136 companies across numerous industries addressed difficult problems with the help of AT&T by entering into IoT agreements.[15]

AT&T CUSTOMER SUSTAINABILITY COLLABORATION EXAMPLE
HydroPoint, a leader in smart water management solutions targeting the area of greatest waste in urban water use landscape irrigation, uses an IoT, machine-to-machine solution in its WeatherTRAK smart irrigation collectors, which connect irrigation control points and sensors with climate analysis to determine exact water needs. The company chose AT&T to provide the wireless network,

Figure 3.3. Internet of things

Source: Google Open Art

customized network access, and a self-service management platform to support the data transport requirements. Each smart irrigation controller has its own subscriber identification module (SIM) card for each device, so each can be individually contacted for control and data collection. As a result of its solution, HydroPoint saved customers more than 15 billion gallons of water and $137 million in expenses in 2014 alone.[16] In a recent blog, Khan, of AT&T, stated, "These customers are from a diverse set of verticals that include agriculture, automotive, aviation, energy, health care, transportation, security and supply chain logistics. Although the range of our IoT solutions continues to expand and evolve, the purpose for creating them remains the same: to help businesses streamline processes, reduce costs, be more productive, and create new products and lines of businesses."[17]

KEY TAKEAWAYS

- Companies are partnering with customers and aligning their goals and initiatives to maximize synergistic benefits.
- Companies are designing their product and service offerings to meet customers' sustainability objectives.
- Companies must proactively participate in customers' choice promoting, consumer education, and employee engagement activities.
- Industry partnerships are increasingly employing company-customer collaboration to deliver societal benefits.
- B2B companies are realizing value from exploiting underutilized, latent assets across the value chain.

To effectively *drive the top-line growth with triple-bottom-line thinking* with customers, a company should:
1. Understand and strive to align with customers' sustainability mandates and goals.
2. Offer innovative sustainable products and services that help customers grow their businesses.
3. Work with customers to identify and reduce non-value-added supply chain costs.
4. Help customers plan for and make decisions that meet existing and emerging sustainability challenges.

4 Inspiring Employees

In a prosperous society, you really have only two assets: people – their creativity and skills – and the ecosystem around them. Both need to be carefully tended.

  Mats Lederhausen, former senior executive of McDonald's Corporation[1]

Figure 4.1. Sustainability stakeholders framework: Inspiring employees

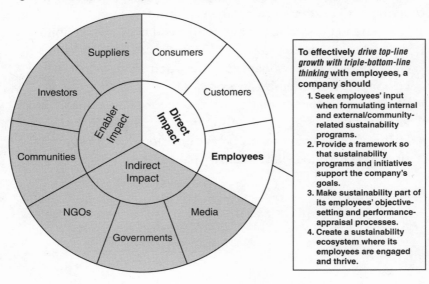

To effectively *drive top-line growth with triple-bottom-line thinking* with employees, a company should

1. Seek employees' input when formulating internal and external/community-related sustainability programs.
2. Provide a framework so that sustainability programs and initiatives support the company's goals.
3. Make sustainability part of its employees' objective-setting and performance-appraisal processes.
4. Create a sustainability ecosystem where its employees are engaged and thrive.

The Business Case for Inspiring and Engaging Employees

In the book *The Happiness Advantage*, Shawn Achor makes a business case for an engaged workforce, reinforcing the first asset that Mats Lederhausen identified in a prosperous society in the epigraph to this chapter. Many leaders intuitively understand the power of engagement, but few have the statistics to convince rationally focused corporate decision-makers to put engagement at the top of strategy discussions.

A study conducted by Anchor concluded that the productivity of engaged employees is 31 percent higher, that they are more accurate in their task by 9 percent, they experience lower turnover, and they use fewer sick days than their less engaged counterparts. Not surprisingly, engaged employees deliver an astounding 37 percent higher sales.[2]

Gallup's research has expressed similar findings. The companies in the top half of Gallup's employee engagement chart experience twice the success of those companies in the bottom half (Figure 4.2). According to an article in the *Gallup Business Journal*, Jim Harter, PhD, Gallup's chief scientist of employee engagement and well-being, was quoted as stating, "Engaged workers, though, have bought into what the organization is about and are trying to make a difference. This is why they're usually the most productive workers." The Gallup article goes on to share that the research showed "work units in the top quartile in employee engagement outperformed bottom-quartile units by 10 percent on customer ratings, 22 percent in profitability, and 21 percent in productivity. Work units in the top quartile also saw significantly lower turnover (25 percent in high-turnover organizations, 65 percent in low-turnover organizations), shrinkage (28 percent), and absenteeism (37 percent), and fewer safety incidents (48 percent), patient safety incidents (41 percent), and quality defects (41 percent)."[3]

Because online technology gives everyone a mouthpiece, a lack of engagement can harm your brand image. For example, a JetBlue flight attendant, Steven Slater, was having a bad day when he was struck by a piece of falling luggage from an overhead compartment

Figure 4.2. Engagement's effect on key performance indicators:
Median outcomes, top- and bottom-quartile teams

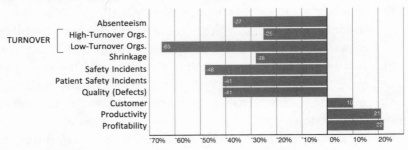

Source: Gallup Inc.

and then was subsequently cursed out by a passenger. The incident only served to bolster his negative feelings about his job at JetBlue; he immediately announced his decision to quit his job over the plane's intercom and then activated the emergency evacuation chute and slid to the ground with a beer in hand. This image, shared on social media, not only embarrassed JetBlue but also took a sizable bite out of its brand equity.

The numbers and the stories vary slightly, but the overwhelmingly high correlation between inspired, energized, and happy employees and businesses profitability is consistent. In addition, negative employee experiences are garnering more and more social media exposure, resulting in lower sales and profitability to associated businesses. By implementing effective employee engagement initiatives and programs, businesses not only improve their employee retention levels but also drive up employee productivity and realize resulting profits. Rather than focusing solely on external business factors to drive competitive advantage, smart businesses are establishing effective internal programs and enjoying the competitive power stemming from their own happy and engaged workforce.[4]

An Ecosystem of Engagement

This brings us to the second asset that Mats Lederhausen identified in a prosperous society: the ecosystem in which the employees operate. Discussing the ecosystem and employees independently by no means makes them separate topics. They are two intertwined parts. The employees are part of the ecosystem, and the ecosystem is essential for the engagement that good leaders want. More and more companies are recognizing that only through addressing both people and ecosystem simultaneously will they see increases in profitability.

One of the most important parts of creating an engaging ecosystem is company sustainability. Employees want to work for companies that voice their commitment to the planet and societies and consistently act on those commitments.

The Harvard Business School conducted research to evaluate the relationship between the level of participation of employees in sustainability-related work activities at Caesars Entertainment and their customers' desire to return to their properties (hotels and casinos). The study determined a high correlation between these two factors. To implement Caesars Entertainment's environmental stewardship commitment to preserve the planet for current and future generations, in 2007, they embarked on an internal sustainability initiative, *CodeGreen*. Through *CodeGreen*, Caesars Entertainment identifies means and measures, manages, and develops programs aimed at lowering their material impacts on the environment. The initiative is implemented locally, with clear annual targets for each property to achieve. A digital platform facilitates collaborative learning and competition among its employees. Gwen Migita, vice president of sustainability and community affairs, believes adding a mobile component further leverages the passion of their employees and encourages more participation while creating fun for employees. It will also engage their guests and suppliers in a meaningful way.[5]

In many companies, employees are the principal drivers of internal sustainable initiatives. In 2013, a survey conducted by Ernst & Young (one of the world's leading professional services organizations) asked company leaders to rank the top three stakeholder groups who are driving their company's sustainability initiatives. As expected, the top spot went to customers, who were cited by 37 percent of the respondents surveyed. The study's biggest revelation was

Figure 4.3. Intel: GHG correlation to employee engagement

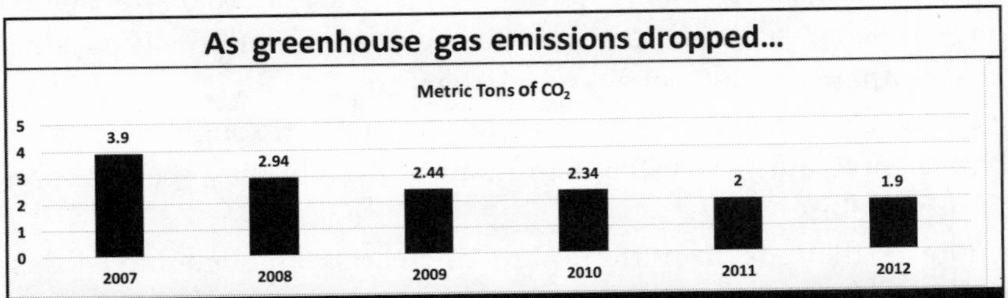

As greenhouse gas emissions dropped...					
Metric Tons of CO$_2$					
3.9	2.94	2.44	2.34	2	1.9
2007	2008	2009	2010	2011	2012

...employees have felt more engaged.					
	2008	2009	2010	2011	2012
I would recommend Intel as a great place to work	73%	74%	80%	83%	84%

Source: Intel Sustainability Report 2012

that employees edged out shareholders for the second spot in the ranking (cited by 22 percent versus 15 percent of the survey's respondents). Following shareholders, policymakers (7 percent) and NGOs (7 percent) completed the field of influencers cited.[6] Smart companies need to pay attention to these findings and harness their employees' energy and passion for sustainability as part of their overall sustainability strategy.

Intel's 2012 Corporate Sustainability Report conveyed a strong correlation between their internal employee engagement measures and progress in their sustainability initiatives. For example, in the five years prior to the report, employee engagement rose more than 10 percent while simultaneously the company realized steady reduction in greenhouse gas emissions (Figure 4.3). Intel leadership appears convinced that engaged employees are the major driver when it comes to achieving the company's environmental strategies and goals. The report states, "Since 2008, Intel has linked a portion of every employee's variable compensation – from front-line staff to the CEO – to the achievement of corporate responsibility goals, primarily related to environmental areas. They believe that including a corporate responsibility component in the overall annual performance bonus (APB) calculation helps focus executives and employees on the importance of achieving corporate responsibility objectives."[7]

A major change has taken place in the working world – the rise of the millennial in the workplace. If leaders aren't already building their internal strategy around millennials, or Generation Y (Gen Y for short), they are likely creating a great risk for their businesses. Gen Y is already 40 percent of the workforce and will be 75 percent by 2025. Gen Y has consistently stated that the environmental sustainability practices of a company are fundamental to their choices of where to work and how to work.

Johnson Controls reports that 96 percent of Gen Y employees want their employer to be environmentally friendly and over 70 percent expect to see concrete actions in the workplace advancing sustainability. Cone Communications, a PR and marketing agency, found that 56 percent of millennials would refuse to work for an employer with a negative environmental reputation.

Sustainability practitioners know that the environment is just one piece of the sustainability equation. Environmental sustainability initiatives are, in many cases, more easily copied by competitors than social or economic sustainability initiatives. For example, it's much easier to institute a recycling program or to buy carbon credits to offset greenhouse gas emissions than it is to significantly change a company's compensation structure or to contribute meaningfully to social equality.

Progressive companies can view this fact as good news. Such companies have an amazing opportunity to demonstrate sustainability leadership and consequently a means to engage their employees with customized and diverse approaches to sustainability. Companies can be innovative in their choices of sustainability initiatives and strategies, harnessing the various pillars of sustainability that are most material to their employees. Companies are most likely able to inspire and enlist their workforce in the achievement of sustainability goals that are truly meaningful to them, instead of creating cookie-cutter or me-too initiatives. This approach provides a clear path to a very real, sustainable, competitive advantage.

So it's important to ask employees what "sustainability" means to them, instead of assuming a definition. When a business's definition of sustainability (and associated initiatives) truly aligns with employee values, the inspiration and motivation to power those initiatives, and the subsequent benefits, come from within. No competitor can take that away. Increasingly, sustainability-educated and empowered employees are playing a critical role in creating and executing successful sustainability programs, giving them relevance and paving the way for organizational institutionalization.

Six Best Practices for Establishing an Engaging Internal Sustainability Ecosystem

Six best practices for creating engaging sustainability ecosystems that lead to a competitive advantage are summarized next, accompanied by real-life examples, which smart leaders are best advised to understand and emulate.

Make Initiatives Strategic

A business's sustainability initiatives, if they are to endure and thrive, must both be hinged to the business's core strategies and garner visible support and involvement from senior leadership. According to C-Suite Network, a private online exclusive community of the VP level and above, "The C-suite must understand and prioritize sustainability and its strategic value to the company." Business leaders must exhibit proof of their commitment to sustainability, not just talk about it. The C-Suite Network typically challenges its members to consider sustainability when making business decisions, and to act individually and as a group, at work and at home, to foster sustainability.[8]

Hewlett-Packard (HP), for instance, takes a strategic approach to employee engagement in sustainability and ties it to its business goals. Among its programs, HP houses an internal Sustainability Network with 30 chapters and over 10,000 members worldwide. This volunteer group engages employees worldwide, driving Earth

Day celebrations, onsite waste collection and community programs that positively impact the business, community, and the planet. HP also offers employees an Eco Advocates program, which provides employees with training modules to learn more about environmental issues. This enables employees to leverage this new knowledge to educate customers and partners on how to best use HP products so as to minimize environmental impact and to instruct suppliers on what's expected of HP's product components from a sustainability perspective.[9]

Making sustainability strategic is best evidenced in decision-making. When it comes down to cost-cutting or protecting a natural resource, which does the company choose? How do those discussions take place? In many cases, acting sustainably saves companies money, and we have seen that engaged employees create successful companies. But effective employee engagement doesn't happen overnight. It requires the ongoing support of courageous executives willing to take action for long-term benefit. If short-term revenue and profit always trump sustainable action and investment, then the company is clearly showing where it stands, at least until the next fiscal quarter. Rising above this short-termism frees good leaders to deliver greater impact for people and the planet.

Gain Internal Stakeholder Buy-in – Make It Personal

Co-creating sustainability programs with both leadership and employees cultivates trust, ownership, excitement, and commitment. The more connected corporate social responsibility and environmental sustainability are to personal values and passions, the more likely employees are to engage and the more likely a company is to reap competitive benefits. Few companies actually poll or interview employees to discover the social, economic, or environmental issues those employees believe are the most important. This step is fundamental to maximizing employee engagement in the company's sustainability program. A leader may do several interviews first to collect enough information to write intelligent survey questions and then survey the entire employee base about social, economic, and environmental issues of importance.

This data can be published internally to help create more engagement. If 70 percent of employees voice concern about the company's greenhouse gas emissions, then the remaining 30 percent will be much more inclined to support the company's GHG-related environmental initiatives. For example, Hyatt Hotels & Resorts created Hyatt Thrive, leveraging the power of peer-to-peer influence and social networking to connect and empower their 300 internal Green Teams worldwide. Employees use a Facebook-like interface to post photos, questions, and even presentations about their local sustainability efforts.

Build in Flexibility

Developing flexibility in the program elements will ensure a higher level of employee participation. A one-size-fits-all strategy may provide scale but not the engagement necessary for employees to own the program. As the program's name suggests, My Sustainability Plan (MSP), Walmart's global employee engagement platform, was developed to enable its over two million employees in 28 countries to create and own their individual, customized plans. The platform framework encourages employees to live healthier and greener lives. The framework is flexible enough so that employees can, in effect, craft their own program by selecting sustainability goals they find most relevant to their own lives. These chosen goals are broken down into manageable and measurable everyday actions.[10]

Make Participation Easy

To encourage employee involvement, Google creates an environment on their campuses that enables them to learn and participate. To illustrate this point, Google provides green transportation to its employees, ensures that the delicious food served on its sites is obtained from responsible sources, and provides work spaces that are fabricated from sustainable materials and feature clean air and natural light. Micro-kitchens, integrated throughout their work-places, are designed to encourage the use of reusable dishes and utensils. Google encourages its leaders to break a sustainability pro-gram into manageable steps that will let all interested employees participate. Google further educates employees about the impact of simple actions on the environment; they stress to their employees how something as simple as turning off their computers at night would impact Google's broader sustainability agenda.[11]

Make Initiatives and Progress Visible

To get the best results, a company can use both recognition and re-ward systems to make employee sustainability engagement visible. Recognition is just as important as incentives, and in some cases it works better for motivating individuals. A company's recognition and reward system communicates to the organization what it val-ues. If all of the internal accolades and compensation are awarded solely based on financial performance, this sends a very clear mes-sage across the ecosystem. On the other hand, recognizing and re-warding sustainability sends an equally strong message.

Companies can consider the following questions as they craft rec-ognition systems. What are an organization's sustainability success stories, and how is everyone learning about them? Have employees helped advance the company's sustainability strategy/journey? How can they be recognized? Are they rewarded in a relevant way?

Recognizing an employee who has demonstrated commitment to sustainability by either introducing or implementing a sustainabili-ty initiative would send a positive message and encourage other employees to follow their lead. Similarly, sending an employee who preaches sustainability and acts accordingly to a sustainability con-ference such as the Net Impact Conference, for example, is a simple reward that is compatible with the effort. It puts that employee in the energizing midst of like-minded individuals. In addition, the employee will be exposed to new sustainability ideas that may ben-efit the company. Good leaders look for these types of highly aligned and very personal forms of recognition.

Integrate into Corporate Culture

Creating an effective program is just the beginning. To encourage ongoing success, companies can treat employee engagement as a reward or as a recognition that can be factored into their performance appraisals. For example, Clif Bar, a family- and employee-owned company that makes "health and lifestyle" nutrition bars, has made sustainability a very big part of the company culture by embedding it in its incentive benefit package, which rewards employees for sustainable behavior.[12] They state, "Happy, healthy people create the best food." Their pay, benefits, and holistic wellness programs create a unique situation, which employees consider meaningful and valuable. Their employee benefits package includes unique features, such as incentives for actions like purchasing a fuel-efficient car and making eco-friendly home improvements. At weekly staff meetings, employees share practical tips for living a greener life, and at yearly award ceremonies, individuals are recognized for excellence according to the company's values.

Implementing the Sustainability Ecosystem with Employees

The tools and techniques for activating employee engagement in company sustainability programs and initiatives vary widely. The best results appear to happen when companies implement the sustainability ecosystem with employees in an authentic way that matches their culture and is compatible with their existing business processes. Here are four effective methods to implement employee engagement that have yielded excellent results.

Individual Engagement

Dale Carnegie's famous quote from his 1936 bestseller, *How to Win Friends and Influence People*, sums up the capability business leadership must have when engaging employees in any business initiative, especially sustainability. Carnegie quoted Charles Schwab as saying, "I consider my ability to arouse enthusiasm among my people the greatest asset I possess, and the way to develop the best that is in a person is by appreciation and encouragement."

At work, encourage "treasure hunts" to identify untapped opportunities to reduce waste and energy use. Hold Earth Day fairs, which include booths set up by organizations to engage and educate employees.

At home, encourage employees to create personal sustainability plans or otherwise incorporate sustainability into their everyday lives. The key here is to support these choices with actions, policies, or products from the company. For example, if employees want to reduce carbon emissions by using their cars less, a company could offer more work-from-home opportunities.

In communities, companies can offer support for employee group activities to clean up parks or plant trees or to help employees raise funds for a favorite charity. The best-in-class companies offer a wide array of volunteer choices to employees, and all these choices are aligned to the company's values and culture. For example, Patagonia offers seven ways for employees to get involved in doing social and environmental good. One unique implementation is an internship program that pays employees to work up to two months for a non-profit environmental organization of their choice. In addition, every June, Patagonia's bicycle-loving employees throughout the company gather to celebrate and encourage sustainable commuting to work.

Employee Communication

Best-in-class companies use a wide range of communication tools both online (intranet, social media, blogs) and offline (newsletters, posters, meetings, lunch-and-learn sessions) to raise awareness and engage employees on sustainability initiatives. These companies use multiple channels, tell multiple stories, and make initiatives easily sharable to maximize impact. In 2011, Unilever Australia conducted a clever experiment. To ensure all employees internalized its recently launched Sustainable Living Plan program, and that every employee felt empowered to truly make a difference, each was provided a name card with their name and the title, "Head of Sustainability." This sparked employee curiosity about and improved their knowledge of the company's innovative sustainability plan. The company further implemented training for employees and bombarded them via promotional posters with sustainability messaging from all directions. These measures ensured that employees became familiar with Unilever's innovative and ambitious sustainability plan and started acting on the tangible opportunities to drive desired change.[13]

Engagement Programs and Tools

Innovative employee engagement programs are capable of energizing younger, Generation X and millennial, employees. For example, 3M staged what it referred to as a *Sustainability Power Pitch* across the entire company. This initiative could be considered a cross between the shows *Shark Tank* and *American Idol*. Employees were encouraged to pitch their best ideas for a sustainable product to a panel of judges and other employees. Winning ideas were awarded a research grant to bring their product ideas to fruition. In a Sustainable Brands' article, 3M's Heather Phansey shared, "Employees, especially younger ones, want to feel that their contributions are respected. If you show them that, you'll be surprised by the novel ideas people are capable of."[14]

Today, cloud-based engagement platforms help companies engage employees on digital mobile devices in real time. The systems allow groups to compete and companies to collaborate and compare. Three companies offering such platforms are WeSpire,[15] GreenNexxus,[16] and CloudApps.[17]

WeSpire provides technology-based engagement programs to inspire employees for measurable impact. WeSpire (formerly known as Practically Green) claims to have developed persuasive technology – combining dynamic content, social levers, and gamification to capture people's imaginations and produce meaningful results.

They position their offering as a method to help companies accomplish critical business goals like innovation, growth, and revenues.

The GreenNexxus platform offers a peer-reviewed, action-based Acts of Good calculator that allows individuals and organizations to determine ways to reduce their environmental footprints. This technology provides measurable results and gives individuals and organizations the ability to "visualize" the difference they are making through their actions.

CloudApps is the provider of Sustainability Momentum (SuMo), a sustainability performance platform that uses advanced game mechanics to make sustainability success transparent across the organization (Figure 4.4). SuMo uses game concepts that include leveling systems, competitions, challenges, points, rewards, and badges to motivate employee engagement. SuMo breaks sustainability targets

Figure 4.4. SuMo for sustainability

Source: CloudApps Inc.

down into manageable actions that allow employees to get involved and contribute. In PSFK's Future of Gaming report, Timothy Ryan shares how SuMo drives employee engagement by making visible the employee carbon footprint in real time and encourages employee participation in the energy use and recycling programs delivering accelerated sustainability performance for the company.[18]

Recognition and Reward

As Peter Drucker famously stated, "What gets measured gets done." Tracking awareness, participation, and performance metrics and communicating these results on a periodic basis is key to engaging employees. Best-in-class companies recognize and reward employees based upon measurable environmental or social improvements.

At General Electric, employee engagement in the Ecomagination program is fostered in many ways. One approach is to recognize performance excellence for those operations that contribute most dramatically to reductions in energy use, GHG emissions, water use, and materials consumption. General Electric's GE Power and Water business has been successfully engaging its employees in its internally branded, Ecomagination Nation program for a number of years. Through this program many GE Power and Water employees and contractors have been participating in community-focused events including coastline cleanups, tree planting, and lighting upgrades in local schools. Through 2015 the impacts of these programs have been substantial, reducing water consumption by six million gallons and electricity usage by three million kilowatt hours collectively at GE and GE-managed customer sites.[19]

Kimberly-Clark's Crystal Tree Award recognizes leadership in sustainability among several internal stakeholder types, including employees, manufacturing facilities, and business units or teams. The award, first presented in 2010, honors outstanding contributions in any of the three classic sustainability focus areas – people, planet, and products. Crystal Tree Award recipients are (1) presented a tree statue fabricated from recycled glass, (2) honored with a donation given in their name to the nonprofit of their choice, and (3) provided an opportunity to collaborate with one of Kimberly-Clark's NGO partners on a project such as tree planting or water replenishment.[20]

Sony Electronics has recently harnessed gamification as part of its green workplace certification to reach its overall "Road to Zero" environmental goal. The certification encourages employees to take steps ranging from eliminating the in-office trash to turning on the energy-saving settings on their computer. Based on steps they complete, they earn one of four badges: seed, leaf, tree, and forest. Employees can also earn "Sony Bucks" along the way.

In an article in the *Guardian* on the subject of employee engagement in sustainability, Susan Hunt Stevens shares how Sony, in the pilot phase of its program, realized an average savings per participant of $85, with less than a $20 investment, a four times return on investment in the first year. Eric Johnson, head of the Sony program, stated, "Small behavior changes add up to big savings, especially when multiplied across a large organization. Building a story about why each action is important and packaging it in a way that is approachable, scalable and most of all fun encourages people to 'own' the actions they choose to take on."[21]

Case Study: Walmart's MSP Employee Engagement Platform

Matt Kistler, current SVP of Walmart's Global Customer Insights and Analytics, headed Walmart's sustainability group in 2006 when its employee engagement program was first conceived and developed. He shared,

> Walmart's *Personal Sustainability Program (PSP)* was developed so that our associates could live healthier, safer lives and so that their associates could successfully translate Walmart's business concept, *Save Money – Live Better*, into their own homes and families. Mr. Lee Scott, Walmart's CEO was a sponsor and a big supporter of the program at that time, and the entire team felt that if their associates got behind the

program, Walmart could propel what they were doing with the business concept in a more holistic way. The sustainability group with strong support from the CEO and top leadership introduced the PSP program in 2007 in order to engage the retail giant's 2.2 million associates, working in nearly 9,600 stores, across 28 countries using an internal video.

The term "Personal Sustainability Plan (PSP)" was owned by another firm, so Walmart's sustainability group contracted BBMG (a sustainability-focused brand development company) to build a gamified platform called My Sustainability Plan (MSP) that rewarded individual Walmart associates for recording and tracking simple goals, which they voluntarily committed to as part of their individual sustainability plans (MSPs). BBMG's branded My Sustainability Plan (MSP) platform was developed with a "freedom within a framework" approach. MSP expanded the scope of the original PSP program, as it went beyond Walmart's traditional focus areas of reducing waste, promoting renewable energy, and choosing more sustainable products to include nutrition and exercise elements. This customizable framework specifies universal icons and toolkits that successfully captured the diversity of small actions that their millions of employees committed to at a local level. Based on employee input, the framework has three key focus areas: My Health (eating healthy, getting active, quitting tobacco, reducing stress), My Planet (saving water, reducing waste, saving energy, enjoying nature), and My Life (learning new skills, managing their money, making quality time, helping others).

The individual goals initially have a timeframe of four to seven weeks, with hopes that they could then be integrated into employees' daily lives. In-store training combined with employee-to-employee encouragement helps to reinforce individual employees' MSPs. "Sustainability Captains" are recruited from the hourly and salaried employee base to assemble meetings and help educate their fellow employees on MSPs. Fresh food was added to the list of products for which associates enjoyed an in-store discount. The

Figure 4.5. MSP (My Sustainability Plan) toolkit

MSP goal framework

Source: Walmart and BBMG

company invested in tools like MSP cards, which encouraged associates in an engaging way to live sustainably in both their personal and professional lives. Employees also collaborate and act at a store level to accomplish sustainability-related goals in their communities. For example, the program encourages associates to set up recycling programs or to clean up wildlife areas in their local communities. The MSP concept is designed to help associates improve their own lives and spread the sustainability to their friends, families, customers, colleagues, and communities.

Within the first few years of implementation, the company saw 20,000 U.S. associates who actively participated in the program kick their smoking habits; recycle three million pounds of plastic; and, as a group, shed 184,000 pounds. As of 2013, over 50,000 U.S. associates had signed up and used the tool, which provides Walmart the ability to measure their associates' level of engagement and collective impact. Walmart does encourage participation in MSP through simple low-cost actions, such as offering employees free smoking-cessation programs and providing healthy and affordable food choices in their cafeterias.

Matt Kistler added that additional business benefits came from the MSP program when Walmart got many great ideas from associates on ways to save money within the company. He said, "The MSP unleashed and provided a catalyst for associates to think differently about things, and to come up with very innovative, often breakthrough ideas, and in other cases very simple ideas that can save Walmart money." He went on to share two examples to illustrate the value of MSP for the company.

- A store manager in North Carolina noticed that the vending machines in their break rooms have lights running all the time, but associates can see the goods being offered without them, so the light is not required. By eliminating the lights in the vending machines in all their break areas, the company saved over $1 million per year in electricity costs. The store manager was recognized by Walmart's leadership and was featured in *New York Times* and *Wall Street Journal* articles.
- The drive within industry on packaging reduction is phenomenal. With packaging, the consumer pays for it twice – first as part of the goods sold and a second time when they pay to dispose of it. Raising employees' sustainability awareness can yield business benefits through packaging reduction/optimization. An associate recognized that Christmas lights had excessive packaging: they were first put in a poly bag and then placed in a box. Eliminating the poly bag not only eliminated the potential waste to landfill but also helped keep the costs lower for consumers.

To broaden the impact of the MSP platform, Walmart, as part of its commitment to the Clinton Global Initiative, shares the intellectual property of the MSP program with any organization requesting a license. More than 35 organizations have used this license, including Unilever, UPS, J.B. Hunt, and United Healthcare.[22]

When asked what advice he would give to any business looking to initiate an employee engagement program, Kistler shared these key insights: (1) engaging employees is the smart thing to do; (2) the programs need to be developed by employees and supported by senior leadership; (3) the programs must promote the values of the business; (4) the programs must recognize and reward employees for participation; and (5) the programs must be refreshed periodically to maintain the momentum. His insights are consistent with the essence of this chapter.

KEY TAKEAWAYS

- Engaging employees in sustainability helps with recruiting and retention, while motivating them contributes to sustainability business metrics that drive business success.
- Creating a sustainable business ecosystem is an excellent way to demonstrate a business's commitment to issues that matter to a company's workforce.
- Companies are most successful when constructing and implementing a business ecosystem in a way that is consistent with existing business processes and goals.
- Investing in individual and group employee engagement programs, proper and regular communication, and adequate metric tracking and measurement are the ways in which companies can build best-practice sustainability programs that drive business results.

To effectively drive *top-line growth with triple-bottom-line thinking* with employees, a company should:
1. Seek employees' input in formulating internal and external community-related sustainability programs.

2. Provide a framework so that sustainability programs and initiatives support the company's goals.
3. Make sustainability part of its employees' objective-setting and performance-appraisal processes.
4. Create a sustainability ecosystem where its employees are engaged and thrive.

5 Nurturing Suppliers

Sustainability is no longer about being incrementally less bad, but it is about transformational change and making business fit for the 21st century.
Steve Howard, chief sustainability officer, IKEA[1]

Figure 5.1. Sustainability stakeholders framework: Nurturing suppliers

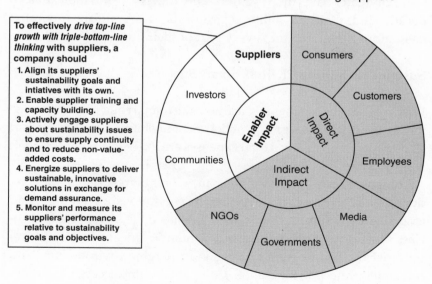

To effectively *drive top-line growth with triple-bottom-line thinking* with suppliers, a company should

1. Align its suppliers' sustainability goals and intiatives with its own.
2. Enable supplier training and capacity building.
3. Actively engage suppliers about sustainability issues to ensure supply continuity and to reduce non-value-added costs.
4. Energize suppliers to deliver sustainable, innovative solutions in exchange for demand assurance.
5. Monitor and measure its suppliers' performance relative to sustainability goals and objectives.

Suppliers   Consumers
Investors   Customers
Enabler Impact   Direct Impact
Communities   Employees
Indirect Impact
NGOs   Media
Governments

Thomas Schaefer, sustainability leader at IKEA (a top-rated sustainable company), shared that because IKEA comes from a region with limited resources, creating more from less and not wasting any resources became embedded in the DNA of the company long before sustainability was born. IKEA has a rich history of working toward sustainability, striving for the highest ethical standards, and being a good partner in society. In the 1990s, the realization of formaldehyde's harmful effects and its prevalence of use in the fiber sourcing market served as a wake-up call that led to IKEA becoming a founding member of both the Forest Stewardship Council and the Better Cotton Initiative. The IKEA code of conduct for suppliers, IWAY, was launched in 2000. According to Thomas, this was the embryo of the supplier-based sustainability agenda that has evolved over time. Their initial focus was on home furnishings, but it has now expanded to all of their 1,000-plus direct suppliers. The IWAY team has recorded over 165,000 environmental and social improvements to date, making a difference in people's lives and the environment around the world. IKEA has maintained successful partnerships with UNICEF, Save the Children, and the WWF for more than a decade. Today, sustainability is part of the IKEA culture and value base and is integrated into every part of their business.

Sustainable Supply Chain Is Smart Business

Why are IKEA's sustainability activities also smart business? "According to the awareness group Action Sustainability, between 60 and 80 percent of a company's total expenses are likely to be spent on their supply chain."[2]

Companies can significantly enhance their own sustainability credentials and reduce major expenses by continuously examining and assessing their supply chains, as IKEA has done. Adopting best-in-class procurement procedures and standards can, at a minimum, reduce risks/exposure from existing and emerging environmental and consumer protection legislation. Companies with successful, sustainable procurement processes and procedures can potentially realize reduced costs, increased sale price, better quality, new customers, and a more talented workforce. Collectively, these benefits will positively impact business results and enhance brand reputation, creating a sustainable business ecosystem composed of healthy supplier/customer partnerships that are mutually reinforcing. This is the crux of a sustainable supplier's attributed competitive advantage.

In a *Harvard Business Review* article, Peter Senge, a faculty member at MIT's school of management, stated, "In most supply chains, 90% of them are still transactional," speaking about the nature of relationships.[3] Parties involved in supply chain agreements see each other as simply providing or receiving needed resources, instead of viewing each other as valued business partners capable of advancing the other's larger company values and objectives. The concept of synergy, where one plus one should result in a value greater than two, is not exploited in the classic buyer-seller relationship. This happens because companies are largely stuck in a "top-down" mentality, where the buyer's focus on the supplier relationships is purely based on cost minimization.

Large manufacturers, distributors, or retailers routinely leverage their scale to literally squeeze suppliers. For example, it's common for them to pressure upstream suppliers to continuously reduce the price of goods or services they require to reduce their input costs and improve profit margins. This creates an environment in which there is very little basis for trust and very little incentive or ability to innovate as partners.

In Suppliers We Trust

In Dov Seidman's bestselling book, *How: Why How We Do Anything Means Everything*, he discussed Jeffrey H. Dyer and Wujin Chu's 2003 landmark study which examined the nature of relationships between a buyer and a supplier at the top eight auto manufacturers from the United States, Korea, and Japan. The study found that trust between the buyers and suppliers is the core determinant of the purchase price and subsequent profitability of the buying company. An atmosphere of trust creates an open, transparent environment where both parties are able to address the real challenges and develop value-added solutions.[4]

It boils down to one word, *trust*. Market forces and leverage do not help bring about trust. Shared values and collaboration do. As a result, values shared regarding sustainability can create much more profitable supplier relationships when those values are put on the table and made part of the relationship. A company can literally watch the investments they've made in sustainability permeate their entire value chain, bringing about greater returns from the process.

Making Supply Chains Sustainable

Unfortunately, many companies are struggling with establishing sustainable supply chains because of their unproductive attempts at enforcement. These companies attempt to ensure supply chain sustainability solely through monitoring policies and compliance, like parents waiting for a child to misbehave so they can eventually scold them. This engenders the same trust issue as other forms of pressure. Only authentic collaboration toward mutual goals ensure the development of an authentic trust-based relationship.

Companies are beginning to realize that simply dictating supplier policies and intermittently monitoring for compliance via auditing of suppliers doesn't add real or lasting value. The true value is created by engaging and collaborating with suppliers as part of a larger sustainable procurement strategy. For example, when IKEA determines that a supplier has not been complying fully with their supplier sustainability standards, they often employ an extensive intervention program, which, in some cases, helps the supplier develop whole new capacities that are more sustainable for their business.

The buyer's recipe for bringing about this collaborative partnership starts at home and not first with external suppliers. Companies need to look inward at their own internal environmental and socially focused practices before requiring or pressuring those they do business with to conform to supplier sustainability standards.

Companies need first to embody their own desired sustainable value-chain agenda. That is, they must install their own robust sustainable policies and then carefully monitor actual practices within their operations.

Advantages of Developing a Sustainable Win-win Customer/ Supplier Relationship

Apart from the many benefits discussed previously that are typically inherent in maintaining sustainable supply chains, partnering with suppliers to enact sustainable supply chains often offers customer businesses distinct, downstream, competitive advantages that emerge within their own operations. After all, the value chain starts with supplier inputs. Robust supplier/customer relationships and more sustainable practices at this stage cascade their benefits all the way down the value chain, through to the end consumer and to future consumers. There are five main benefits to such relationships that merit highlighting.

Protecting Against Reputational Damage

In recent years, stakeholders including investors, shareholders, customers, and nonprofits have significantly increased the pressure on businesses to extend sustainability accountability into their supply chains. According to Ceres, during the 2013 proxy season there were 110 shareholder resolutions filed that related to addressing climate change and supply chain policies, a near record number. These resolutions were filed by a host of stakeholders, including socially responsible pension funds and foundations, and select NGOs focused on religious and labor issues.[5]

In addition, the increasing pervasiveness of social media, resulting in increased and nearly instantaneous public access to information, has prompted most companies to ensure that they are viewed as committed to sustainable and responsible business practices with regard to ethics, labor, health and safety, diversity, and the environment. The publicity backlash resulting from perceived negative sustainability practices could be highly material; this is not a new phenomenon.

As far back as 1996, television personality Kathie Lee Gifford authorized a clothing company to market a line of clothing named after her. Gifford faced a firestorm of criticism when the news media learned that the clothes were being produced in Guatemala using child labor. Gifford apparently had not known the conditions under which the clothes were being produced. Regardless, the ensuing media firestorm significantly damaged her reputation and brand value.

The Nike Company serves as another notable example of supply chain sustainability risk. Almost everything the company sells is actually sourced from another company outside of the United States. Throughout the 1990s, Nike kept on encouraging their contract manufacturers to move sourcing to the locations that offer lower production costs, countries such as Korea, Taiwan, Indonesia, China, Vietnam, Bangladesh, and Honduras. They became the global standard for abusive labor practices when workers' wages, safety, and working conditions became hot news items. A real shift happened in the late 1990s when CEO Phil Knight recognized that this was impacting the brand image and began to take ownership for the practices at its suppliers. Their initial attitude of denial (e.g., they don't own the factories and thus don't control what goes on there) was transformed to Nike actively monitoring their suppliers' workplace standards on a daily basis – similar to how quality was being managed.[6]

Nike created a Fair Labor Association (FLA), a nonprofit association of like-minded FMCGs (fast-moving consumer goods) to establish and monitor labor wages, safety, and workplace standards. The FLA conducts labor audits for companies and for universities that license manufacturers to produce merchandise with university logos. Nike contracts with the FLA to audit a small percentage of Nike's factories each year.[7]

A tragic event that occurred in 2014, which involved a catastrophic fire, building collapse, and subsequent loss of many lives at their Bangladesh garment factory, sparked new urgency and raised red flags regarding the safety standards used by the offshore garment factories of high-profile apparel brands including Gap, Nike, Kohl's, and Target. While this issue was front-page news, John Liu, New York City's comptroller, recognized that though suppliers need to address the workplace code of conduct, they first need to become more transparent by filing sustainability reports. To compel suppliers to do so, he filed several related resolutions so that the City of New York stayed at the forefront of these issues.[8]

Recently, Apple, which manufactures the products most consumers love, found itself on the defensive when labor practices at their extended supply chain contractor, Foxconn, were exposed on the *60 Minutes* news show. Apple faced a tsunami of criticism for issues at Foxconn related to lower wage rates and poor workplace conditions that resulted in some workers committing suicide at the Chinese subcontractor's Shenzhen factories. Apple's Tim Cook, who headed the global operations for Apple then, promised to conduct an audit and place corrective measures during an interview on the show. As a result, Apple joined the FLA, agreeing to follow the FLA's Workplace Code of Conduct in all their supply chains.[9]

Reducing Environmental Impact and Costs

As companies engage suppliers, apply science, and conduct environmental and labor studies across a product's life cycle use, they not only are able to reduce environmental impact but can also reduce costs and improve quality.

In the retail and service industries, whose direct footprint is relatively small compared to the footprint of their supply chains, it's imperative that they engage their suppliers to lower the environmental and social impacts of the products they sell. When retail giant Walmart announced their hefty sustainability-related goal to reduce their corporate GHG (greenhouse gas) emissions by 20 million tons per year by 2020, they realized that reductions in their own internal footprint would have a minuscule impact. Walmart needed to engage with their core suppliers if they were to have any chance of accomplishing their stated goal. Walmart worked to distribute the goal among major suppliers with clear accountability.

"Because the Walmart supply system is many times larger than the company's direct footprint, in many cases, the biggest, fastest, most economical efficiency gains and GHG reductions are not at the retail-level, rather up or down the value-chain of consumer products, either in raw material extraction, product manufacturing, transportation, customer use, or end-of-life," said Lea Jepson, Walmart's director of sustainability for Private Brands in a 2013 GreenBiz article.[10]

Improving Continuity of Supply

In today's complex web of sourcing, given the speed of product copycats and the rapidly changing business environment, it's necessary for companies to ensure ongoing, on-time delivery of supplies to remain as competitive as possible.

The auto industry learned this lesson when the 2011 floods in Thailand brought a halt to the auto parts supply industry, causing idling factories around the world. Working with key suppliers in the wake of the flooding, the auto industry ensured that its supply chain is now much more diversified, which has resulted in benefits for suppliers as well.

In another example, food giant Heinz found that the soil in China's Xinjiang region had been devastated by decades of poor soil management. The company began training local farmers on sustainable agricultural practices, including the efficient use of fertilizers and pesticides, better irrigation, and more appropriate machinery. As a result of the program, Heinz reported a 58 percent improvement in the region's farm yields and a revitalized agricultural community.[11]

Innovating Products and Services

Innovation is at the top of executive agendas across the globe, yet very few companies effectively involve their suppliers in this endeavor. Suppliers often represent a gigantic pool of untapped innovation potential.

The array of company innovation needs is vast. Companies know that they can benefit from technical innovations, management innovations, process innovations, and cultural innovations. By engaging suppliers in addressing the many challenges a company faces, companies are often able to solve some of these innovation challenges collectively. If suppliers understand a company's vision and long-term plans, they may be able to suggest changes and upgrades to the products or even their own processes and resulting material inputs, which have the potential to improve many areas of a company's operations. In short, suppliers can be powerful allies to companies striving to accomplish innovation goals.

The city of Istanbul and one of its suppliers, Siemens, serve to illustrate a great example of this collaborative innovation approach to problem solving. Istanbul needed innovation to significantly improve its water infrastructure and, through discussions, learned that Siemens wanted opportunities to advance their own technology and share it with the marketplace. Water is a precious resource for Istanbul's growing population. The company and the city worked together to install a failure-free water system. Siemens placed ultrasonic-level sensors throughout the city's water system and connected each pumping station to a central control-desk system. This allowed for continuous monitoring of the water and wastewater infrastructure. This high-profile project has benefited Siemens' brand and allowed the city of Istanbul to project an image as a forward-thinking modern city.[12]

Creating Partnerships or Global Industry Standards

Companies can advance their knowledge of the footprint of their products by partnering with NGOs or working to create global industry standards, allowing them to stay ahead of any legislation or negative consumer sentiment that could impede their operations, and it can make them more competitive in the marketplace.

Companies often need to look beyond their own footprint and engage other expert stakeholders in order to meet their sustainability objectives. A classic example of this occurred a few years ago when Coca-Cola, which is highly dependent on clean and plentiful water as a principal ingredient in their beverages and processing, was looking for ways to cut 20 percent of the water it uses to make a liter of Coke, from 3 liters to 2.5 liters. After examining its broader value chain they discovered that the "low-hanging fruit" existed upstream from their bottling plants – i.e., the 200 liters of water it took to grow the sugarcane that yielded the sugar that went into that liter of Coke. Reducing water usage at the sugarcane plantations was possible only by teaming up with water experts at World Wildlife Fund (WWF), who had the capability to analyze the water footprint across the value chain. As a result, Coca-Cola started promoting and educating farmers on drip-irrigated techniques to save water along the chain.[13]

In 2011, a group of major apparel and footwear brands and retailers made a shared commitment to lead the industry toward zero discharge of hazardous chemicals (ZDHC). The group's vision was to develop sustainable chemistry and work practices to protect all: the users, the makers, and the environment. They published an ambitious Joint Roadmap that outlined pathways so that industry could achieve ZDHC for all products. The signatories to the Joint Roadmap include six founding brands (Adidas Group, C&A, H&M, Li-Ning, Nike Inc., and Puma SE) and an expanded new members roaster of companies like Esprit, G-Star Raw, Gap Inc., Inditex, Jack Wolfskin, Levi Strauss & Co., Limited Brands, M&S, New Balance Athletic Shoe Inc., PVH Corp., and United Colors of Benetton. Each signatory defines its own goals and time commitments in an attempt to realize their shared goal of ZDHC.[14]

In this case, collaboration has crossed company boundaries, improving sustainability, operational efficiency, and marketing clout via a global standard that will move the industry forward.

Creating a Strategic and Sustainable Procurement Organization

Once a company gets its "own house in order," the foundation has been set to examine and potentially alter the nature of the existing company/supplier relationships. Companies can then begin to move from a tactical approach of top-down monitoring and leveraging of scale to a more impactful and strategic collaborative approach, aimed at advancing mutual goals and generating much more value. The emerging best practices for building these relationships include the following seven steps to sustainable procurement:

Align Sustainable Procurement and Core Business Strategies

Ian Heptonshall, director of Action Sustainability, advises companies to ensure that all sustainable procurement initiatives they undertake have a business case and that all such initiatives be evaluated across the value chain so as to avoid any perceptions of "greenwashing."[15]

The greatest value emerges when there is a strong business case behind a company's supply chain initiative, which can then be clearly articulated. This can change the focus of supply chain management from simple resource procurement to a set of reinforcing capabilities that have the potential to generate value for the business – whether the business value is direct, like cost reduction, or indirect, like customer loyalty.

Pursuing this strategic approach also allows alignment to be built across all levels of a company's organization, from CEO to the individuals in its supply chain department, so that everyone speaks with one voice in a common sustainability language.

For example, Walmart's efforts to drive sustainability initiatives like green power, greener products, and zero waste down their supply chains are totally aligned with their own stated environmental goals and their stated business purpose, "Saving people money to help them live better."[16]

Institute Sustainable Procurement Policies

Once a company's sustainable procurement strategy is aligned with its core business strategy, sustainable procurement procedures and policies help institutionalize these ideas and put them into practice.

These policies work best when they are endorsed and signed off on by those at the top of the organization, ideally the board of directors, so they will have a stabilizing and lasting influence that will allow value to accumulate over time. By developing and implementing the following three tools, a company can establish a base for a sustainable procurement program.

- *Supplier Sustainability Code of Conduct* – These documents reflect the basic tenets of responsible management. They typically cover key elements including labor, health and safety, environment, ethics, and management systems. They are reviewed and updated regularly to continue to reflect best practices and account for emerging issues. Adherence to these codes of conduct is mostly self-reported by suppliers, but these codes help set standards and expectations in the customer/supplier relationship.
- *Zero-Tolerance List* – These lists include minimum standards and thresholds of performance a company expects suppliers to attain. They typically reflect the values near and dear to the company. We recommend companies follow the guidance provided in the document titled, "Supply Chain Sustainability – A Practical Guide for Continuous Improvement," to develop their own supplier code of conduct, especially with regard to labor practices. This is a comprehensive framework jointly developed by the UN Global Compact and Business for Social Responsibility (BSR). It integrates the UN Global Compact's principles into supply chain relationships.[17] Non-compliance with the zero-tolerance standards often results in termination of the supply contract and business relationship.
- *Supplier Diversity Policies* – Diversity in business and portfolios mitigates risk. Further, these policies are established to give a company a competitive advantage and meet customer and government requirements. The policies can spell out in the broadest terms the philosophy that diversity is good for the business. It also articulates the need for regional (to access global skills and markets), cultural (to offer different viewpoints and styles), and

social (to benefit different communities and local economies) diversity. Building diversity into a company's procurement policy will give procurement managers more flexibility, empowering them to work with new and more sustainable suppliers.

Create a Sustainable Supplier Roadmap

Many companies do not have a comprehensive understanding of the sustainability impacts of their supply chain. In this step, a company inventories its suppliers and develops a sustainable supplier roadmap. Companies can categorize suppliers by their level of influence – both from the risks and opportunities perspective, both inside and outside of the company. Some of the suppliers will be large and sophisticated, while others may be better characterized as "mom-and-pop shops." Upon investigation, some suppliers may even be further ahead in their sustainability journey than the company itself, creating new opportunities for learning. Conversely, other suppliers may be behind in their journey and can be pulled forward for added value.

Similar to other well-considered and well-designed expansion strategies, it's recommended that any new supplier sustainability initiative should be first pressure-tested in the form of a pilot test involving select stakeholders. Only a finely tuned program should be expanded across the broader supply chain. Larry Loftus, director of purchasing capability and strategy at P&G, confirmed the rollout strategy in a GreenBiz article by warning, "Don't start with too many suppliers; learn from the right sized group." P&G did exactly this by first engaging only 30 of their key suppliers in their new sustainability procurement program during the first year. Only after evaluating and improving the efficiency and effectiveness of the program did they expand the program to their top 400 suppliers in subsequent years.[18]

Engage Supplier Management in Goal Setting

Companies may wish to engage supplier management, as high up as possible, when developing clear sustainability goals. Becoming more sustainable is typically good for both parties. The suppliers may have publicly stated or internal goals that can best be advanced by leveraging the company's initiatives, activities, or networks. Companies that do this well often hold a top-level summit with key suppliers and even consider drafting and signing a joint commitment letter, outlining how all parties will work together to promote sustainable practices with both clear goals and clear accountabilities. In this way, companies can begin to build a community or ecosystem contributing sustainable value.

Document Baseline Performance

In addition, as with any goal setting, it is important to determine and record a company's starting point or baseline before establishing a meaningful trajectory of where a company wants to end up. For example, if a company seeks to reduce its collective suppliers' carbon footprints, it must first know what its suppliers' current emissions are. Only then can a company develop solid goals and strategies for driving and delivering improvement. The choice of what companies ask suppliers to report on is also a strategic one. Companies do best when they ensure that the data they are asking suppliers for is material to address the company's own goals. Care should be taken not to compromise the proprietary aspects of the relationship or cause great expense to the supplier that might end up being passed on to the company. A company may be well advised to utilize existing data collection and reporting systems, such as the CDP or the Sustainability Consortium, when possible, to help gather and track sustainability data/progress.

Enable Training and Capacity Building

Training and capacity-building initiatives will take buyer/supplier relationships to the next level, impacting both businesses in a positive manner. For sustainability areas in which a company capacity is strong, it may be possible to build supplier capacity by leveraging company expert resources for supplier training and support. While suppliers can advance and become more-sustainable companies on their own, they will likely do it a lot faster with the support of their buyers. Supplier capacity building aims to train suppliers on both the general and the company's specific sustainable management practices. Capacity building can also support the implementation of specific, desired sustainability practices and standards. In some cases, the door swings both ways. Companies can also learn from suppliers' sustainability competencies. This reciprocal training and capacity-building arrangement can be the crux of the supplier meetings and engagement strategy, catapulting the relationship far beyond the typical transactional level. It often develops into a partnership that adds value to all parties and creates a mutual loyalty that serves as a competitive advantage.

Monitor and Measure Supplier Performance

Without making the effort to monitor supplier progress versus expectations, it is very difficult to see success or the lack thereof. After establishing a baseline, companies can establish ongoing measurement processes such as a cadence of regular, face-to-face check-ins (e.g., twice a year) with their suppliers. This level of accountability helps ensure efforts undertaken in good faith produce desired and expected results. For that reason, many companies have designed scorecards that clearly spell out expectations, track sustainability results, and maintain a collaborative process for continued improvement and dialogue.

To promote collaborative, trusting relationships, a company may choose to assemble all of its suppliers in the same room and have open discussions about mutual goals and measured progress. They can talk candidly about what's working really well and, conversely, what isn't working so well. This provides suppliers and buyers alike a chance to network and help each other achieve their joint and individual business goals.

In summary, embedded supply chain sustainability comes from closely working with suppliers in a very strategic way. Companies that communicate their requirements, monitor supplier compliance, and track performance derive levels of greater value from their supply chain than do companies that refrain from these activities. Companies should ensure that their suppliers have management systems in place to help mitigate potential risks, ensure continuity of supply, and improve overall value chain sustainability to effect a positive impact in the marketplace and with consumers.

Case Study: Supplier Sustainability at IKEA

IKEA's journey was not without bumps or rough rides, but through consistency, integrity, and constant learning, IKEA is leading the sustainability agenda. These are the key components of the IKEA's strategic sustainability efforts.

IWAY

In 2000, IKEA introduced IWAY – simply an IKEA way of doing things right in their supply chain. This was a code of conduct focused on IKEA's sustainable values. Initially, the program was focused on home furnishings. By 2002, after dealing with several challenges, IKEA believed all their home-furnishing suppliers were following the IWAY code of conduct. When they began digging deeper, however, it was revealed that many suppliers did not actually meet the IWAY standards.

To address the issue, IKEA employed 100 auditors around the world to implement and verify that suppliers meet IWAY standards. This required auditors to work with the suppliers, to educate and train them. It took almost 10 years, but in that time, IKEA has been able to ensure that all of its direct suppliers, more than 1,000, are complying with their sustainability guidelines.

If a potential new supplier doesn't agree to the IWAY standard, they cannot be an IKEA supplier. On the other hand, new suppliers who do agree are given time to meet the standards. If they fail after that time, they cannot become an accredited IKEA supplier.

IKEA is now applying IWAY standards to business partners who provide services, as well as expanding them across the value chain.

IKEA proudly reports that 18,000 registered secondary suppliers meet IWAY MUST standards. IWAY MUST standards are the zero-tolerance policies of IWAY. They address working hours, minimum wages, minimum safety practices like smoke detectors and fire exits, and avoidance of child/bonded labor. Delivery from any supplier who violates IWAY MUST is stopped immediately. Business relationships with suppliers who have two violations are terminated immediately.

Democratic Design Principles

IKEA leaders believe that form, function, design, costs, and sustainability go hand in hand in designing a new product. The company will not compromise on IWAY standards but may compromise on the price. This order of priorities has sent a clear signal to all suppliers and business partners about where top management stands. There is flexibility and room for suppliers to contribute their own ideas and request adjustments on certain variables, whereas IWAY MUST policies remain nonnegotiable.

Responsible Sourcing

In the 1990s, formaldehyde was connected to a host of health risks; this brought IKEA's focus to their wood-fiber and cotton sourcing practices, which often involved formaldehyde during processing. The focus on this one area of responsible sourcing was then expanded to the sourcing of sustainable palm oil, and now IKEA is exploring further transparency in wool, leather, feathers, and even food sources.

SEEP

The Supplier Energy & Efficiency Project (SEEP) was initiated in 2007, as IKEA began to focus on energy use reduction both inside and outside of their operations. The intent was to work closely with suppliers and motivate them to make the right energy-efficiency decisions. Working with the glass industry, the IKEA team was able to demonstrate a 50 percent improvement in the efficiency of fuel furnaces used in glass production. This illustrates how companies and suppliers can both improve sustainable performance and reduce costs.

Range Development

To further expand their sustainability agenda, IKEA developed a Sustainable Product scorecard for all the products they carry. The scorecard was based on 11 criteria and used basic LCA (life cycle assessment) principles that address energy efficiency, manufacturing performance, and handling of resources, water, and waste. This structured approach has provided a roadmap for supplier sustainability improvement by showing where supplier product lines currently stand and how IKEA can further improve their product score rating. The scorecard was further refreshed in 2015 by applying learning from the past few years – in keeping with the constant improvement and journey philosophy of IKEA.

Innovation

IKEA has recently announced some gigantic goals. For example, IKEA plans to be using non-fossil plastics for all their products and produce more energy than they consume – both by 2020. This has opened doors for open innovation with suppliers. For example, IKEA is working on renewable mattress foam using post-industrial foam material in a pilot plant, as well as collaborations with biopolymer suppliers. There is clear recognition in the company that only by engaging openly with suppliers can these big, audacious goals be attained.

Creating "Impossible" Change

IKEA leaders believe that by integrating sustainability into the business agenda, it is possible to achieve what once was considered impossible. The best example of this is IKEA's efforts to apply IWAY standards for working hours in factories in China. IKEA, like many leading multinationals, made the decision that by 2012 they will limit working hours in supplier factories to 60 hours per week. Working together with suppliers in China, this was accomplished with both efficiency improvements and minor capital upgrades, while holding the product cost and workers' wages steady.

This was not easy for all suppliers, and IKEA did lose many who were not able to meet this new standard. Those who met the standard, however, are now more competitive than their peers, and IKEA's supply network is in turn more sophisticated. IKEA then embarked upon further reducing the working hours per week to 49 by 2015, thus meeting China's own laws and helping China's government with compliance issues. Not many other companies have joined this tough journey. This initiative will require re-examining the entire business process and touching every aspect of the manufacturing process. It will not be easy to keep costs and labor take-home pay steady while reducing worker hours. Most other businesses see this change as crazy or impossible, yet IKEA wisely sees these activities as the core of their competitive advantage and part of the reason they are such a dominant force in the market.

Communication Challenges for IKEA

IKEA's survey of customers found that 85 percent were interested in reducing their environmental footprint, but only 50 percent were aware that IKEA offered product solutions to help them with the challenge. This is what Thomas Schaefer, sustainability leader, identifies as a great challenge. He believes that IKEA is doing so many good things but is not proactive enough in promoting its hard-won sustainability credentials. IKEA uses its brand label as the only marker that stands for all the principles behind the product. This has made the brand both extremely strong and not as easily transparent as other brands that use various sustainability certification logos. Schaefer believes that the company's consumer opportunity is to find new and creative ways to close the gap in consumer perception. This will only serve to complement IKEA's supplier sustainability strategy and grow its competitive advantage in multiple directions.

KEY TAKEAWAYS

- Companies are seeking supply-side-focused sustainable initiatives as they often offer a high potential to reduce costs and risks.
- Companies are increasingly acting collaboratively with suppliers rather than in a transactional mode when implementing sustainability-related programs or initiatives.
- Companies are developing and implementing sustainable procurement policies.
- Companies often share supply chain sustainability goals, metrics, and policies with suppliers.
- Companies that partner with suppliers to develop win-win relationships involving sustainability reduce costs and risks – delivering competitive advantage to both entities.

To effectively *drive the top-line growth with triple-bottom-line thinking* **with suppliers, a company should:**
1. Align its suppliers' sustainability goals and initiatives with its own.
2. Enable supplier training and capacity building.
3. Actively engage suppliers regarding sustainability issues to ensure supply continuity and to reduce non-value-added costs.
4. Energize suppliers to deliver sustainable, innovative solutions in exchange for demand assurance.
5. Monitor and measure its suppliers' performance relative to sustainability goals and objectives.

6 Investing in Communities

In a free enterprise, the community is not just another stakeholder in business, but is in fact the very purpose of its existence.

Jamsetji N. Tata, founder, Tata group, 1868[1]

Figure 6.1. Sustainability stakeholders framework: Investing in communities

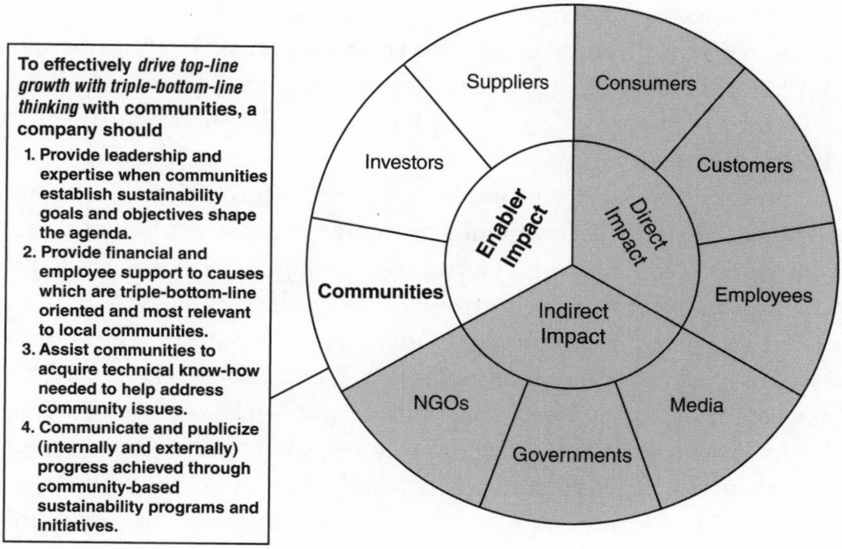
To effectively drive top-line growth with triple-bottom-line thinking with communities, a company should
1. Provide leadership and expertise when communities establish sustainability goals and objectives shape the agenda.
2. Provide financial and employee support to causes which are triple-bottom-line oriented and most relevant to local communities.
3. Assist communities to acquire technical know-how needed to help address community issues.
4. Communicate and publicize (internally and externally) progress achieved through community-based sustainability programs and initiatives.
Suppliers
Consumers
Investors
Customers
Enabler Impact
Direct Impact
Communities
Employees
Indirect Impact
NGOs
Media
Governments

Companies and communities have a symbiotic relationship. There is an unwritten social contract, a social bond, which necessitates them to support each other, both in good times and in bad times. When companies decide to expand their business into new communities, they seek communities that can offer them the requisite employee talent pool, investment incentives, and a safe social environment for their employees and their families. In return, communities are interested in the employment opportunities that a given business can provide its citizens, the revenue it can collect from direct and indirect taxes, and the potential reservoir of social leaders who will ensure that the community continues to thrive.

An old debate about the real reason companies exist has been revived recently with the collapse of firms like Enron, Arthur Andersen, WorldCom, and Lehman Brothers. All these firms were proudly practicing the shareholder maximization model. Views that run counter to this model are now gaining the upper hand. Will Hutton, a British newspaper columnist, challenges companies to be transparent in their purpose, clearly articulating how the company delivers social and economic benefits to society. In his book, *How Good We Can Be*, Hutton coined his call to action as the "Companies Act for the 21st century." Colin Meyer, a professor of management at Oxford University, argues that businesses and their boards must disclose their higher social purpose, similar to how they now are required by law to disclose other material information. He points out that some of the companies recognized as the world's best, including Bosch, Carlsberg, Bertelsmann, and Tata, are owned by foundations with the sole purpose of delivering public good.[2]

The Tata group is among the world's top 50 groups based on market capitalization and reputation. In Tata companies, every single employee shares in the deep values of the founding leader. The Tata group has evolved stronger connections between their values and their business by finding mutually beneficial bridges between them. In 2003, Tata, a company renowned for their business processes, introduced a framework they named the Tata Index for Sustainable Human Development. The framework provided a guideline to Tata companies to channel all their social responsibility efforts. Going forward, all Tata group companies are expected to direct, measure, and enhance their community work under this common framework.[3]

Several cases of effective community programs, implemented by companies in the emerging markets, are shared in an article titled, "B2B Branding in Emerging Markets" by Jagdish Sheth and Mona Sinha, published in October 2015 in *Industrial Marketing Management* journal.[4] These include the following three:

1. By 1995, after a prolonged 17 years of civil war, Mozambique, a poor African country, had begun recovery but faced many social challenges. Malaria was still a rampant heath issue and AIDS was becoming a formidable health challenge. BHP Billiton, a large diversified company, which had invested $1.18 billion in setting up an advanced aluminum smelter plant in 1998, recognized that their investment in the country will only thrive if the people of Mozambique were both successful and heathy. They started to collaborate with the Mozambique government to address the potential health challenges; they invested more than $140 million over the next 12 years to promote community health, distributing netting material, sewing machines, and insecticides. The joint business/government efforts resulted in reducing the incidence rate of malaria from 85 percent to less than 20 percent. In addition, BHP Billiton partnered with the local community to set up a secondary school for 1,800 students, built a community theater and police station, and improved the infrastructure for roads, bridges, waste management, and electricity.[5]

2. Maisa is a Chilean company and market leader in wood boards for furniture. To promote sustainable wood products and increase the demand for their products, they trained 30,000 carpenters, who use this sustainable wood to make furniture for Maisa's Western customers. The company was recognized for creating economic opportunities for low-income families and integrating them in the value chain. The program was subsequently rolled out to Argentina, Brazil, Mexico, and Venezuela, copying the successful model in Chile.[6]

3. Tanzania's Lake Victoria became highly polluted due to increasing amounts of raw sewage being dumped into the lake as the population grew. Along with the rapid environmental degradation came the rise of associated diseases. Barrick Gold Corporation, which had invested heavily in four Tanzanian mining sites, faced a hostile business environment created by local stakeholders, so it actively initiated community engagement to begin to address this challenge. They partnered with local governments to create an environmental awareness program and to better manage issues related to land degradation and toxins in the rivers and the lake. They helped the community set up an Integrated Mining Technical Training program, educating locals on sustainable mining practices. In addition, Barrick contributed funds to upgrade local hospitals' capabilities to effectively treat malaria and yellow fewer patients.[7]

These programs not only helped solve societal challenges but also created an environment in which companies could survive and thrive.

Companies and Communities Have Become Physically Disconnected

In the early industrial age, this community-business relationship took the form of a virtuous cycle in which the community supported and sustained its businesses and, in turn, businesses were committed to delivering the sustenance required for the development of the community. With the growth of globalization and suburban living, this cycle was broken. Products are now created piece by piece in several countries to be shipped to their final destination, and people began long commutes to their own work.

The willingness of business to address societal challenges in the communities where they exist or serve is both threatened and enabled by the burgeoning of the Internet and the emergence of the "virtual" versus the traditional, consolidated workplace. The Internet increasingly disengages employees' personal life and identity, moving both away from a central building or location.

Thus, our notions of the communities where we do business are no longer rooted in the physical domains or in close proximity to an organization's assets. Even with this changing work-home environment, there is recognition by companies that healthy communities depend on healthy businesses and, conversely, healthy businesses continue to rely on healthy communities.

ISO, the International Organization for Standardization, maintains an International Standard that provides guidelines for social responsibility, named ISO 26000. ISO has developed a working definition for "social responsibility" as follows: "Social Responsibility is the responsibility of an organization for the impacts of its decisions and activities on society and the environment, through transparent and ethical behavior that is consistent with sustainable development and the welfare of the society; takes into account the expectations of stakeholders; is in compliance with applicable law and consistent with international norms of behavior and is integrated throughout the organization."[8]

Overall, corporate social responsibility is a company's promise to effect a positive change in the world, wherever and however they operate. This does not mean they do not have a profit motive; it merely means they are willing to demonstrate that they care about the world in which they are trying to make money and about the communities that allow this profit to happen, from the bottom to the top of the organization. This is a recipe for sustainable competitive advantage and profits.

Stakeholders, Drivers of Community Programs

In addition to the pressure applied to companies to create additional value in a wider circle, stakeholders are also driving a shift in businesses toward even more and better community-focused social initiatives. Customers, suppliers, employees, investors, and activist organizations are taking companies to task for their predominantly net negative impacts and are increasingly expecting positive business contributions to society.

- A *consumer* survey conducted by Environics International, involving 1,000 respondents across 20 countries, found that an increasing number of consumers base their purchasing decisions upon their perception of a company's ethics; more than 20 percent of consumers reported that they have either purchased or rejected a company's products based upon the company's perceived social performance.[9]
- *Investors* are starting to behave similarly to customers. More and more university endowment funds and large state retirement funds like CalPERS are choosing to invest in companies that take responsible actions to protect the environment and human rights. In addition, a survey by Environics International confirms the fact that more and more consumers are buying or selling company shares based upon their perception of the companies' ethical behavior across the globe. In the United States, where a large percentage of consumers own stock, over 25 percent of consumers exhibit this behavior. Businesses are sensing this growing investor trend and now are monitoring as well as reporting on ethics-related criteria in their performance metrics.[10]
- *Employees*, especially Gen X and Gen Y employees are increasingly looking beyond paychecks and benefits and are seeking out employers whose philosophies and operating practices best match their own values.
- *Suppliers* differentiate themselves from their lower-cost competitors and effectively defend against offshore companies, where lack of regulation and oversight are commonplace. Suppliers are recognizing that ethical behavior and social not only are responsible business practices but are also beneficial in retaining and winning new business. Great suppliers both effectively market and share their ethical practices and capabilities with like-minded customers, often partnering with them to effect even greater good.[11]
- *NGOs* are monitoring companies' ethical performance and demanding corrective actions via social media and shareholder resolutions or proxy proposals. They have increasingly realized

that much-needed access to funding, required to address their chosen causes and associated programs, can best be obtained from businesses and their charitable foundations. Even contentious NGO and business relations can be transformed with discussion about solid, community-focused partnerships and collaborative efforts, as discussed further in chapter 10.

- *Government* is challenged with tighter budgets and ever-shrinking resources. This situation, coupled with an increase in public distrust of government bodies, has led to the rise of voluntary and non-regulatory initiatives instead of more regulations. A case in point would be certified sustainable palm oil or FSC-certified wood products.

The Business Benefits of Successful Community Programs

Many business leaders might view the stakeholders' interest in community programs with concern and see them as threatening their business interests or bottom lines. More enlightened business leaders, however, see stakeholder-initiated community programs not as a threat but as a cooperative opportunity that brings forth sustainable benefits and potential points of differentiation.

Well-executed community programs create a positive image for a business and can have realizable impacts on the actions of the stakeholders driving its performance. By proactively addressing the drivers of sustainability with appropriate action and decision-making, companies can create advantages in key areas with the following three key stakeholders:

- Customers – By collaborating with customer community social programs and initiatives, a company can expand its base as more and more consumers rally to support businesses that do well for their community. PetSmart, a major pet supply chain that doesn't sell dogs or cats, established PetSmart Charities in 1994 as a nonprofit animal-welfare organization that facilitates 1,000 pet adoptions every day. Free-roaming cats and dogs present several health problems. They are a health threat to people and pets. Rabid dogs are the number one cause of rabies deaths in humans. For example, over 20,000 people die of rabies in India every year, many of them children, and most contract the disease from dog bites. Free-roaming cats and dogs also negatively impact the environment and animals in the wild. Pet product companies can join forces with PetSmart Charities, thereby attracting and retaining new consumers.

- Investors – Similarly, community program activity can enable a company to expand its investor base, as more investors and institutions seek to put their money in socially responsible investment (SRI) vehicles. Companies listed on SRI funds and indices attract additional investment from like-minded investors. (This is discussed more thoroughly in chapter 7.)
- Employees – Companies with successful community program stories attract and retain high-quality, top-talent employees. More and more, workers wish to be a part of a company where they can maximize their collective impact on societal issues. A *Forbes* magazine study involving executives of 59 large companies confirmed that companies are widely seeing benefits from their CSR efforts. The survey showed that 86 percent of companies reported happier employees and that 76 percent said they have better employees as an outcome of their CSR programs and initiatives. Improved talent attraction and retention result when companies engage in programs close to their employees' hearts.[12]

In short, a company that practices good CSR will win over more customers and investors; will attract and retain happier, better employees; and will generate more profit.

There are, of course, benefits to the communities in which these businesses operate or serve as well, resulting in more goodwill and a mutually reinforcing cycle of development. A well-executed community program can enhance communities in three very important ways:

1. Specifically, businesses can *advance social programs* that increase a community's opportunity to tackle major social issues and to foster harmony among its members. Kimberly-Clark's Water for

Life program provides a platform on which it collaborates with NGOs to provide clean drinking water, sanitation, and hygiene education to communities around the world. Successful projects have included communities where K-C's production facilities exist and where its workers and their families live.

2. Businesses can *achieve economic prosperity* by revitalizing neighborhoods, helping people achieve self-sufficiency and enhance their quality of life. Historic Lansing's restoration and revitalization effort is a classic, successful example of how best to revive an older U.S. city. The project, started in 2006, reinforces the contention that preserving historic city buildings not only helps retain and create jobs but also attracts the new investment necessary to spur the revitalization of the city. Lansing preserved three historic buildings during the first phase of the project, creating 500 new jobs while ensuring that the city retains the 932 existing jobs at these sites. Overcoming the headwinds associated with the sagging economy, this project yielded over $190 million in new private investments to downtown Lansing.[13] In addition, General Motors employee volunteers are partnering with Habitat for Humanity Lansing today to help finalize construction and interiors for the new Allen Market Place, located in Lansing's Neighborhood Center. The teamGM Cares volunteer project is funded by General Motors Foundation. As another example, JPMorgan Chase identifies itself as a community development bank and as "a national leader in community development," providing loans, investments, and community development services. Their focus has been on financing affordable housing and community development programs. The bank has reportedly provided $2.6 billion in loans to the low- and moderate-income communities in the United States for development projects.[14]

3. Businesses can *promote environmental sustainability* by supporting programs that promote regenerative society and enhance and protect the planet's natural resources. Most major supermarkets and grocers are committed to, and now have in place, strict policies regarding sustainable seafood sourcing. Overfishing

and pollution challenge the industry to sustain sourcing and sales of this commodity in both the short and the long term.

Steps to Developing Successful Community Programs

Upon examination of real-world community programs, the programs that bring value to the businesses that run them, and also deliver positive contribution to the communities in which they exist, have three distinct steps. The successful programs are set apart from the rest based on how well they execute the following three steps.

1. Selecting and Supporting Right Community Projects

The best-in-class companies have a two-pronged approach to selecting and supporting projects. They identify "signature projects" and "team projects" ensure maximum leverage and mobilization of both business leadership and its employee base. Without this support base, such projects will remain uninspiring and ultimately unsupported.

SIGNATURE PROJECTS
These are the projects that are intricately related to the core of their business, products, and brands and are led by business leadership. They are linked to societal needs and deliver solutions for betterment of the community. Both Coca-Cola and Pepsi have in place major programs to become "water neutral." The two companies understand that clean, accessible water is essential to the health of communities and also essential for their business continuity. In a similar vein, Kimberly-Clark recognized the importance of sustainable forestry to its tissue businesses and broadly supports the FSC-certification label on its iconic tissue brands.

TEAM PROJECTS
These are the projects selected by employees themselves, which will benefit the community they live in. Many companies let their employees select the community projects they want to work on and devise means to support them via funding or by providing

employee volunteers time off or other creative incentives. Examples include supporting local community programs such as the United Way, community development projects, or healthcare awareness projects (breast cancer, ALS, diabetes, etc.).

2. Marketing and Communicating Projects

Best-in-class companies market all of their community projects both internally and externally, to maximize stakeholder awareness and impact. Hence, they require some level of branding and communication. For signature projects, it is best to explicitly link external communications about such projects or campaigns to the corporate brand or brands they support. Some good campaign examples are "Let's Can Hunger" by Campbell's Soup and "Every Little Bottom Counts," by Kimberly-Clark's Huggies brand.

For team projects, internal branding and communication can be just as important as, or even more important than, external communications or PR. Internal branding and communication demonstrates corporate commitment and creates energy around community initiatives to help extract the greatest benefit. For example, AkzoNobel (a Fortune 500 chemical company headquartered in Europe) recognized that serving the communities where they operate and sell is paramount for their own success. So in 2005, they started a Community Program to encourage and assist employees in local community participation. By 2015, the Community Program expanded to over 50 countries with more than 9,000 active volunteers serving their local communities. The program has supported a great variety of projects, from educating and supporting underprivileged groups impacted by the economic crisis to creating awareness in the community about the importance of a clean environment. These projects deliver threefold, as they provide much-needed assistance to the communities, value to the company, and excitement to their employees. The company started a tradition by holding an annual contest where employees vote on the project that has made the best contribution to the community. This event has created a competitive environment for employees to strive in as well as learn from each other.[15]

Another great example illustrating how companies can create effective community engagement programs was generated by a consulting firm, West Monroe Partners (a multinational management and technology consulting company headquartered in the United States). Their novel 1+1+1 Program is a CSR initiative through which they commit to donate 1 percent of their time, 1 percent of their treasure, and 1 percent of their talents each year to organizations in their communities. The concept is simple and memorable for all stakeholders. Gary Beu, managing director of the firm, shared, "Since kicking off our 1+1+1 Program, West Monroe Partners has collectively matched 1,500 employee volunteer hours, completed nearly 4,000 hours for pro bono projects across the United States, and donated over $250,000 to non-profit organizations."[16] Think of the phenomenal level of impact possible if most businesses simply gave back 1 percent.

3. Monitoring and Reporting Projects

As shared previously in this chapter, the employees at AkzoNobel vote annually to select the program that exemplifies contribution to the community as part of their Community Program. In 2014, the prize went to a team of employees from Decorative Paints, Functional Chemicals and Powder Coatings located in Langfang and Tianjin, China. For many years, the local AkzoNobel employees engaged in helping 80–100 children housed at the Shepherd's Field Children's Village center. In 2013, the employees ratcheted their involvement to a new level when the team volunteers refurbished the facility's Rehabilitation and Skills Center. The children at the center are taught the skills needed to earn a decent living in a safe and clean environment. These types of programs and associated competitions empower and encourage socially minded employees to make a difference in their local communities.[17]

Community Development Partnership Examples

Grameen Bank began providing loans to low-income groups while generating reasonable financial returns, something many in the banking industry said could not be done. In the process, Grameen Bank has helped improve the lives of many people. To continue the social experiment, the Grameen Foundation USA (GFUSA) was formed and tasked to address social issues. The foundation recognized that most schoolchildren from low-income homes do not have access to nutritional meals, so they teamed up with Danone Foods to develop a low-cost meal called "Shakti," a yogurt formulated to improve nutrition. Not only has the drink improved the lives of millions of Bangladeshi schoolchildren, but the benefits are felt by stakeholders across the entire value chain. The milk for making the yogurt is purchased locally from micro-farmers, thereby ensuring them a livelihood. In addition, local women are hired for door-to-door selling of yogurt so they earn living wages. In summary, apart from proving nutritional meal to millions of schoolchildren in Bangladesh, the Grameen Danone Foods project has created a livelihood for over 1,600 people adjacent to the plant.[18]

Case Study: Tata Group

We chose Tata for this case study because of their scale and unique structure. Based in India, the Tata group is a large multinational conglomerate operating in more than 80 countries. It comprises more than 100 Tata companies, spanning six continents, whose combined revenue was $108.78 billion in 2014 and whose combined global workforce is over 610,000. Dr. Mukund Rajan, who is a member of the Group Executive Council at Tata Sons Ltd., serves as the Tata brand custodian, chief ethics officer, and chairman of the Tata Global Sustainability Council. He shared with us the founding history of the company and the reasons why their commitment to community is so unique.

The Tata group is almost 150 years old but has had only six leaders in that time, thereby providing consistency of purpose and reinforcement of values. The founder, Jamsetji N. Tata, was an inspirational leader whose values are still etched in the company's DNA. He believed that the purpose of an enterprise is the improvement of the quality of life of the community it serves. His definition of community was broad and included investors, customers, and employees as well as community in a traditional sense. He pioneered the JN Tata Endowment in 1892 to fund higher education for talented young Indians, arguably the first such fund globally to acknowledge the importance of education in building the country and community. Reflecting Jamsetji's inclusive instincts, a woman was selected to be the first awardee for this scholarship. Soon after, Jamsetji proposed the establishment of a university dedicated to higher education in modern science and left a significant part of his personal fortune toward the creation of what became known as the Indian Institute of Science in Bengaluru.

He dreamed of a modern city that would be inclusive and exhorted his sons to ensure such a city would have "wide streets planted with shady trees of a quick-growing variety. Plenty of space left for lawns and gardens. Large areas reserved for football, hockey and parks. Areas earmarked for Hindu temples, Mohammedan mosques and Christian churches."

His sons Dorab Tata and Ratan Tata turned that concept into reality by creating the city that is known today as Jamshedpur. They further expanded this concept of inclusiveness to the labor practices adopted at Jamshedpur, offering benefits such as pensión, gratuity, provident fund, free medical aid, schooling facility for children, leave with pay, profit-sharing bonus, and an eight-hour workday to name a few; all of these benefits were transformed into laws in India several decades later.

Both of Jamsetji's sons left their entire wealth to two trusts whose mandate is to give back to society. The Tata Trusts currently own 66 percent equity in Tata Sons. Ensuring corporate governance in line with doing the best for society, Jamsetji Tata's sons introduced the concept of trusteeship to the corporate world.

The Tata group is an enterprise like no other in the corporate world. Their legacy, ownership structure, and business mission set them apart as one of the best examples of a corporation whose core purpose is to improve the quality of life of the communities it serves.

Does this work as a business model? According to Richard Foster of Yale University, in 1920 the average lifespan of a U.S. company in the S&P 500 was 67 years. That number has dropped dramatically over time, and in the year 2012 the average lifespan was 15 years.[19] Tata group has been a healthy company for 150 years. Their longevity, size, and continued growth are testament to the success of their model.

Dr. Rajan further shared the work his group has undertaken in reframing the organization's mission in 2014. It builds on the founding values to define the kind of world Tata wants to create. The mission states, "The Mission of Tata is to improve the quality of life of the communities we serve through long term stakeholder value creation based upon leadership with trust."[20]

Over several decades, Tata's social sustainability work has become as diverse as its many business units. At the group level, therefore, they have tried to create more focus around a limited set of crosscutting themes, which also helps smaller and newer companies to adopt such initiatives. To accomplish that, Tata Sons initially created a nodal agency, the Tata Council for Community Initiatives (TCCI), comprising CEOs of over 50 major Tata companies; this recently morphed into a new governance structure, the smaller Tata Global Sustainability Council, supported by an executive body called the Tata Sustainability Group (TSG).

The way this body governs is rooted in a framework Tata has been developing for almost 20 years. In 1997, TCCI began to work on an approach to understand how all the social work undertaken by Tata companies leads to improving the quality of life of communities.

An inquiry document led to a compilation of case studies. This was refined into a set of Community Guidelines in 2000. In the following years, major Tata group companies signed on to the Global Reporting Initiative (GRI) and to the UN Global Compact (UNGC). The TCCI forged an innovative partnership with the UN Development Programme (UNDP) to combine the power of business processing, a democratic and systematic way to build consensus and aggregation, with the main objective of going beyond "results" or "outcomes" to measure "impact." Impact was defined as a resultant positive change in human life, which is sustained and long term. In

2003, a yearlong effort went into developing correlations between HR and business model initiatives. From this effort, the Tata Index for Sustainable Human Development was created to ensure that the goal of all initiatives is assessed in terms of Tata's vision of human achievement and human excellence (Figure 6.2).

In 1995, around the same time TCCI was formed to look at social impacts, the Tata Business Excellence Model (TBEM) was also introduced by then chairman Ratan Tata to bring Tata companies together, to define their common purpose and philosophy, to inspire them to seek global excellence, and to strengthen the Tata brand (Figure 6.3). The model has provided Tata companies with a framework for assessing their businesses holistically and adopting measures to improve their competitive strength, financial performance, and operational efficiencies.

The TBEM initiative led to the "stitching together" of Tata companies at different levels, connecting chief executives, business leaders, and line managers of the many group companies. TBEM plays another important role as the vehicle for seamlessly integrating the group's global acquisitions and aligning them to the Tata culture.

The group combined the learning from the Tata Index for Sustainable Human Development into the TBEM by incorporating climate change and social development programs. The new TBEM assessment criteria are built on 11 core values and concept systems:

1. Visionary Leadership
2. Customer-Driven Excellence
3. Organizational and Personal Learning
4. Valuing Workforce Members and Partners
5. Agility
6. Focus on the Future
7. Managing for Innovation
8. Management by Fact
9. Societal Responsibility
10. Focus on Results and Creating Value
11. Systems Perspective

Figure 6.2. Tata Index for Sustainable Human Development

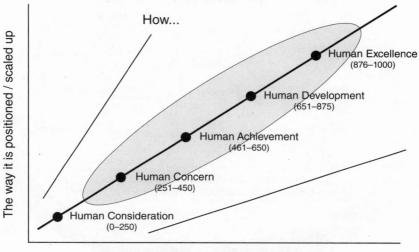

A TATA Program Is a Journey towards Human Excellence

Source: Tata & Sons

Essentially, TBEM highlights the importance of governance and societal responsibilities within the leadership category by asking senior leaders how their organization fulfills its legal, ethical, and societal responsibilities and supports its key communities. In addition, climate change (an aspect of environmental sustainability) is woven across TBEM to assess the following:

- Leadership commitment to climate change and active involvement in enabling processes;
- Integration of climate change challenges and opportunities in the strategy planning process;
- Climate change aspirations and action plans;
- Capturing of customers' "green" expectations;

Figure 6.3. Tata Business Excellence Model (TBEM)

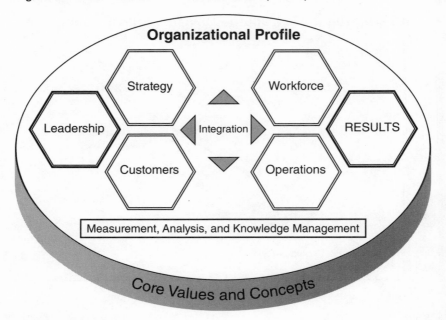

Source: Tata & Sons

- Development of "green" products/services/business models;
- Appropriate climate change governance structure and review mechanisms;
- Development and sourcing of current and future climate change capabilities;
- Incorporating a "low carbon" perspective while designing and improving processes.

The objective of the Tata Sustainability Framework, which will be integrated with TBEM in 2016, is to mainstream sustainability to achieve simultaneous economic, social, and environmental benefits. The core principle is the need to strike the right balance between the various constituents of environmental and social sustainability while maintaining a sharp focus on economic value creation for all stakeholders. For this to happen, it is imperative to focus in four ways, which Tata has described as four directions:

1. Deep: integrate and embed sustainability into the company strategy and standard operating practices;
2. Wide: engage and leverage the value chain (all stakeholders);
3. Long: short-term focus to long-term objectives;
4. Local: shared responsibility that needs local action and commitment.

The Tata Sustainability Framework is so structured that it will help Tata companies assess their maturity on these dimensions, monitor their sustainability progress over time, and provide ideas for improvement to achieve leadership positions in sustainability.

Tata continues to advance its own world-leading practices on combining excellent corporate performance with life-changing community impact.

Dr. Rajan's position with the group as brand custodian, chief ethics officer, and chairman of the Tata Global Sustainability Council is itself quite unique and highlights the Tata way of doing business. By combining Tata brand stewardship, ethics, and sustainability under one person, the group continues to demonstrate its progressive way of thinking. In addition, it ensures that ethical business practices, concern for the environment, and giving back to society will all continue to be embedded in the brand and nurtured. This will help further grow the brand and image of Tata in the community.

Dr. Rajan shared with us that Tata's integration of profit and service to the community has allowed them to attract different kinds of business opportunities. For example, high numbers of high-performing millennials specifically seek out Tata for employment, helping to ensure productivity and leadership for the future. He shared that this talent is often willing to join Tata companies even if the pay on offer is not necessarily the highest because of the longer-term benefits the companies offer; their engagement scores are also typically high. In addition, Tata is often the destination partner when it comes to foreign multinationals looking to expand in Asia. When India's aviation market opened to privatization, Singapore Airlines specifically choose Tata for the joint venture that launched a new, successful airline, Vistara. Dr. Rajan attributes these wins to one concept – trust. Tata's unwavering commitment to improving the quality of life of communities across the globe has given them a reputation that opens up many opportunities completely closed to other business groups.

KEY TAKEAWAYS

- Companies and communities can enjoy a symbiotic, sustainability-centered relationship in both good times and bad times.
- Business leaders increasingly view caring for community as an opportunity to gain a competitive advantage.
- Company programs often help communities address social issues, enhance quality of life, and improve the environment.
- The most robust company community programs effectively relate to business objectives.
- Company community programs' progress is best measured and reported with both frequency and transparency.

To effectively *drive the top-line growth with triple-bottom-line thinking* with communities, a company should:
1. Provide leadership and expertise when communities establish sustainability goals and objectives and shape the agenda.
2. Provide financial and employee support to causes which are triple-bottom-line oriented and most relevant to local communities.
3. Help communities acquire the technical know-how needed to address community issues.
4. Communicate and publicize (internally and externally) progress achieved through community-based sustainability programs and initiatives.

7 Attracting Investors

CEOs change on an average every 3.7 years, while you want to see sustainability initiatives to go on for 3.7 decades.

Mindy Lubber, president of Ceres

Figure 7.1. Sustainability stakeholders framework: Attracting investors

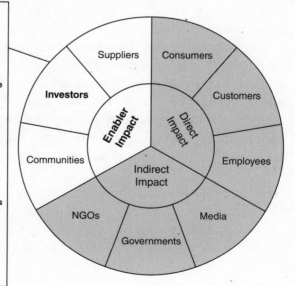

To effectively *drive top-line growth with triple-bottom-line thinking* with investors, a company should

1. Demonstrate that, in the long run, sustainability-related initiatives benefit shareholders more than those that are non-sustainable.
2. Move toward carbon neutrality and show how it contributes to the bottom line in the long run.
3. Hold workshops that serve to educate the investor community about the business impacts of sustainability issues.
4. Engage in sustainability initiatives that will enhance its brand's equity and its reputation.
5. Make sustainability challenges an aspect of its risk profile and their management the responsibility of its board of directors.

Suppliers · Consumers · Investors · Customers · Communities · Employees · NGOs · Governments · Media

Enabler Impact · Direct Impact · Indirect Impact

Ceres is one of the most influential sustainability advocacy groups in the world. Mindy Lubber in a recent interview shared the conundrum and frustration faced by the sustainability-minded investment community for investment decisions as they face the seemingly competing forces of short-term results and long-term goals.

According to Lubber, the tension in this time frame is actually not as great as the tension caused by leadership that does not walk the talk of sustainability. The real challenge, she explains, is that companies often take inconsistent or extreme positions. What they say and what they do often don't match, and what they support in their public policies runs counter to their behind-the-scenes agendas. Sitting in those boardroom meetings are stakeholders who have become much more aware of the eroded value caused by this tension and who have a major influence on company activities: investors.

Banks, insurance companies, private equity funds, and other institutional investors are now making the sustainability connection and have begun evaluating companies' performance from the triple-bottom-line perspective (profit, people, and planet). It is important for investors to ask companies for their sustainability credentials when it comes to water, carbon, governance, and supply chain issues.

When Mindy Lubber was asked which companies have done well on the sustainability journey, she offered that highly successful companies – such as Unilever, Nestlé, Intel, Marks & Spencer, and IKEA – are considered strong leaders in most sustainability areas. And others have done well in one or two specific areas but still have skeletons in the closet: for example, Pepsi has done well with water and waste initiatives, but their base product has strong links to obesity.

Sustainability Is a Good Investment

There is growing recognition that the social and environmental conditions in society can have a direct impact on the business operations of a company and its long-term viability. For example, a beverage company like Coca-Cola must protect its sources of potable water to manufacture its product in both the short and long term. Technology companies like Google and Facebook must have a reliable electrical grid and access to affordable power sources. In addition, the way a company like Apple protects the health and safety of its workers and the communities where it operates helps investors understand management's practices and ethics.

The investment market is increasingly taking note of the sustainability practices and positions of businesses. There are six factors that illustrate the trend of connecting investment potential with company sustainability.

Shareholder Resolutions

Shareholder voting patterns provide convincing evidence of investors' belief that a company's social and environmental policies correlate strongly with its financial performance. Jackie Cook, of Fund Votes' *Proxy Season Roundup*, summarized the votes on 502 resolutions submitted by shareowners in 2013. Her analysis of shareholder resolutions shows that the majority relate to corporate governance concerns, including executive pay, shareholders' rights, election of directors, and the like, and that the average support for such resolutions was found to have decreased from historic highs. In contrast, the average level of support for environmental and social issue–based resolutions, constituting the balance of the remaining resolutions, was at a 10-year high.[1]

Steady Growth in Sustainable Investment

The growth over the past 15 years in sustainable capital investments or socially responsible investments (SRIs) is noteworthy. As a matter of fact, the growth in sustainable asset investing is outpacing the broader category of conventional investment assets under professional management. Currently in the United States, SRIs account for nearly one out of every six dollars under professional management or 18 percent of the $36.8 trillion in total assets under management tracked by Cerulli Associates.[2]

According to Daniel Schmid, a contributor to CSRWire, in 2014, NASDAQ OMX estimated that nearly $1.9 trillion was invested in SRIs globally, accounting for 10.3 percent of the capital market. To provide perspective, this compares to 5.9 percent of the capital market invested in SRIs in 2010.[3]

Taking note of the significant growth in funds focused on environmental, social, and governance (ESG) over the last few years, the large Wall Street financial giants Morgan Stanley, BlackRock Inc., and Goldman Sachs have decided jump on the SRI bandwagon. Morgan Stanley has educated investors, teaching them that doing good and realizing competitive market returns are not binary choices, while BlackRock Inc. and Goldman Sachs opened the BlackRock U.S. Equity Fund (BIRAX) and Goldman Sachs Imprint Capital Advisors Fund, respectively, to provide investors attractive ESG-focused fund choices. In a *Wall Street Journal* article, Fiona Reynolds, managing director of the Principles for Responsible Investment (or PRI, a UN-supported initiative whose signatories pledge to incorporate elements of sustainability into their financial decisions), states, "When you have some of the largest players in the financial-services sector taking ESG seriously, it sends a powerful signal to the markets." According to the article, Reynolds shared that there has been a large jump in the ESG-focused funds amounting to $59 trillion, about half of all institutional assets worldwide the investors are managing.[4]

Correlation between ESG and Financial Performance

Analysis done by the Carbon Disclosure Project (CDP) in 2014 clearly shows that the companies considered leaders in climate change management among S&P 500 members by and large deliver superior results compared to their low-scoring peers, both in terms of profitability (18 percent higher) and stability (50 percent lower volatility). As a result, these climate change management leaders have been able to consistently increase dividends for shareholders, thus making them an attractive investment for many equity investors.[5]

The 2014 Climate Disclosure Leadership Indices (CDLI) included three companies that have been on the list since its inception in 2003: BMW, Bank of America/Merrill Lynch, and the National Australian Bank. The study report states, "Listed companies tend to show reduction over time in their overall carbon emissions (Total of Scope 1 and Scope 2 emissions reported to CDP in 2014), as well as reductions over time of a metric CDP refers to as 'financial intensity,' calculated as Metric tons CO_2e (Scope 1 and 2 emissions) per unit of revenue (US $ million)."[6]

Sustainability Staffing at Institutional Investors

The huge sum of potential investment dollars at stake has led large financial services firms to establish their own sustainability research departments. The Sustainable Investment Research Analyst Network (SIRAN) now supports more than 260 North American sustainable investment research analysts from more than 50 investment firms, research providers, and affiliated investor groups. These analysts use a variety of approaches to benchmark companies within their peer groups, including screening for "best-in-class" examples of sustainable practices. The CFO of Kimberly-Clark, Mark Buthman, discussed with us his observation of a growing desire on quarterly earnings calls and investor analysis road shows to connect a company's financial performance to its social and environmental impact.

Better Analytical Tools

Accelus is a comprehensive toolkit made available by Thomson Reuters for managing business risks by providing a platform that delivers market-leading solutions for a host of governance issues (bribery, corruption, financial crime, board, and disclosure) and regulatory issues (environmental risk, compliance management, global regulatory intelligence, and due diligence). In addition, Thomson

Reuters offers related training and e-learning modules.[7] MSCI offers ESG Impact Monitor, which allows investors to analyze a company's social and environmental impacts and the company's ability to manage them. Bloomberg's new ESG Valuation Tool enables users to apply a financially based methodology to assess and value the impact of ESG factors on a company's earnings before interest and tax (EBIT) performance and share price. Better metrics will mean better-informed investors, which will encourage a further escalation of the sustainable investing trend.

Growing Interest among Institutional Investors

A Harvard study conducted in 2011, examining the web hits for Bloomberg ESG data, found increasing investor interest in ESG data, with sell-side firms (brokers and dealers) primarily interested in greenhouse gas emissions data and buy-side firms (hedge funds, money managers, etc.) interested in a broad range of ESG information. It is speculated that the reason for this difference in interests of the two types of firms is the belief that analysts are more comfortable integrating the impacts of GHG emissions in their valuation models and profit projections, while buy-side firms view the broader ESG data as an indication of sound inevitability.[8]

Progressive companies are quietly differentiating themselves by upgrading their sustainability reporting processes and systems using the GRI's G4 and participating in the CDP and the Dow Jones Sustainability Index (DJSI). In 2012, CDP requested climate risk disclosure on behalf of 655 institutional investors holding $78 trillion in assets under management. This represents an 18-times increase in both numbers of signatories (35 in 2002) and assets ($4.5 billion in 2002) over the previous 10 years.

The Role of Investors

The preponderance of data shows that more and more individuals and institutions want to invest in a manner that is consistent with their specific beliefs and values. Some hold that private-sector capital can and should play a key role in driving large-scale solutions to the most critical challenges to global prosperity and well-being. As mentioned, nearly one in six dollars under professional management in the United States follows investment strategies that consider corporate responsibility and societal concerns. The SRI slice of the pie has been growing and is forecasted to continue to do so. The Vision 2050 WBCSD document estimates that the global business opportunities in health, education, agriculture, and other sustainability-related sectors which promote sustainable living could total as much as $10 trillion annually by the year 2050 in today's constant dollars.[9]

In an uncertain world, we tend to invest as an act of faith in the future, with the belief that we can shape the future and be better off because of our investment. When headlines consistently reflect seemingly insurmountable challenges, smart investment takes a long-term perspective and uses the vision that extends well beyond balance sheets and stock prices.

The earliest approach to sustainable investing by institutional investors screened out "sin sectors" that used practices like blood mining or sold products like cigarettes. Soon afterward, sustainable investors began rewarding companies who improved natural resource efficiency (energy, water, waste) or who practiced sustainable procurement.

The long-term environmental and social sustainability issues are gaining prominence, as they often bear directly on companies' risk profiles, their reputations, and their financial performance. Though the SEC (Securities and Exchange Commission) requires that all publicly traded companies disclose risks that could impact a company materially, not all companies are doing so, especially for water-related risks. To encourage disclosure of water shortages and associated sustainability risks to the shareholders, in 2015 Ceres, along with 60 institutional investors who manage $2.6 trillion in assets, challenged one dozen food and beverage companies to openly share the water risks they face. The companies included large multinationals

Kraft Heinz Company, Tyson Foods, Monster Beverage, Fresh Del Monte, and Dean Foods. Some of these companies already had experienced business disruption during tough summer months because of water scarcity. For example, Tyson Foods closed one of its meat processing plants during the summer of 2015 because of diminished cattle stock in southwestern states.[10]

These sustainability risks will have far-reaching economic implications that savvy investors include in their investing decisions. They will challenge businesses and affect investment returns across all asset classes. As recent economic bubbles and crashes have shown, simply waiting to respond can lead to great losses.

Assessing Risks and Sustainability Rankings to Attract Investors

Unprecedented risks to the global economy make this a challenging time for the twenty-first-century investor, most of whom have multigenerational obligations to beneficiaries. Yet many challenges remain before sustainable investing is truly open to any investor. One of the biggest is that there isn't yet one agreed-upon definition of what makes an investment "sustainable." The question of what is a sustainable investment remained unanswered in 2015 in the absence of guidance from regulators. Before the October 2015 ruling by the U.S. Labor Department, the ESG factors were not considered in investment decision-making by pension fund and 401(k) plan managers. The ruling, while groundbreaking, neglected to identify precisely what is considered sustainable. To make matters worse, businesses are not required to disclose ESG factors. Although the ruling is considered a step in the right direction, much work is required before audit systems could be in place that enable consistent assessments of ESG risks and associated sustainable investments.[11]

To further complicate the issue, there are over 140 sustainability rating agencies, each of which prioritizes different metrics. This makes investment decisions all the more challenging for an investment house. Since no single rating is comprehensive enough, most companies look for ratings from the top three or four rating agencies, like the

DJSI, the Centers for Disease Control and Prevention (CDC) rating, and that of Corporate Knights.

The leading resource for any institutional asset owners and their investment managers is Ceres's Blueprint for Sustainable Investing. According to its authors, "This Blueprint is written for the 21st Century investor ... who needs to understand and manage the growing risks posed by climate change, resource scarcity, population growth, human and labor rights, energy demand and access to water – risks that will challenge businesses and affect investment returns in the years and decades to come." Ceres has analyzed 680 of the top Russell 1000 Index companies for engagement at the board level, compensation of senior leadership, transparency, goals established and their performance against the goals, supply chain sustainability, and position on public policies.

Institutional investors have started to offer platforms for individuals, pension funds, and insurance companies to choose impact investments as part of their portfolio. For example, Morgan Stanley's Institute for Sustainable Investing platform claims to provide a multitude of resources to those seeking to integrate sustainable investments into their portfolios. These include a sustainably vetted product matrix that includes over a hundred exchange-traded funds, mutual funds, and other investment vehicles; an Impact Framework to classify funds by type of impact; and access to white papers, educational materials, and global analyst teams that are well versed in sustainability and responsible investing[12]

Because sustainability issues are interconnected and intertwined, the key to assessing the future is to understand how one issue impacts another. For example, how does climate change impact disease migration? What impact does the climate have on urbanization and demographic trends? How then does this impact water scarcity? The future of sustainable investing will focus on these interconnected, longer-term positive impacts. This will be aided by new valuation methods for sustainable technologies, like regenerative solutions, as resources become more finite. The sustainable investing picture will continue to get more robust and more lucrative.

Building the Sustainability-Investor Connection

The barriers to explaining the advantages of sustainability to investors that are not already accustomed to such considerations can be overcome. By understanding what has worked in the real world, and by taking advantage of current trends, companies can highlight and build their own sustainability advantage for the investment community by answering these four questions:

What Are the Most Material Issues?

Businesses can conduct an analysis to identify the issues that are of highest concern to investors. This will help companies identify their key issues, the ones that are both important to stakeholders and have the highest impact on the company's performance. The process to develop a prioritized list of issues that are the most material for a specific company or sector is referred to as a materiality assessment.

In a 2013 GreenBiz article, Mark A. Serwinowski, the president and founder of MetaVu, defined the purpose of materiality analysis in the context of sustainability as follows: "The materiality assessment is an exercise in stakeholder engagement designed to gather insight on the relative importance of specific environmental, social and governance (ESG) issues. The insight is most commonly used to inform sustainability reporting and communication strategies, but it also is valuable to strategic planning, operational management, and capital investment decisions."[13] Materiality assessments have become best practices for many large, sustainably minded corporations, such as Kimberly-Clark and Nestlé.

How Does Materiality Connect with Growth, Productivity, Risk, and Brand Image?

Companies need to develop specific commercial strategies to address critical issues that impact business revenue growth, productivity, costs, supply chain risks, and reputational risks for the brand.

In 2014, Nestlé engaged Accenture, a leading sustainability consulting firm, to study their materiality analysis and help them fine-tune their commercial strategies to address these risks. Accenture further helped Nestlé build these strategies into Nestlé's Creating Shared Value commitments. Nestlé believes that successfully meeting these commitments will ensure that the company will be able to deliver superior shareholder returns and help people improve their nutrition, health, and wellness.[14]

How Can Operations Better Drive Value for These Issues?

After identifying material issues, companies need to prioritize and initiate actions on them by integrating them as business practices throughout the organization. For example, AT&T not only monitors the issues identified as material to them but also reports on the progress they have made on these issues annually. Issues determined to be of higher importance by stakeholders require more frequent engagement and communication with relevant stakeholders. On the other hand, the issues identified as top priorities by the business will require broader management engagement in all business units. All priorities, internal or external, would have clear relevant goals, KPIs (key performance indicators), and detailed program plans. Implementation of prioritized issues ensures value is created for the business.[15]

How Do Sustainable Operations Compare with "Normal" Operations in Value Creation?

Companies can communicate to investors using metrics and ratios of the performance of sustainable activities versus "normal" activities to demonstrate that caring for these issues contributes to the top and bottom line and helps the company to mitigate risk and maximize opportunities. The Mitsubishi Chemical Holdings (MCHC) Group recently implemented a materiality assessment while taking into account the perspectives of their stakeholders. The materiality

assessment identified the issues that the group believes are important and prioritized material managerial issues that need to be addressed. The company reported that they will use the assessment
results to develop and formulate management policies and incorporate them in their *KAITEKI* values so MCHC continues to be
viewed as a trusted company by shareholders and is able to contribute sustainable development of people, society, and Earth, without
being influenced by economic volatility.[16] According to the 2011
McKinsey survey, Dow Chemical saved close to $9.8 billion in water
and energy savings while investing less than $2 billion to improve
the company's resource efficiency since 1994, thus creating value for
the shareholders.[17]

Sustainability has become one of the most important and defining
challenges of our time. It is redefining societal expectations, public
policies, regulatory frameworks, and, as a result, business environ-
ments and investment outcomes. Such challenges create new opportunities and risks that smart companies will address today to
remain competitive tomorrow. Companies that successfully translate these challenges to their advantage can expect to outperform
their peers in the future.

Many companies appear to appreciate, at some level, the importance of sustainability to various stakeholders, yet most businesses
have struggled with how to measure and track the impact of their
sustainability activities on core business metrics such as revenue
growth, cost reduction, risk management, and reputation. As a result, many companies have difficulty explaining the benefits of a
sustainable business strategy to investors.

David Lubin and Daniel Esty argue in the 2014 *MIT Sloan
Management Review*, "Given that the expected steady increases in the
impacts of climate change, regulatory pressures and evolving consumer attitudes are likely to make sustainability strategy even more
important going forward, we believe mainstream investors will reward companies that demonstrate business gains from sustainability
– provided investors can easily spot the sustainability winners."[18]

Case Study: DuPont Promotes Sustainability with Investors

DuPont is one of the best-in-class examples of how to communicate the triple-bottom-line results to investors and shareholders. Ellen Kullman, chair of the board and chief executive officer for DuPont, in a 2014 GRI report articulated the company vision as follows: "At DuPont, sustainable growth is integral to everything we do as a company, as we work to enable greater food security and safety, create high performance, cost-effective and energy efficient materials across industries, and deliver renewably sourced bio-based materials and fuels. We define sustainable growth as creating shareholder and societal value through all of this work, while reducing the environmental impact of our value chains."[19] The vision resonates well with investors and stakeholders while addressing all three pillars of sustainability, namely economic, environmental, and social. Highlights of DuPont's sustainability progress, as communicated in its 2014 GRI report, are summarized here.

Economic Progress

- $2.5 billion, or close to 6 percent of total revenue in 2013, came from products that reduced their total GHG emissions versus the benchmark reduction of $100 million or 0.3 percent in 2007.
- $11.8 billion, or 30 percent of total revenue in 2013, came from products using non-depletable resources versus the benchmark of 20 percent in 2007.
- Recognized as an industry leader by being listed in *Fortune* magazine's World's Most Admired Companies, 100 Top Most Powerful Brands, and Newsweek's 100 Green Ranking, DuPont continues to improve their standing on most of these rankings and indices, further enhancing the brand image.
- DuPont more than doubled its R&D spending to $0.9 billion, innovating products that reduce environmental impact.

Environmental Progress

- DuPont achieved its stated 2015 footprint stewardship targets two years ahead of plan by reducing the absolute impact while growing the business.
- They reduced net Scope 1 and Scope 2 GHG emissions from 18.8 million metric tons in 2007 to 16.5 million metric tons in 2013.
- Absolute water consumption was reduced from 24.2 million cubic meters in 2007 to 19.9 million cubic meters in 2013 for sites in water-stressed or water-scarce locations.
- Dramatically improved air emissions were achieved by reducing SOx from 28.3 metric tons in 2007 to 9.0 metric tons in 2017 and NOx from 9.0 metric tons to 7.0 metric tons for the same period.
- They reduced hazardous waste from 449,000 metric tons in 2007 to 388,000 metric tons in 2013.
- DuPont reduced cumulative (customers' and consumers') absolute GHG emissions by 45.7 million tons of CO_2 from 2007 to 2013.
- ISO 140001 certified 100 percent of DuPont legacy sites.

Social Progress

- Total recordable injury rates at DuPont facilities were reduced by over 23 percent between 2007 and 2013.
- DuPont introduced 1,964 new products that make people safer globally.
- The company spent $1.3 billion in R&D investment through 2013 to help feed the world.
- They improved the livelihood of 205,000 family farmers and their rural communities.
- DuPont engaged over 770,000 youths in educational opportunities.[20]

KEY TAKEAWAYS

- Investors are increasingly evaluating a company's performance from the triple-bottom-line perspective.
- Trends in the business world show a marked growth in value and sustainability-based investing.
- Companies are conducting materiality analyses to identify the sustainability-related issues most relevant to stakeholders and their future.
- Companies are developing and implementing strategies to address material issues that add the greatest value.
- Companies are learning to package and communicate progress on sustainability metrics using terms investors are most familiar with and understand the implications of.

To effectively *drive the top-line growth with triple-bottom-line thinking* **with investors, a company should:**
1. Demonstrate that in the long run, sustainability-related initiatives benefits shareholders more than those that are non-sustainable.
2. Move toward carbon neutrality and show how it contributes to the bottom line in the long run.
3. Hold workshops that serve to educate the investor community about the business impacts of sustainability issues.
4. Engage in sustainability initiatives that will enhance its brand equity and its reputation.
5. Make sustainability challenges an aspect of its risk profile and their management the responsibility of its board of directors.

8 Leveraging Media

In today's environment where social channels are available to everyone, every brand is a media company.

Megan Cunningham, CEO of the Magnet Media Company

Figure 8.1. Sustainability stakeholders framework: Leveraging media

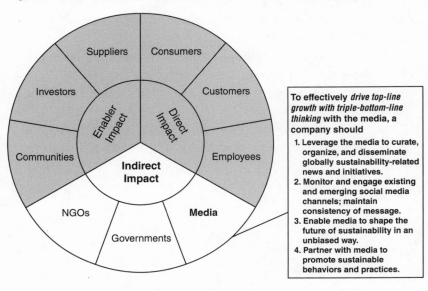

The Magnet Media Company is a strategic studio providing creative content solutions. The company specializes in telling Fortune 1000 brands' stories through developing, producing, and syndicating content across the digital landscape to engage target audiences, drive action, and measure results. Cunningham's message embedded in the above statement has serious ramifications for businesses and brands.

Cunningham speaks with businesses about the evolving consumer attention, which has shifted from billboards, press, and linear television experiences to multichannel or omnichannel consumption, where everyone has all forms of media in their pocket. Until the 1990s, advertising/PR agencies helped develop the content while media companies like NBC and the *New York Times* provided the media distribution. Now with the growth of YouTube, Facebook, Twitter, Tumblr, and Pinterest, brands can create their own content and distribute to their own audiences, creating an entire experience either outside of or completely connected to all other forms of media.

The old-school approach is still very much alive. The $500 billion annual global advertising industry has encountered increasing criticism for promoting unsustainable consumerism, promoting unhealthy habits, and wasting resources. Of course, this industry is getting paid to do so and will continue to get support as long as its means are effective and its reach is broad. So it appears that traditional media engagement will always be sought out by sustainable and not-so-sustainable companies alike, and this engagement is likely here to stay.

To the sustainability-minded businesses, Cunningham's advice is simple: "To capture the imagination of customer influencers, one needs to supplement the 'old school Public Relation (PR) approach' with the use of 'new social media tools' synergistically. This will help progressive businesses galvanize the community through a movement, which in turn will give them a competitive advantage."

That's why achieving sustainability goals will require a partnership between sustainable companies and media to shape the future of company-directed TV, print, online content, social networks, and web applications. The modern scope and opportunity of the media world and the modern sustainability movement make near-perfect partners when they utilize their respective roles in support of each other.

Roles of Media in Sustainability

For this book, "media" is defined as inclusive of the traditional forms of print, radio, and television (network and cable), as well as the burgeoning Internet presence and rise of social media. The media's role will be to educate consumers about unsustainable consumerism, unhealthy habits, and resource waste in an effective way. Savvy sustainable businesses can leverage the following four critical roles of media to increase the engagement in and impact of the company's sustainability goals.

Screener

The U.S. media, in aggregate, can be classified as "content agnostic," as it typically presents both sides of the coin on almost every issue. That's typically viewed as a good thing. This pursuit becomes a problem, however, when presenting both sides of an issue as "equal" does not reflect the known "facts" about a given issue. Climate change reporting is one example. The media's intention to pursue objective reporting has, in practice, actually skewed the facts. In an effort to present a balanced account of both sides of the issue, the media has underrepresented the preponderance of scientific evidence, of which 99 percent falls on one side of the debate.

A scientific study conducted in 2004 at the University of California by Maxwell T. Boykoff and Jules M. Boykoff found that media has given more coverage than merited to the "denial discourse" (i.e., the contention that climate change is in fact not a real global threat supported by a preponderance of sound scientific opinions). The journalistic norm, that of "balanced reporting," results in the media giving equal space to air suppositions of both viewpoints. Inadvertently, "balanced reporting" may actually have delayed any needed action on climate change in the United States for reasons of "uncertainty." At times, the media either consciously or unconsciously screens out select facts for the supposed purpose of conveying objectivity. The problem is, however, that humans aren't inherently objective and the choice of how to be objective is itself a subjective one. That's how "balanced reporting" can become highly unbalanced.[1]

Survey data collected in 2014 by the American Association for the Advancement of Science (the world's largest general scientific society) involving American adults uncovered a large discrepancy between what scientists believe and what the public believes regarding global warming or climate change. A large majority, 87 percent, of scientists attribute human activity as the major contributor to climate change; compare this to 50 percent of Americans. The discrepancy is even more pronounced when the two groups are queried about the seriousness of this issue; the gap almost doubles (77 percent of scientists versus 33 percent of the public). This difference in perception by the public versus the scientific community raises a question about the origin of this disparity. Could it be that media bias, evident in media copy and coverage, which arises as it strives to provide a balanced point of view, is driving the public's false perception?[2]

Companies, with their vast resources and intimate knowledge regarding the impacts and technological levers available to address sustainability challenges, can help educate the media with facts that can in turn educate the public.

Media, in print, radio, digital, or mobile formats, bombards today's consumers, resulting in the challenge of information overload. When faced with an abundance of information, media consumers will often choose either to ignore media completely or to selectively seek out and trust a very limited number of media sources. In effect, this has a potentially negative impact on people's ability to entertain multiple perspectives and to fully participate in a democratic and plural society.

Even for media creators and providers, it is challenging to discern between what is a fact, what is an opinion, what is advertising, and what is entertainment. So one can only imagine the plight of the media users. "Media literacy" is the term coined for the art and skill of separating fact from fiction so that the end consumer of the media can access and understand the real information communicated to them. This is a necessary skill because no matter the intention, subjectivity always creeps into the media.[3]

People are often labeled either knowledgeable or ignorant, but in journalism "strategic ignorance" is a widely recognized term. Linsey McGoey, in the *British Journal of Sociology*, illustrates how ignorance can be strategically leveraged by people and companies as a productive asset, enabling them to command resources, shed liability from disasters, and assert leadership in unpredictable cases.[4]

As people in most societies are continuously bombarded with subjective and biased information, provided through various media sources, media literacy skills have become absolutely fundamental to citizenship today. This is more than browsing the news; those in the know may, through knowledge, enjoy more empowered lives, as they are able to comfortably navigate the wealth of available options, both conceptually and practically. From social networking to getting directions, understanding both sides of any issue, deciphering food labeling, and getting the best insurance deal, being media literate is becoming a critical skill.

In order for sustainability credentials to be deemed relevant and credible, media content providers must be constantly examined by their sources and each of us as consumers must actively or passively screen input ourselves. This constant media screening process results in the ability to separate facts from conjecture and bias. Companies can work with the media to acknowledge this screening effect and be transparent about its consequences, thereby authentically enhancing public awareness. Professor Sonia Livingstone, head of the Media Department at the London School of Economics, identifies how media literacy could help companies: "The promise of media literacy, surely, is that it can form part of a strategy to reposition the media user – from passive to active, from a recipient to a participant, from consumer to a citizen."[5]

Supporter

On the other side of the spectrum, when the mutual goals of multiple societal institutions align around the facts, the media can flex its informational power to provide the support those institutions need as they attempt to advance sustainable goals to benefit everyone involved.

A recent example of how media can play an active supporting role in promoting societal good comes from the 2014 Clean India campaign. India's prime minister, Narendra Modi, kick-started this campaign to address the chronic lack of sanitation in India, which contributes heavily to the human health burden and also creates a negative image of the country as a whole. General media is typically critical of government actions, but in this instance, media recognized that they themselves have a major role to play in promoting this campaign and effecting positive societal impacts. The media provided wide publicity to the cleanliness campaign and, in doing so, inspired the public to take part in it. Modi even recognized the media's contribution in a friendly way when he publicly thanked the journalists for turning their "pens into brooms" in order to contribute to the national cause.[6]

WPP, the world's largest advertising and public relations company, based in the United Kingdom, believes that marketing and communications services can play an important role in driving progress toward a more sustainable society. They work with clients on many aspects of sustainability, including marketing commercial sustainability campaigns with a social or environmental dimension, marketing social campaigns to raise awareness or create behavior change on issues such as public health, safety, or the environment; and offering cause-related marketing campaigns. They also provide communications services to charities for little or no fees and negotiate free media space to run their campaigns. This pro bono work offers exciting creative opportunities for their people and supports their development.

Every year, 30,000 people in the United Kingdom experience cardiac arrest. Only 10 percent survive. The British Heart Foundation (BHF) believed these numbers could improve if more people were confident enough to administer cardiopulmonary resuscitation (CPR). The improvements will result in lower costs and better social services to people at large. To address this, in 2012, Grey Advertising, a member of WPP Company, developed an effective advertising campaign for the BHF, showing Brits how to perform CPR on those having cardiac arrest and ultimately save lives. The campaign created a TV, direct-mail, press, and online campaign showing British soccer "hard man" Vinnie Jones demonstrating how to perform hands-only CPR to the rhythm of a Bee Gees group classic, "Stayin' Alive." Grey also created an online training video, which received over one million views during its first week and resulted in a grassroots petition, signed by 100,000 people, to make emergency lifesaving courses compulsory in school curricula.[7]

Susan McPherson, a contributor to ForbesWoman, conveyed the power of Twitter hashtag (#) campaigns to raise awareness and galvanize action to address injustices. She cited the example of the UN #WomenShould campaign that successfully initiated a major global discussion regarding gender equality by exposing the negative sentiments against women.[8] This is another great example illustrating where social media has become an incredible tool for those individuals and institutions seeking to gain support for a cause – in this case, empowering women and girls across the globe.

Fortunately, media can act as a supporter if it wishes for virtually all aspects of sustainability. So why doesn't the media wholeheartedly support all sustainability causes? Often the reason for less widespread media support on sustainability issues comes from reliance on the viewer or reader ratings rather than on the facts. It is therefore up to companies and their consumers to appreciate that their collective future hangs in the balance and to engage and encourage the media to support mutually beneficial outcomes on important sustainability issues.

Practitioner

Media companies themselves can be strong sustainability practitioners. They can demonstrate sustainability leadership by addressing climate change and other sustainability issues within their own value chain. Media can promote sustainable business practices and transform the ways in which energy, materials, and other resources are used throughout the advertising and publishing life cycle.

Timberland, the manufacturers of Earthkeeper brand boots – high-end products designed with sustainable materials, targeted at outdoor enthusiasts and environmentally conscious consumers – sought out a media agency capable of staying true to Timberland's core values. They contracted Mullen's Mediahub to create a carbon-neutral electronic media plan that would drive retail sales while concurrently representing the product promise. Mullen undertook a comprehensive environmental impact audit of their proposed media plan's elements, including office and equipment usage, transportation-related energy, consumption of materials, and impacts from media infrastructure and broadcast. Their impact assessment showed that the largest environmental impact of the proposed media campaign came from the electricity consumption required to power the media plan over its entire life cycle, from in-house creative work to final deployment in TV, radio, and web. To offset the carbon dioxide emissions associated with the campaign's electricity consumption, Mullen purchased clean wind power credits from its electricity provider. In addition, the campaign employed novel ways to recycle and reuse advertising billboards and other print media as well as promoted use of mass transit to Boston residents. The campaign was the first of its kind in the United States; it won *Ad Week*'s "Media Plan of the Year" in its category and ultimately resulted in Timberland's desired outcome, which was driving up sales of Earthkeeper boots.[9]

Educator

Across the world, consumer trust in companies has been falling for the last three decades; the brands are not delivering what people want. Instead, they're trying to deliver what they always have – the same old combination of faster/bigger/newer – while the world yearns for brands that are meaningful.

To take up this emerging brand image challenge, media creators will need to develop and employ new processes and strategic tools to help clients understand the new landscape and discover a purpose for the brand that's beyond simply maximizing profit.

A new index known as Meaningful Brands – created by Havas Media Group, one of the world's largest global communications groups – is the first global analytical framework or index to connect human well-being with brands at a business level. The top 25 brands as determined by the Meaningful Brand index (i.e., those that improve the well-being of people's lives in a tangible, significant, and fulfilling way) also deliver a comparably higher and impressive (12 percent) return to shareholders.[10]

Apart from helping brands find their purpose, media creators can drive the sustainability conversation with consumers, especially when it comes to the topic of sustainable consumption. Sustainability experts have argued that unless we, as a human race, change our consumption patterns, there will not be enough resources on this planet to meet human needs. The advertising business, in particular, is typically brilliant at persuading people to change their behaviors, and that's what is needed for all of us to overcome the challenges that threaten our collective future and companies' profitability. Companies need to leverage agencies to change consumption behavior to sustainable consumption, if only to protect their own long-term success.

One best-in-class example of a successful green campaign is Patagonia's full-page 2011 ad in the *New York Times*. The ad was placed in advance of the traditional Black Friday shopping bonanza and featured a picture of one of their jackets with the copy, "Don't buy this jacket." The ad basically discouraged sales on the biggest shopping day of the year, an unconventional move for a for-profit organization. Because this ad was consistent with Patagonia's company purpose and was so radically different from all the noise in the consumer world, it had the effect of further differentiating Patagonia and thereby increasing both their brand appeal and customer loyalty.[11]

Use of Media: Case Studies

Sustainability is no longer only of interest to the niche stakeholder; it's now of interest to all of the key stakeholders, including consumers, investors, employees, media, NGOs, and customers. To continually engage these stakeholders, companies are looking for an "always on" and "always accessible" channel for sustainability communication. Smart companies, those who understand the four critical media roles, are evaluating media options that align with their sustainability strategies. Three effective ways companies can effectively leverage the media are here illustrated with examples.

Communicating Sustainability Strategies and Stories

Companies are faced with the challenging task of effectively communicating their sustainability strategies, fact-based accomplishments, and challenges to a large and diverse audience who wants this information delivered in both an engaging and compelling manner. Information is most memorable when delivered in an exciting, emotional, and relevant way. Companies also want their message to be delivered in a credible and timely manner that will affect consumer decision-making. That's a lot to ask for in a media campaign, but it's completely possible with modern media's opportunities.

To deliver their sustainability strategy or stories in an engaging and impactful way, the smart companies are using omnichannels of communication. That entails going beyond customary media delivery by employing new and emerging social media platforms, along with reimagining the traditional media platforms of press and TV. Social media has driven a profound change in how sustainability is communicated, as both social media and sustainability are bound in common foundational values including authenticity, transparency, community, innovation, and creativity.

According to SMI-Wizness's Social Media Sustainability Annual Index, which provides an in-depth analysis of best practices in social media sustainability communication, the number of companies that use social media to communicate sustainability has grown exponentially. The index showed that among the companies included in their sampling, the inclusion of social media platforms like YouTube, Facebook, and Twitter in their media plans doubled from 2010 to 2011. This trend has continued to date as the social media platform palette has further expanded with the emergence of Snapchat, Instagram, Pinterest, and others.[12]

According to SMI-Wizness, companies like General Electric and IBM continue to be on the top-10 lists of companies leading with best practices in sustainability strategy communication. IBM's Smarter Planet website showcases, via compelling storytelling to bring the point home, how IBM is collaborating with companies and communities around the globe to promote sustainability.[13]

General Electric is actively leveraging social media to crowd-source ideas, hoping to identify innovative solutions to pressing sustainability challenges. GE created its Ecomagination Challenge to uncover clean energy ideas. In 2011, Ecomagination Challenge winners received a $200 million capital investment by GE and its partners. As this investment was tiny compared to the total investment GE Energy makes in innovation research, GE applied the learnings from this program internally, making Ecomagination a way of doing business by engaging over 8,000 GE employees to help reduce its own footprint.[14]

In another best-practice example of a company using social media platforms and crowdsourcing to innovate solutions for sustainability challenges, Starbucks initiated a BetaCup Challenge in 2009, addressing the exorbitant amount of waste associated with the 58 billion disposable paper cups it sells with its drinks each year, to the Jovoto online community. The Jovoto platform website crowdsources ideas from the creative public and was recruited in an attempt to find a sustainable alternative to the disposable coffee cup. Starbucks received many creative ideas to address the issue and implemented the Karma cup, which promoted reusable cup usage by awarding every tenth reusable user a free drink, thus effectively reducing the total number of cups going to waste.[15] Like AT&T, more and more companies are recognizing that websites like Causes provide them platforms to discover, support, and find solutions for sustainability issues that impact them and their communities.[16] There are so many new media opportunities for companies to consider.

Corporate social responsibility occurs when a company's policies and programs push forward the common interests of all stakeholders, including investors, customers, employees, the community, and the environment. In large numbers, consumers now expect companies to create and implement programs that give back to society in one way or another.

Adobe turned to Magnet Media to integrate the Adobe Youth Voices program into the fabric of the company. The Adobe Youth Voices program highlights issues around the globe that youths care about through production of videos addressing these issues. Since 2006, more than 190,000 youths have participated in this program. The value that this program yields is best summed up by Linda McNair, communications lead at Adobe: "The team at Magnet Media brought Adobe's social purpose to life, and the results go beyond views and shares. The way people feel and react when they view these videos is what it's all about. Employees express their pride to work here. Everyone wants to take action. They ask how they can help further the cause. We can't help but believe these sentiments are also felt by our customers, partners, and the public."[17]

Managing Crises

For many companies, the media does more than boost their sustainability profile; it is a necessary tool to manage their brand. Social media is a powerful way for consumers to speak out against corporate actions and, conversely, for companies to engage with their dissenters. Companies recognize that social media tools, on one hand, can help boost a company's sustainability credentials; on the other hand, if these sites are not well managed, they can very quickly damage a company's reputation. An event in some remote part of the world can rapidly come into the global limelight on these sites, thus the need for careful management. Shortly after the infamous Gulf of Mexico oil spill disaster in 2010, a Facebook group was created called "Boycott BP," and almost overnight 791,000 "likes" destroyed BP's brand reputation.[18] Why should BP have taken notice? For one simple reason. According to 2013 Pew Research, on average, every Facebook user has 338 "friends." Thus in the case of BP, the 791,000 "likes" could create a total of 267 million potential exposures to the idea of boycotting BP.[19]

This modern media form can also be used to a company's advantage in a crisis. Megan Cunningham of Magnet Media points out that traditional media will offer companies a 30-second sound bite and the narrow audience awareness and judgment that come with it. She advises brands and companies to follow a four-pronged strategy to avoid this trap.

1. Step back and investigate what really happened to get the internal facts straight.
2. Engage social media monitoring tools to gauge the pulse of the community and its reactions.
3. Think of potential channels of distribution, then respond quickly in a strategic and responsible way.
4. Partner with media creators to essentially create an appropriate context using Facebook posts, Twitter feed, blog posts, and YouTube videos to get the word out and supply facts in a transparent way.

Many case studies can serve to highlight how to best handle a business crisis so as to minimize reputational damage. Johnson & Johnson's Tylenol and DuPont's Teflon PR crises are great examples. For illustration purposes, we will examine the DuPont Teflon PR crises and the lessons companies can learn from this case.

In the early twenty-first century, many studies linked PFCs in Teflon, a high-performing and profitable chemical product, to human health issues. Chemical suppliers, product manufacturers, and retailers have been working to replace PFCs in their products. DuPont employed a specific type of PFC in the production of their Teflon product, perfluorooctanoic acid (PFOA), linked to various types of cancers. As a result, the negative PR story was building and consumers were demanding action. DuPont needed to react quickly to find a safer chemical alternative and to manage the transition to it across the globe without irreparably hurting the brand. Amy Westervelt shared the key lessons learned by DuPont in her 2012 GreenBiz article. The five key lessons learned can be summarized as follows: (1) Don't wait for negative media to snowball before acting; (2) Identify partners and suppliers who are on the same page and can help address the crisis; (3) Comprehensively examine the business case including the impact on reputation; (4) Go public with your plan of action and be transparent on your progress; and (5) Engage and seek buy-in from your customers.[20]

Partnerships

When a company and its partner media agencies have alignment on values, they have the potential to develop sustainability magic in the form of purpose and profit, because each sustainable campaign or initiative reinforces both of their brands.

Successful companies like Procter & Gamble (P&G) recognize that though they have a great team of innovators and marketers, by opening up innovation and collaborating with the right partners they can create more and faster value for their shareholders. P&G started open innovation in 2001, and their program is still going strong. The key to P&G's success purportedly lies in choosing the right partner, one whose values are closely aligned with P&G's, and subsequently exploiting collective capabilities to create the right synergy. P&G recognizes that by continually seeking ways to better align their needs with external capabilities, they will build a win-win situation and lasting partner relationships.[21]

The following example illustrates how a sustainable company needs a creative partner who also thinks sustainably to effectively reach consumers. Hewlett-Packard (HP) selected the Oliver Russell agency in the early twenty-first century for the task of communicating its complex, closed-loop recycling process in a simple and compelling way to the consumers. HP was a recognized leader in recycling and its closed-loop recycling of ink cartridges was the first of its kind in the industry. The Oliver Russell agency, working closely with HP, simplified the complex 15-step HP closed-loop recycling process diagram into a simple 6-step diagram with many easy-to-understand images. The Oliver Russell agency not only delivered on HP's environmental sustainability initiative but also cemented their relationship with HP and substantially grew both HP and their own sustainability practice. They now have enjoyed more than 12 years of partnership with HP.[22]

KEY TAKEAWAYS

- Collaboration between companies and the media creators yields a more sustainability-focused culture.
- Companies are learning to balance legacy media tools with new online and mobile media in engaging ways.
- The media plays several important roles in promoting sustainability, including screener, supporter, practitioner, and educator.
- Companies can best leverage the media's power when managing a sustainability-related crisis by communicating sustainability stories in an engaging, authentic, transparent way.
- Companies can develop values-aligned partnerships with media to create a competitive advantage.

To effectively *drive the top-line growth with triple-bottom-line thinking* with the media, a company should:
1. Leverage the media to curate, organize, and disseminate globally sustainability-related news and initiatives to the media.

2. Monitor and engage existing and emerging social media channels; maintain consistency of message.
3. Enable media so as to shape the future of sustainability in an
unbiased way.
4. Partner with media to promote sustainable behaviors and
practices.

9 Engaging Government

Democratic government is accountable to shareholders with different values. Public values. Social well-being. Environmental and ecological integrity. Security.
Paul Hawken, environmentalist, entrepreneur, journalist, and author[1]

Figure 9.1. Sustainability stakeholders framework: Engaging government

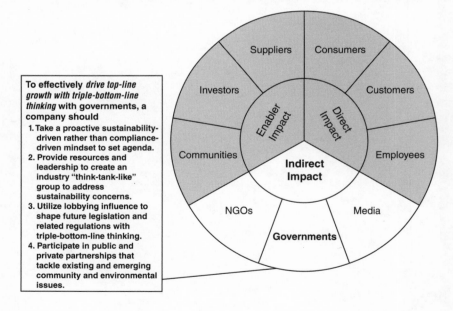

To effectively *drive top-line growth with triple-bottom-line thinking* with governments, a company should
1. Take a proactive sustainability-driven rather than compliance-driven mindset to set agenda.
2. Provide resources and leadership to create an industry "think-tank-like" group to address sustainability concerns.
3. Utilize lobbying influence to shape future legislation and related regulations with triple-bottom-line thinking.
4. Participate in public and private partnerships that tackle existing and emerging community and environmental issues.

Suppliers Consumers
Investors Customers
Enabler Impact Direct Impact
Communities Employees
Indirect Impact
NGOs Media
Governments

Government's baseline purpose is to protect and promote the best interests of the people it governs. There are certainly a few disagreements about how this should play out, but the fundamental goal is the same – to be of service to those governed, not a hindrance, and that includes the realm of business.

To fulfill this aim, it's important for governments to invest in strategies that promote the types of development that work for the highest overall good of those being served. The past 20 years have seen a growing realization that the current model of development is unsustainable. Politics is filled with short-term thinking that runs on election cycles. But, in the long run, the success of Western governments today will be judged on how much they contributed to a sustainable world. A government's long-term success for the humans it governs involves ensuring that societies are sustainable and that businesses grow and have a sustainable future.

The responsibility to create a sustainable future jointly rests on the shoulders of governments, society, and businesses, as no single stakeholder can deliver it alone. It's paramount that partnerships between government and business be created and fostered to contribute to maintaining and sustaining the earth and the future generations that will inhabit it. To this end, such partnerships will then guide and drive all necessary activity and infrastructure investment.[2]

We are currently trapped in an economic system based on the one-time use of natural resources, and we are reliant on finite fossil fuels. With the global population expected to pass nine billion in the near future, we have a major imbalance on our hands, where the humans on one side living their lives in the current way outweigh what the planet can sustain on the other side.

Some believe there is hope in the form of new sustainable technologies and techniques that we have not yet seen. By developing and deploying sustainable technologies, we can create a renewable resource–based circular economy. This is where business can play its greatest role. We simply cannot continue consuming non-renewable materials and dumping the waste on our land or in our seas, or we will remain trapped and burdened by an unsustainable future. Embedded in this dire forecast is a potentially huge business opportunity.

Lasting Change Is a Collaborative Process

The necessary, dramatic transition from a waste-based (single-use, disposable, and nonrenewable fossil-fuel-centered) economy to a more sustainable, renewable circular economy will require joint private- and public-sector partnerships.[3] Short-termism is just as prevalent in business as it is in government. The idea of business success is based almost solely on quarterly results. This model is also unsustainable.

Thus, governments and businesses need each other and need to work together to mutually support a longer-term view. We see a very necessary and powerful link between businesses and governments in bringing about the future that we all need to thrive.

Eradicating extreme poverty is one of the UN Sustainable Development Goals (SDGs). At the World Economic Forum, the World Vision challenged governments, the private sector, and civil society to work together and deliver on this ambitious goal by 2030. World Vision made the case that with a "business as usual" mindset, eradicating extreme poverty would be impossible to achieve and applying collaborative breakthrough thinking is a must. They encouraged global leaders to pool their financial, technical, and political resources and apply the inclusive principle to investments and innovation focused on the "have-nots," those who have missed out on the broad-based growth.[4]

This link between government and business interests is good for business. For example, in the United States, federal government agencies like the Environmental Protection Agency, the Food and Drug Administration, and the Department of Transportation all provide incentives for companies to make more sustainable choices. Those incentives are gradually contributing to a shift in behavior, but it is up to business to take a leadership stance on government initiatives that derive the biggest benefit and, therefore, competitive advantage. Businesses can influence governments in many ways.

The Environmental Protection Agency (EPA) incentivizes the implementation of combined heat and power (CHP). The EPA believes that CHP technology enables businesses and institutions to create an efficient, clean, and reliable energy source that yields significant environmental and climate change benefits. There are financial incentives available to businesses at both state and federal levels, such as financial grants, tax incentives, low-interest loans, rebate programs, and feed-in tariffs. The applied focus of CHP efforts within the EPA is promoting CHP in electric and gas utilities, wastewater facilities, large hotels, and ethanol-producing mills, where they believe businesses and the environment would see maximum positive impacts.[5]

The Government's Role in Creating a Sustainable Future

Understanding government's role will help the companies shape their strategies, better deploy their own resources, and use government resources to further their own sustainability initiatives.

Looking at sustainability in a broad context, the government's role applies to all three main aspects of sustainability – social, financial, and environmental. To implement their role successfully, most governments attempt to balance the short- to medium-term goal of preventing harm and promoting the common good with the medium- to longer-term goal of creating a sustainable future. Let's look at each of these time-based views in more depth from the perspective of businesses that want to take advantage of government action.

Establishing Short- to Medium-term Goals

PREVENTING HARM

This approach happens when the government relies on laws and regulations to establish minimum standards, and in some cases penalties, designed for businesses to prevent destructive practices.

There are several simple examples of how government uses regulatory authority to set the boundaries of behavior. Minimum-wage standards establish a compensation floor for workers. The recently published U.S. Federal Trade Commission (FTC) Green Guides outline the practices to prevent consumer deception in environmental claims. Emission limitations establish acceptable discharge levels to prevent an unhealthy environment. Land use regulations and rights minimize destruction of ecosystems. And the Securities and Exchange Commission established financial reporting requirements to prevent fraudulent and misleading information to the public.

Contrary to popular belief, sustainable businesses can influence and benefit from government regulations. A progressive, ethical, and savvy business can use these regulations to level the playing field in its favor.

For example, the 2008 amendment to the Lacey Act prevents illegal logging of forested areas. Forestry businesses that were using sustainable resources as a means of differentiation suddenly had another weapon in their arsenal to fight against cheap imports flooding the market with raw material sourced by illegal logging. The consumer products giant Kimberly-Clark worked with industry associations and NGOs to successfully discourage retailers from buying products sourced from illegal and unsustainable logging operations in Indonesia. This helped K-C level the playing field, helping mitigate their unfair, unsustainable competition.

Today, the average consumer is confused by all the green labels and claims seemingly placed on every product. As a result, businesses that truly have sustainable products tend to lose any advantage with environmentally minded shoppers at the shelf. Working behind the scenes at the policy level can give collaborative businesses the upper hand. For example, the FTC's Green Guides (developed with input from industry, government agencies, and NGOs) provides guidance regarding proper use of "green" advertising claims and labeling. Sustainable businesses and sustainably positioned products or services can reference the guide to determine the required support and appropriate claims language to showcase and differentiate their products to consumers.

PROMOTING THE COMMON GOOD

This is the flip side of preventing harm in the short to medium term. With this goal, government tries to use regulations and laws to promote the common good beyond current standards.

The U.S. government routinely deploys incentives to promote behavior change and voluntarism. Incorporating sustainable procurement requirements and promoting sustainable development practices through programs/certification schemes such as Leadership in Energy and Environmental Design (LEED), a rating system devised by the U.S. Green Building Council and Energy Star, and providing tax credits for energy-efficiency retrofits are current examples of incentivizing behavioral change. In addition, governments can eliminate barriers to open up opportunities, such as eliminating or providing exceptions to restrictive land use requirements.

Once again, business has a great opportunity to influence and benefit from these incentives. Retailers like Walmart took advantage of the energy-efficiency tax credits by eliminating incandescent lamps from their stores and replacing them with more energy-efficient alternatives, which also provided them a platform from which to promote their own sustainable behavior and leadership.

The U.S. government is the world's single largest buyer of goods. The EPA's *Guidance on the Acquisition of Environmentally Preferable Products and Services* includes sustainable procurement guidance for such items as paper goods. Its procurement standard prescribes a minimum recycled fiber content for various paper products. These regulations have helped sustainable paper companies do more business with the federal government and entities that receive federal funding.

A few years ago, when gas prices hit $4 per gallon at the pumps, consumers' demand for electric cars made by Tesla and Nissan skyrocketed. This demand was further fueled by tax credits offered to consumers at federal and state levels. Additionally, these companies received millions of dollars from the State of California indirectly through the sale of California zero-emission vehicle credits to other car companies. Specifically, as Tesla only manufactures electric cars, it has been able to earn seven zero-emission vehicle credits that translate to nearly $35,000 per car in earnings when selling the credits to automakers that have not been able to meet the mandated average fleet mileage regulation.[6]

Establishing Medium- to Longer-Term Goals

To build a sustainable future for businesses and society, governments put planning and resources behind longer-term projects. In addition, governments will foster an environment where businesses are encouraged to make that effort and assume investment risks associated with sustainability-focused actions. Here are five areas in which government and business can combine forces for mutual long-term sustainability benefits:

DEVELOPING HUMAN CAPITAL

Most businesses and governments agree that twenty-first-century workers require different skill levels than those of the past. Businesses need to find the right talent locally, but as the business and technology change, retraining existing workers to have requisite new skills often requires massive efforts and investment. That's where government can play an enabling role. Keeping jobs local is critical for the politicians as well.

To prepare the workforce for tomorrow, the California legislature introduced a bill to create a Clean Technology and Renewable Energy Job Training program. This program was made available to businesses interested in transitioning their workforce to a green one. There are similar government-sponsored schemes available for companies all over the United States. These programs help businesses defray the cost burden of retraining the workforce and instead create a talent pool with competitive, long-term skills required for a sustainable future.[7]

FUNDING SUSTAINABLE SCIENCE AND PROVIDING INCENTIVES
FOR PRIVATE INVESTMENT

Investment in sustainable science often comes with high risks and costs, which many businesses are not willing or able to accept. For example, the need for alternate energy solutions to reduce dependency on fossil fuels and the need for cradle-to-cradle solutions to manage and recycle our waste stream will require investments with high risks and longer-term returns on investment. These two factors serve as a barrier to long-term action. That's where a public-private partnership can create a win-win solution.

Government support, coupled with business ingenuity and creativity, can create a unique asset to develop a competitive leadership position in sustainable technologies for both the government and the business. Governments have all the power they need to take the longer view in building the technological base for a sustainable economy by funding research programs and providing government grants and long-term research tax credits. Smart businesses can take advantage of this power.

The U.S. National Science Foundation (NSF) provides investment dollars for science, engineering, education, and technology research that has led to many discoveries and new innovations around the world. One such successful example is NSF's funding of the MIT-founded company Altaeros. The company received two NSF Small Business Innovation Research grants to develop (a) a low-cost, high-performance fabric and (b) a modular, inflatable, and easy-to-install wind turbine for power performance. Altaeros's novel Buoyant Airborne Turbine (BAT) turbine concept was developed to capitalize on the fact that at higher altitudes wind is denser and faster. BAT operates at almost four times the altitude of a normal turbine and delivers twice the amount of energy for the same rated turbines. This case clearly demonstrates how governments can channel their resources to create innovative renewable solutions to address the green power challenge.[8]

FUNDING INFRASTRUCTURE

In the nineteenth and twentieth centuries, the U.S. government played a large role in job creation and economic growth by commissioning infrastructure projects like waterworks and highways. In the twenty-first century, governments must build the infrastructure of our time – renewable energy, digital communications, and waste and water management. This again will require public-private part-nerships. Constructing and operating these facilities will likely be the lucrative work of private firms, but the vision and financing will need to come from taxpayers and their governments.

PROMOTE COMMON SUSTAINABILITY METRICS

As management guru Peter Drucker famously stated, "If you can't measure it, you can't manage it." One needs to establish a base-line benchmark in order to evaluate if actions are making things better or worse. This also holds when reporting sustainability per-formance. Consumers and analysts are demanding companies gen-erate and communicate their baseline data to confirm that the improvements companies are making and claiming are credible. As governments are among the largest customers for many businesses around the globe, governments as customers have begun to exert their influence on supplier companies, requiring transparency and for suppliers to report on their sustainability performance.

Additionally, various governments working with relevant stake-holders are driving the development of common reporting standards across businesses and geographical boundaries.[9] Governments are also recognizing that widespread sustainability reporting practices can help markets function more efficiently by providing important non-financial information to drive progress toward sustainable de-velopment goals.

Sustainable businesses can help themselves get access to more capital and talent by influencing and encouraging the government to promote common standards as these measures are implemented and published. The Financial Accounting Standards Board (FASB) standards now require companies to report on CO_2 emissions, there-by identifying embedded liabilities on companies' balance sheets. Most sustainable companies are using the latest global GRI G4 stan-dard for reporting, which ensures that management discusses and takes actions related to issues that are most important for the sus-tainable future of the company.

The Government of Finland is at the forefront when it comes to creating and developing a publicly available and transparent sustainability information source. They have passed a resolution requiring all state-owned companies to report their sustainability performance alongside their financial performance. This resolution is a continuation of the government's push to divest state-owned enterprises to private enterprise. Of note is a similar shift in state-owned enterprises and sustainability reporting practices in Sweden, Spain, China, and India.[10]

Businesses can make their own measurement tasks slightly easier on themselves by adopting these frameworks and publishing their results in the market. This is at once an act of both differentiation and customer engagement.

TRANSFERRING TECHNOLOGY TO THE DEVELOPING WORLD

The developing world will have a massive influence on global sustainability. As their economies grow and churn, as their consumers become more sophisticated and desire the lifestyle enjoyed for years by many in the West, the developing world will significantly accelerate their usage of resources. The planet does not have the capacity to provide enough resources for every person on the planet to live like the average person in the Western world. The best-available technologies the developed world is implementing to become more sustainable will need to take root in the developing world at a much earlier time in their development cycle – ideally, right now.

Transferring Western or best-available sustainability-related technologies to the developing world is good not only for the developing world's prosperity and longevity, but for the planet's sustainability as a whole. The cost attributable to climate change is real, as evidenced by the rising insurance claims reported by companies because of climate change. According to a 2008 article on the Natural Resources Defense Council (NRDC) website, "New research shows that if present trends continue, the total cost of global warming will be as high as 3.6 percent of the world's GDP. Four recognized global warming impacts – hurricane damage, real estate losses, energy costs, and water costs – will alone come with a price tag of $1.9 trillion annually (in today's dollars) by 2100."[11]

In summary, developing nations require adequate incentives to employ and invest in the new, more sustainable technologies instead of more-affordable conventional ones. Mitigation of climate change will require not only the adoption of new or best-available sustainability technologies by the developed world, but also an effective technology transfer and financing support mechanisms. Smart, sustainable companies can tap into these incentives to grow their own businesses and investments in the developing world.

Business's Role in Influencing Government's Sustainability Agendas

We have highlighted areas in which business can influence and benefit from government activities that are already part of the governmental agendas around the world. But why not proactively influence and shape the government's sustainability agenda itself?

One example of note is the Wipro Foundation's Wipro Applying Thought in Schools social initiative in India. This initiative is designed to build capacity for and reform India's educational system. Wipro is a large multinational IT products and service provider based in India with thousands of employees worldwide. Wipro's focus on education is premised on the simple idea that education or knowledge is not only the catalyst for required social change but, in addition, will create an equitable playing field for all classes of society. By reforming and building Indian school capacities in communities around where Wipro operates, the Wipro Applying Thought in Schools initiative will allow the foundation to sow and nurture their values and develop a large talent pool for the future.[12]

With this strategic approach, Wipro believes that the private sector can have a much larger and even more important role to play in the much-needed global transition to a sustainable economy. It is the private sector that produces the goods and services upon which modern life relies. As there are multiple businesses competing for the same prize in any market, an effective competition requires rules, referees, and meaningful penalties for antisocial and criminal behavior. Only governments can effectively create these rules and guidelines for an efficient market.

Businesses can initiate both short- and long-term actions on their own to influence the overall government guidelines and agendas to their own advantage. Here are five areas in which businesses can successfully influence government at the agenda level.

Generating Public Opinion

Politicians mostly work on laws and regulations that are important for the betterment of the society they represent as new needs are expressed. At the end of the day, politicians get their cues and direction from the constituencies they represent. Companies can use their financial and marketing power to influence the public opinion.

For example, many believe that business influence is sorely needed in the area of climate change legislation. Most companies have realized that climate change is impacting their bottom lines in more than one way. The effects include supply chain disruptions, closure of plants, loss of productivity, and in many instances, reduction in product or services demand. Companies have an obvious business case for influencing public opinion and, indirectly, the opinions of their governments. The collective global leadership can hopefully act in a timely fashion and make a difference in the trajectory of climate change. Those in the know hold that the failure to act soon on climate change mitigation will only translate into more catastrophic business losses down the road and a tragic legacy our grandchildren will deal with for their entire lives.

Creating Industrial Groups to Address Global Challenges

In the year 2000, a UN gathering of 170 world leaders resulted in the announcement of its ambitious (2015) Millennium Development Goals (MGDs). Unfortunately, the world was far from achieving those goals as outlined by the original target date, so in 2015, more than 190 world leaders committed to 17 Sustainable Development

Goals (SDGs) to help us all end extreme poverty, fight inequality and injustice, and fix climate change. There is growing realization that governments and businesses need to work together in deeper ways, across borders and across sectors, to solve these global development challenges. Brands have the operational power, marketing know-how, and financial resources to bring together both friends and alleged adversaries to address these issues while simultaneously benefiting their business.

One best-in-class example is the UN Women Private Sector Leadership Advisory Council, which taps several major corporations' CEOs, including Unilever's Paul Polman and Coca-Cola Company's Muhtar Kent. The council's focus is to accelerate economic and social progress for women and girls worldwide by sharing information and pooling member resources and know-how to achieve greater results.[13]

Another example of note: many companies have joined the UN's Global Compact to promote better global labor practices. Becoming signatories and adopting recommended practices ensures that these companies act as good corporate citizens and mitigate the risks associated with becoming a campaign target of labor-focused NGOs.

In another example, many businesses are members of local or national chambers of commerce. These groups are powerful resources to promote sustainable policies and influence government regulations or repeal unnecessary regulations. In India, the National Chamber of Commerce recently influenced governments to adopt business-friendly labor practices.

Sustainable Consumption

For Planet Earth to be a place where every person enjoys the basic necessities of life, we will need to re-examine what and how we consume in the developed world, and we will need to re-examine what will be offered to the developing world. In the developed world, we continue to consume and waste much more than the incremental needs of the developing world. Changing this condition could offer staggering results. It has been calculated that if the amount of food wasted in the developed world is reduced by half, the food saved would provide all the food needed for the growing developing world's population for years to come.

There are many business opportunities embedded in resource-shifting opportunities. For example, it's ironic that in the developed world, eating healthy food is more expensive than eating highly processed food. In America, a bag of grapes costs around $6.00 and a pound of tomatoes around $4.00, while less nutritious, high-calorie, fast-food items often cost just $2.00 each with unlimited soda at many fast-food restaurants. This situation is inarguably part of the many poor-nutrition-related health problems that have reached epidemic proportions in the United States. This health epidemic carries huge costs for governments, consumers, and companies.

Trader Joe's, a successful and trendy U.S. grocery retailer, has unlocked an opportunity to address the high price and limited accessibility of sustainable produce while simultaneously turning a healthy profit. Trader Joe's leverages its scale and supply chain partnerships to greatly reduce its costs for, and increase the availability of, organic and local products. While winning consumer dollars and loyalty as a result, and promoting local economies, Trader Joe's also delivers more than three times the sales per square foot than the industry average (Trader Joe's averages $1,723 sales per square foot versus $521 for industry average).[14]

In summary, smart businesses need to collaborate with and lobby governments to bring forth legislation and incentives that promote sustainable consumption in a way that helps rather than hinders their ability to thrive.

Collaboration and Partnerships

As our world gets more complex and interconnected, so do the challenges that all of our businesses deal with on a daily basis. Developing partnerships and industry collaborations can have a tremendously positive impact on the sustainability of businesses by providing an increased ability to handle and capitalize on these challenges.

In an effort to provide every U.S. consumer access to recycling infrastructure where and when they need it, consumer companies like Coca-Cola, Pepsi, Unilever, Procter & Gamble, and Johnson & Johnson teamed up with Walmart and Goldman Sachs investment group to start a Closed Loop Fund. The fund was launched at Walmart's Sustainable Product Expo in 2014, where plans to invest $100 million in recycling infrastructure over the next five years by offering zero-interest loans to cities and make investments in progressive waste-management companies were announced. Once again, this demonstrates how companies who compete for the same consumers can work together with the broader stakeholder community to address societal needs and to spur the required behavior changes.[15] Voluntary industry collaboration and partnerships targeting key sustainability challenges can get out ahead of or mitigate the need for potentially detrimental government actions that can inhibit businesses' growth or their very existence.

Investing in Developing Markets

Most businesses have experienced slowing growth rates in their own developed markets, as both penetration and consumption levels are now reaching their peak. For businesses to continue to grow and prosper, they will need to strategically invest in the developing world economies where there is population and consumption growth. Pursuing traditional business models will not necessarily ensure continued success in developing markets. These new markets often need innovative or modified business models. Companies will have to consider adopting business models that pursue circular economies and the use of renewable resources to have a long-term impact, benefit, and success in these markets. That's where businesses can work with governments to encourage sustainability-focused investment incentives, tax breaks, agenda setting, and policymaking to create a win-win solution in the developing world.

KEY TAKEAWAYS

- A government's success is reflected by its ability to grow and develop sustainable societies, inclusive of businesses.
- Government's role, from a long-term perspective, is to develop human capital; to fund science, innovation, and infrastructure; and to provide incentives for investment.
- Companies can shape government sustainability agendas by lobbying as an industry, providing technical know-how, and partnering with government to address societal issues.

To effectively *drive the top-line growth with triple-bottom-line thinking* **with governments, a company should:**
1. Take a proactive sustainability-driven rather than compliance-driven mindset to set an agenda.
2. Provide resources and leadership to create an industry "think-tank-like" group to address sustainability concerns.
3. Utilize lobbying influence to shape future legislation and related regulations with triple-bottom-line thinking.
4. Participate in public and private partnerships that tackle existing and emerging community and environmental issues.

10 Partnering with NGOs

We have no permanent friends and no permanent enemies. It's not about what you've done but what you do next that's important.

Scott Paul, Forest Campaign director at Greenpeace (2012)

Figure 10.1. Sustainability stakeholders framework: Partnering with NGOs

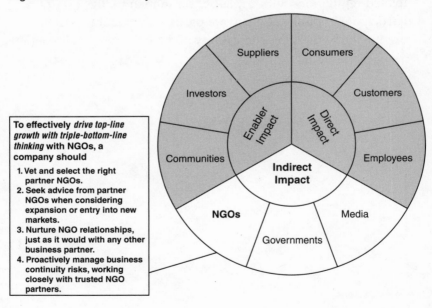

The debate has gone on for decades in the business world – are NGOs friends or foes? The question is profound and important for leaders on both sides to ponder. Scott further elaborated, "Any valuable relationship requires transparency, cooperation and willingness to listen to other perspectives." As leaders in the business world, how can one best embrace this statement? What steps should we take to ensure that we are always cognizant of the changing nature of NGO-industry relationships and of the vast potential value these relationships can bring in the future? What if these relationships are antagonistic?

In a CNN article by John Black, titled "Two Enemies Discover a 'Higher Call' in Battle," the author recounts an extraordinary story that occurred during an air battle in the midst of World War II.

> The pilot glanced outside his cockpit and froze. He blinked hard and looked again, hoping it was just a mirage. But his co-pilot stared at the same horrible vision. "My God, this is a nightmare," the co-pilot said. "He's going to destroy us," the pilot agreed.
>
> The men were looking at a gray German Messerschmitt fighter hovering just three feet off their wingtip. It was five days before Christmas 1943, and the fighter had closed in on their crippled American B-17 bomber for the kill.
>
> The B-17 pilot, Charles Brown, was a 21-year-old West Virginia farm boy on his first combat mission. His bomber had been shot to pieces by swarming fighters, and his plane was alone in the skies above Germany. Half his crew was wounded, and the tail gunner was dead, his blood frozen in icicles over the machine guns. But when Brown and his co-pilot, Spencer "Pinky" Luke, looked at the fighter pilot again, something odd happened. The German didn't pull the trigger. He nodded at Brown instead. What happened next was one of the most remarkable acts of chivalry recorded during World War II. Years later, Brown would track down his would-be executioner for a reunion that reduced both men to tears.[1]

This story, while extraordinary, is not unique. In a business world version of this dramatic story, the environmental nongovernmental organization (ENGO) Greenpeace and the Fortune 500 multinational consumer products manufacturer Kimberly-Clark Corporation once had an extremely antagonistic relationship, but it would not stay this way. Greenpeace called into question K-C's wood-fiber sourcing practices required to supply their global paper business, claiming K-C was partly responsible for the destruction of the high-conservation-value Canadian boreal forests. The five-year-long campaign (2004–9) was creatively branded as the *Kleercut* campaign, a clever manipulation of K-C's highly recognized Kleenex brand. Greenpeace alleged that K-C was clear-cutting forests in Canada and the United States, endangering the ecosystem and threatening wolverine and woodland caribou habitats. Though the protracted and exhausting campaign was a serious public relations nightmare for K-C, it produced little tangible results for Greenpeace and was highly resource intensive. When we examine the changes that took place from this confrontation, it becomes clear that both sides wanted a different outcome than a continued campaign and fighting that served no one.

Greenpeace and K-C had no desire to destroy each other, so they started talking. Against all odds and after years of resentment, they adopted the opposite approach to confrontation – collaboration, which has, by all accounts, yielded beneficial results for all involved. Greenpeace and K-C have long since reconciled by finding a way to mutually reinforce and advance each other's strengths and goals. The two adversaries now consider themselves collaborators to promote sustainable fiber sourcing practices that contribute to the success of both organizations. The relationship with Greenpeace helps K-C sustain and build its tissue businesses.

This was made evident when Robert Abernathy, K-C's former group president of North America, shared with employees that "K-C is a better company because of Greenpeace." This type of symbiotic relationship is potentially available to all businesses as long as they recognize the value of strategic NGO-industry relationships. In any case, there appears to be vast potential for healthy growth in NGO-business collaboration.

Another great example of how confrontation was transformed to cooperation is Clorox's story about Greenpeace. In 2001, in the wake of the September 11 terrorist attacks in the United States, a new movement began forcing companies into safer manufacturing prac-tices. Clorox had already begun planning a move away from manu-facturing its bleach-based products using chlorine gas, the process used to make Clorox bleach since the company was founded in 1913 – instead using a fully sustainable electrolytic process that converts the brine in seawater into bleach.

While Clorox was privately putting in motion its process to elimi-nate chlorine gas from its supply chain, Greenpeace contacted Clorox demanding a letter from their CEO explaining what the company was doing to prevent chlorine from sullying the oceans. Kathryn Caulfield, vice president of corporate communications and crisis management at Clorox, urged that the company choose to engage with Greenpeace rather than ignore them. Their first step was to ob-tain a non-disclosure agreement from Greenpeace. They then met with the activists to announce Clorox's intent to eliminate chlorine from its manufacturing process, a project that couldn't be made pub-lic for another 10 months.

When Greenpeace became aware of Clorox's proactive sustainabil-ity-related plans, those at Greenpeace decided to forgo their inten-tions to do battle with the formidable consumer product company. Instead, Greenpeace offered up the support of its resources, including its website and volunteers, to help publicize Clorox's new sustain-ability efforts.[2] That is marketing Clorox could never have bought with advertising dollars.

A Definition of NGOs

Nongovernmental organizations pursue a public interest agenda rather than a commercial agenda. The first-ever international NGO was the Anti-Slavery Society formed in 1839, followed by the Red Cross, a movement that arose at the end of the nineteenth century and is still going strong. Most of the other NGO movements were founded after the two world wars and were primarily humanitarian in nature.

According to the United Nations, "a non-governmental organization (NGO) is any non-profit, voluntary citizens' group which is organized on a local, national or international level. Task-oriented and driven by people with a common interest, NGOs perform a variety of service and humanitarian functions, bring citizen concerns to Governments, advocate and monitor policies and encourage political participation through provision of information. Some are organized around specific issues, such as human rights, environment or health."[3]

- A *social* NGO is a nongovernmental organization that facilitates achievements in human development, promotes community development, and deals with social impacts of business activity. Social NGOs focus on a wide array of issues including labor practices, child labor, education, community welfare, and the rights of indigenous people.
- An *environmental* NGO is a nongovernmental organization that deals with issues concerning the environment, including the depletion of natural resources, global warming, conservation, and the like. ENGOs focus on a wide range of issues like acquiring and managing endangered land, performing field research, lobbying government institutions, and creating information campaigns to raise public awareness. ENGOs often collaborate with governments, academia, and corporations to draft environmental policy, or they simply provide oversight to governments and/or industry assuring compliance with existing or prior agreements (e.g., the Kyoto Protocol).[4]

The Growth of Corporate and NGO Partnerships

As both societal and business challenges become increasingly complex, it would follow that there will be increasing opportunities to develop beneficial relationships between corporations/industry and NGOs. In many instances, these collaborations have become absolutely necessary for sustainable business and society.

The C&E Advisory, a UK-based international cross-sector business and society consultancy that helps clients create sustainable value, polled 129 leading companies and NGOs and conducted roundtable discussions with senior practitioners from both sectors. They leveraged the output from the poll and roundtable discussions to publish their 2015 Corporate-NGO Partnerships Barometer report, to predict the future viability and effect of such partnerships. The C&E Advisory concluded that they had uncovered strong support suggesting the value for both sectors intensifying their long-term, strategic collaboration. According to the report, "A full 93 percent of corporate and 79 percent of NGO respondents said that collaborators have helped to enhance business understanding of social and environment issues. Some 84 percent of businesses and 96 percent of NGOs are confident that partnerships between the two sectors will become more or much more important over the next three years. And 46 percent of corporate and 40 percent of NGO respondents said that cross-sector collaborations have helped to improve business practices for the better."[5]

NGOs are often enablers for corporations striving to develop new markets and required innovation. Corporate-NGO partnerships are in a unique position to ally to address global environmental and societal challenges that governments are often ill equipped to solve.

As the UN Millennium Development Goals (MDGs) concluded at the end of 2015, the United Nations launched its 2030 Agenda for Sustainable Development aimed at realizing its 17 Sustainable Development Goals. These goals address pressing societal and environmental issues, including ending poverty and hunger, improving health and education, making cities more sustainable, combating climate change, and protecting oceans and forests. Should these ambitious goals be actualized, companies would benefit from the growing customer base resulting from a more prosperous society. In the developing world, the role of NGOs is often critical. NGOs provide essential services that governmental agencies or institutions supply in developed countries.[6] Companies have the opportunity to partner with NGOs and governments (discussed further in chapter 9) to help the UN realize these post-development goals.

While addressing global/societal challenges doesn't prompt action in the boardroom, competitive advantage usually does. NGOs are often highly knowledgeable and locally connected with respect to environmental or social issues, thus bringing business value. In the current business environment, very few products or services remain unique for long, as copycat companies and competitors have never been faster. This partially explains why the Corporate-NGO Partnerships Barometer report found that 67 percent of businesses cited innovation as one of the leading reasons for partnering with an NGO.

Lisa Morden, senior director of sustainability at Kimberly-Clark, summarized it well: "Common views on common problems may not result in the innovation thinking one needs." It is through ideological tension that new viewpoints can emerge. Once formed, a company's exclusive partnership with a leading NGO is much harder to replicate than a product design or service. NGO partnerships can result in a form of innovative competitive advantage.

NGO partnerships don't have to be complicated. A simple financial donation coming from a corporation's foundation to an NGO to address societal or environmental needs is perhaps the simplest form of the partnership. While playing small and staying small brings small rewards, full-fledged partnerships, combining both entities' resources, have been shown to bring forth the greatest mutual benefits. These full partnerships maximize the favorable impact on business results while addressing desired societal challenges. Developing full-fledged strategic NGO-industry partnerships may represent to corporations an area of often-untapped advantage, but they are not without their challenges.

Challenges Inherent in NGO-Corporate Partnerships

On one hand, many corporate leaders may find it conceptually difficult or awkward to bring their NGO partners into business decisions.

At the same time, many NGO leaders are wary of addressing their mission through their corporate partners' business channels.

In addition, NGOs are generally concerned with longer-term (10-plus years) horizons and seek transformative change, while business tends to focus on the shorter (1–3 year) horizon and are largely content with evolutionary or incremental change. Business leaders often concern themselves with the additional expense and time associated with the pursuit of socially or environmentally focused endeavors and their perceived deleterious effect on profit margin. NGO leaders and supporters often worry that collaborating with purely profit-generating business objectives will warp their mission. This, however, varies by NGO. For example, Greenpeace rejects corporate donations, while the World Wildlife Fund depends on corporate money to perform its mission.

Both parties, NGOs and for-profit companies, often believe that their respective goals and agendas will in some way be significantly compromised if they attempt to fully accommodate their partners. Adding to the challenge and complexity of forming NGO-corporate partnerships is undoubtedly the lack of a common language. For instance, try getting your typical corporate or NGO leader to say the words "profit" and "social impact" or "return on investment" and "environmental reduction" in the same sentence.

This apparent inconsistency in goals is often an insurmountable barrier to developing full NGO-business partnerships, when in fact, the logistics, the terms, the obstacles may all be navigable with proper effort. The benefits are waiting to be uncovered. What may stop such partnerships are not these elements but instead the mindset. It is up to forward-thinking business leaders to take on a new belief that, just like in any other relationship, good communication, negotiation, and compromise can lead to a win-win result.

Might businesses and NGOs achieve their goals by rising above this legacy way of thinking? A growing number of consumers are less likely to buy from businesses solely concerned with making money, with a disregard for the resulting social and environmental impacts of their business. In the NGO arena, sustainability advocates will increasingly support NGOs that collaborate with in-dustry for maximum positive impact. The mutual benefit of corpo-rate and NGO partnership has never been more relevant to the success and sustainability of both parties.

The limiting beliefs of business leaders that block deeper partner-ships actually appear to exist on a spectrum of unproductive atti-tudes. On one end of the spectrum, there are companies with a "know-it-all" attitude, and on the other end of the spectrum are companies that are reluctant to engage because they don't know where to start. There are companies in the middle that have not "seen the light" – experienced a productive NGO partnership or been exposed to the stories illustrating mutual benefit – so they do not see the value in forming an NGO partnership and are content to sit on the fence.

For companies with a know-it-all attitude, it is hard to acknowl-edge that there could be knowledge gaps or flaws embedded in their plans or in the implementation of their policies, as these plans and policies are often considered internally as being amply progres-sive and sustainable. This attitude can be a perilous blind spot. If this attitude were applied to customers, a business would quickly lose touch with their sources of revenue. The NGO partnership is like any business consideration; corporate leaders get the best re-sults by remaining consistently open-minded and searching for the best facts and information regardless of their source (specifically when it is NGOs).

Kimberly-Clark experienced this firsthand when Greenpeace al-leged that K-C's third-party fiber suppliers were not following K-C's responsible fiber sourcing policies. K-C initially rejected this idea, not believing at the time that their supply chain was Greenpeace's business. But in the end, what Greenpeace found (that one or more of their suppliers were sourcing wood fiber from an endangered area) was right. If K-C had paid more attention to the details and been open to listen and respond to criticism, it might have avoided the years of negative campaigning against them.

Companies at the other end of the spectrum, those who are reluc-tant to engage in NGO relationships because of inhibition and fear of being too late to the game, don't know where to start and are afraid to put their reputation and business in peril. They may be overwhelmed by the perceived challenges of playing catch-up.

Just like starting any new habit or project, the conventional wisdom suggests that businesses take one small, methodical step at a time. Leaders can examine the pros and cons of NGO partnerships, conduct research to refine the pool of strategic NGOs by doing a stakeholder mapping exercise (this may be done internally or with the help of networks or intermediaries specializing in brokering NGO-corporate relationships), and then start building relationship(s) in small ways. There are NGOs who are open to working with companies at the early stage of development, as long as they see a sincere interest in environmental or societal improvement on the part of the business.

Most of the companies in the middle of the spectrum (those that do not "see the light") exhibit behavior similar to what was pointed out by Kanal Consulting: these companies often avoid contacting an NGO because they have not yet been the direct negative target of NGOs.[7] They do not yet see the value of forming any partnership, nor do they see what value these organizations actually bring to the table. Unfortunately, when an underestimated business problem turns into a crisis, it's already too late to avoid the PR consequences. In this situation, success also comes from baby steps. Leaders can start to establish relationships with strategic NGOs by targeting matters or issues that are the most material to the company both now and in the future. Over time, these relationships, if properly managed, may bear fruit and contribute to the company image and result in competitive advantage.

Two Key Areas for Business Collaboration with NGOs

There are two broad areas where cooperation between companies and NGOs is often most fruitful: nature conservation and community development.

1. *Nature conservation* is one area in which businesses and NGOs should have a clear mutual interest. Companies often depend

on resources provided by nature to sustain business. The responsible/thoughtful use of natural resources helps ensure that a continuous source of required raw materials and services remain available to the company now and in the foreseeable future. This concept is also commonly referred to as "resource stewardship." Many corporations struggle to understand how best to reduce their own and society's collective impact, or how to positively impact the supply of natural resources on which they rely. NGOs may hold the key to this mystery, and companies can learn how to benefit from viewing the natural ecosystem in a sustainable way. Also, NGOs' reach and vision is often global and not constrained by arbitrary political borders. The Nature Conservancy (TNC) collaborates with stakeholders, including businesses, to address conservation issues. TNC and Dow Chemical Company are working together on a breakthrough collaboration that strives to help Dow incorporate the value of nature into its company-wide goals, strategies, and business objectives, giving Dow a sustainable edge over competitors.

2. *Community development and welfare* is the second broad area of cooperation. Business and NGOs maintain a mutual interest in the social and economic well-being of the community. Companies' depend on the community for critical resources, including qualified employees, and as a market for their products and services. NGOs can provide local know-how, understanding of local laws, and the best ways to communicate with and promote to local populations. This knowledge can help companies become more competitive by allowing them to expand into new markets or deepen their roots and influence in existing ones. CARE International routinely works with businesses around the world, supporting more than 900 poverty-fighting development and humanitarian-aid projects, such as girls' and women's rights and empowerment, in 87 countries.

These two broad areas by no means cover the full extent of NGO partnerships. There's an NGO for virtually every cause or critical issue. That's good news for companies.

The Roles NGOs Play

There is no one perfect template for business/NGO partnerships. Business may derive maximum benefit for several different configurations. NGOs can play at least nine roles in the partnership from which businesses can potentially benefit.

1. *Advisor:* NGOs can be a source of guidance regarding compliance with the local laws and about how to operate with the least impact on nature and the environment. They can assist a company's efforts to effectively conduct business within local cultural and regulatory norms, helping avoid costly pitfalls and missteps such as restricted market access, wasted time, and fines/legal fees.
2. *Expert:* NGOs can offer expertise in wide number of areas, such as energy, food, water, agriculture, waste, and natural resources. They can explain the ecological, economic, and in some cases the financial value of ecosystems and ecosystem services.
3. *Credible Advocate:* NGOs bring competencies and resources to such partnerships, including market expertise; legitimacy with clients/customers, civil society players, and governments; and access to local expertise. Partnerships with NGOs can provide stakeholders with the perception that large corporations are indeed genuinely interested in societal or environmental issues. Coca-Cola has a long-standing relationship with WWF to help conserve the world's freshwater resources. Together, they engage the company's value chain; involve additional partners to achieve greater scale and impact; and spark commitments from businesses, governments, and consumers to take action to value, conserve, and protect the planet's natural resources.
4. *Lobbyist:* NGOs can help lobby within governments, for green taxes and other regulations that also serve as incentives for responsible production/business. The ENGO works, uniquely and by design, in the space between governments, businesses, communities, innovative thinkers, and individuals – forging partnerships and developing groundbreaking initiatives to help the businesses use resources more sustainably. They have

strong relationships with government decision-makers, with business leaders with the ability to influence powerful supply chains, and with individuals through their highly respected consumer campaigns.

5. *Third-Party Certifier:* By working with NGOs, some companies have adopted certification for their products, thereby generating a level playing field for their products versus other environmentally or ethically positioned products, potentially outpacing their competitors altogether. For example, like-minded NGOs like WWF, Greenpeace, and others partnered with leading forestry companies to solve the forest certification issue. Their efforts established a comprehensive forest certification, FSC, to ensure sustainable forestry. This is now the gold standard for forest stewardship. The certification is becoming widely leveraged by retail outlets and suppliers. The industry benefited from this innovative new certification, which communicated their products' sustainability to consumers.

6. *Innovation Partner:* NGOs have a wealth of expertise in sustainable development issues and consumer and environmental welfare. By way of example, the NRDC has for several years maintained an office near Walmart headquarters, partnering with Walmart to establish sourcing policy.

7. *Networking Resource:* Companies can tap into NGO networks to address sustainable development issues "on the ground" in countries where their suppliers are operating and to identify novel ways to expand their businesses. Oxfam (an international confederation) works with people in more than 90 countries to create lasting solutions that save lives, develops long-term solutions to poverty, and campaigns for social change. Oxfam recognizes that every organization has its own strategic objectives, markets, audiences, and visions for the future. They state that their partnerships start with exploring common ground and developing innovative initiatives that work for everyone: your company, Oxfam, your customers, and their supporters.

8. *Risk Mitigation Partner:* Negative press and social media exposure travel fast. NGOs can serve to provide an "early warning sys-

tem" as well as valuable advisors on emerging reputational risks. Greenpeace serves this function for Kimberly-Clark in that there are regular communications in which K-C is transparent with sensitive commercial information; together, K-C and Greenpeace have established trust that allows K-C to share this information and receive candid feedback and early warnings about issues K-C might not otherwise spot.

9. *New Market Co-creator:* Corporations often lack the tangible resources or intangible knowledge needed to address challenges when entering new markets. Working with NGOs, corporations can adapt their business models to meet local markets' cultural, economic, institutional, and geographic needs. NGOs can help broker cross-sector partnerships, where parties contribute complementary capabilities along each stage of the value chain to develop products or services that the parties could not produce alone, thus creating and delivering value in novel ways while minimizing costs and risks. One excellent example is the Shakti brand of protein yogurt, which has risen to popularity in Bangladesh, manufactured and distributed by a collaborative venture between Grameen Foundation and Danone.

Partnering with the Right NGO

Every NGO-corporate partnership will be different in execution, but one strategic element will always be present – matching the NGO with issues material to the company's sustainability and business objectives. Companies that have clarity on these issues will uncover what expertise and help they need and could garner from a partnership. So in the end, this is a business strategy relationship that forms like any other.

For example, Lisa Morden, senior sustainability director at Kimberly-Clark, shared with us, "There are five material issues K-C has identified where it could benefit from NGO partnerships. On the environmental side – forest protection and the circular economy (post-consumer waste) are critical for the company, while on the

social side – health and sanitation, active aging and the empowerment of women are major themes important for the company.
Attaining this type of clarity will help corporations focus in on the
appropriate NGO pool that can best help the corporation prosper
and meet its current and, more importantly, emerging/longer term
business challenges."

Partnerships in the world of business might best be described as
marriages with conditions. This is definitely the case with NGO-
business partnerships, as finding the right partner requires proper
due diligence and consideration, as well as clear articulation of mutual benefits and expectations.

Having experienced many NGO collaborations in our corporate
lives, and having extensively researched these partnerships, we've
created a list of best practices, lessons for forging and managing
these valuable partnerships for maximum success. These lessons
should be applicable to all business leaders, whether their expansion goals focus on home or abroad, and may help business leaders find the competitive edge they are looking for in NGO
partnership. Forward-thinking leaders start walking the path of
profitable and productive NGO-business partnerships by following a nine-step process.

1. For each critical/material issue in your business, list the pros
   and cons of accessing the external expertise and help available
   through NGO partnerships. What are the associated costs and
   value? These pros and cons need to be evaluated on their ability
   to affect business objectives. For example, joining the UN Global
   Compact (with over 12,000 corporate participants and other
   stakeholders from over 145 countries, making it the largest
   voluntary corporate responsibility initiative in the world)
   provides member companies access to their wide spectrum of
   work-streams, management tools, and resources designed to
   help advance sustainable business models and markets.
2. Identify the list of potential NGOs actively working in that area.
   As mentioned previously, this can be done internally or with the

help of networks or intermediaries specializing in brokering NGO-corporate relationships. For example, the nonprofit UniversalGiving Corporate provides strategy, operational support services, and high-quality nonprofit partners to scale a company's community relations programs in more than 120 countries.

3. Short-list the potential NGO partners that are a great match for the pros and that minimize the cons. For each NGO on this shortlist, get to know their priorities, mission, tactics, partnerships, and collaboration activities. You want to achieve the closest match possible with one or more of your critical/material issues. In addition, some NGOs are more open and collaborative with business; as such, they may appear to be easier or more approachable partners. Business leaders do well to make sure these NGOs are willing to appropriately challenge their company's practices and direction as well, to improve them. On other hand, some NGOs require large upfront fees as a prerequisite to joining sector groups and supply chains. For example, The Sustainability Consortium (TSC) develops transparent strategies and tools to drive a new generation of sustainable products. A corporation can engage either as a Tier I or Tier II member. Each engagement option has different rights and fees (which can be as high as $100,000 per year). Once again, a company needs to look at the merits and demerits of joining a particular sector group with fees. Lastly, some NGOs may have a predominant image of being an "activist" or "extreme" NGO (e.g., Friends of the Earth), but depending on the competitive environment and urgency of the material issues, that may be exactly who a company needs to partner with to stay ahead of the pack. Treat these NGOs like prospective executive candidates. Examine the NGOs' current working relationships with other companies to determine partnership feasibility. Reach out to these companies and interview them as if they were references for that NGO. Reach out to the NGO leaders and interview them as well. Attempt to understand the NGOs'

full motivations and future goals, approach to tackling their issues, and style of operation. In the end, the best partnership results come from a match in agenda, benefits, and also style and philosophy.

4. Select one to five NGOs that have made it this far through the vetting process. (As each NGO has a different expertise and focus area, it's acceptable to work with a set of NGOs.) In the case of Kimberly-Clark, the team chose four NGOs to help them work on responsible fiber sourcing issues – FSC, as they had best practices for standards; Greenpeace, as they stretched the company's point of view; WWF, to drive the broader forestry agenda; and Forest Dialogue, for forestry policy issues.

5. Start with small-scale engagement. Once you have narrowed down the list and chosen the NGO (or NGOs) to partner with, start small. Work with them on a small project of mutual interest to test the partnership. This will provide a firsthand opportunity to become familiar with each other's culture, further assess compatibility, and begin to establish mutual trust. Trust built this way can help create the lasting foundation for a partnership's success. Lasting trust relies on shared culture or complementary mission, respect for the partner's potential contribution, and ability to meet mutual commitments. For more than a decade, Kimberly-Clark and MedShare International have forged a partnership to bring critically needed medical supplies to health facilities around the world. Since K-C's original grant to help launch MedShare in 1998, the company has funded the shipment of $18.5 million worth of supplies to 13 countries in Latin America. In addition, K-C employees have worked thousands of volunteer hours to help pack the shipping containers with life-saving equipment.

6. Embrace and celebrate differences. Recognize and respect the differences between your company and the partner NGOs. Without the differences, there would be no reason to collaborate. Differing perspectives can make collaboration uncomfortable at times but also valuable, as each side's knowledge, expertise, and

capabilities complement the other's. One strategy increasingly employed to help better understand these differences is to hire some employees directly from the NGO sector. Some companies are employing NGO veterans to help guide their interactions with NGOs. As a corollary, NGOs are looking to the private sector to hire industry veterans who can help them better navigate their relationships with companies. These types of connections or translators can provide immediate understanding that smooths partnership formation.

7. Establish clear win/win goals for both parties. The collaboration must help both parties to meet their goals and address their stakeholder needs. Make sure these goals are SMART goals (specific, measurable, attainable, relevant, and time-based).

8. Assign a business champion. Both NGOs and corporations need to designate their respective partnership champion and give them the appropriate authority, leadership, and decision-making capability with regard to the partnership and within their perspective organizations. There are doubters, and in some cases even saboteurs, in both camps. Because NGO partnerships may represent a new way of doing things, an effective and often well-networked champion is necessary to overcome inertia and get things done. Ensure that you select an experienced businessperson as the partnership champion, with a solid track record of successful negotiations, as doing so will allow small issues to stay small and big issues to be handled with grace and inclusion and in a timely manner. Establish a communication hotline between the two champions, so all inevitable issues are addressed early on, before they become insurmountable or out of control.

9. Commit to regular governance. Establish a regular cadence of meetings, with both parties tracking progress against both their goals and continually assessing the ongoing usefulness/health of the partnership. Build reflection into the process, and modify the relationship, projects, or terms as needed to keep the partnership effective and healthy. Incorporate this governance

process into the initial agreement or memorandum of understanding so that both sides expect that the relationship will require maintenance and periodic reassessment.

Fostering the Relationship

Over time, make NGO engagement part of the core business. Partnerships should gradually be integrated into the responsibilities of business units and functions, rather than being maintained separately by a central support function or stand-alone sustainability group. Partnerships are most successful when each participant fully leverages their core capabilities and expertise and strategically contributes resources at the right times and to the right extent. This is how the partnership or relationship becomes more than just the sum of its parts.

Plan for the relationship to evolve and grow over time. Start with a project or initiative that is small and manageable and then plan to scale up over time. The initial project or initiative should be of mutual interest for the two groups and have clear metrics and deliverables that are not too far in the future. Environmental conditions, business interests, and positions will inevitably change, and these changes will influence or even dictate the future course of the partnership. Just be prepared for, and be responsive to, these changes. If you've properly installed regular governance processes, this evolution will progress more seamlessly.

Case Study: Kimberly-Clark and Greenpeace

Background

Greenpeace confronted several companies alleged to be sourcing, directly or indirectly, wood products or fiber from the ancient Canadian boreal forests, which Greenpeace sought to protect. K-C was among these companies, and its leaders were convinced that their practices were environmentally sound, so they reacted defensively by ignoring the Greenpeace request. Greenpeace saw that their concerns had little effect, and they realized that K-C had recognizable consumer brands with which they could target an influential campaign. In 2004, Greenpeace, working with the NRDC, launched their *Kleercut* campaign, tweaking the Kleenex branded tissue's familiar cursive logo, to draw public attention to K-C's wood-fiber sourcing practices. The publicity effort went on for five years. During this campaign a variety of Greenpeace tactics and creativity were brought to bear. Activists decorated trucks as tissue boxes and parked them outside corporate headquarters. They printed a doctored version of *USA Today* and distributed it at the World Tissue Convention. They attended shareholders' meetings and launched a group called the *Forest Friendly 500*, urging universities, companies, and other major purchasers to boycott K-C's products. They demonstrated in front of mills and chained themselves to train tracks. They pranked a man-on-the-street shoot for a Kleenex spot, sending activists one by one to pose as passersby and denounce the tissue as cameras rolled, and then released their own video of what happened. Greenpeace fully harnessed their energy behind their passion for this cause. There were pauses in the campaign, including a several-month hiatus in 2007, when they negotiated with K-C. At other times the campaign was dormant for tactical reasons.

At one point, as K-C's CEO, Thomas Falk, prepared to deliver a speech at his alma mater, the University of Wisconsin, activists managed to access the audiovisual equipment, swapping out his PowerPoint deck for slides focused on the *Kleercut* campaign. An unhappy Falk cut the talk short, and guests were ushered into a luncheon, where they were greeted at their table settings with satirical menus further hammering home Greenpeace's message.

After five years of active campaigning, the financial impact of all this activity on K-C seemed to be mostly negligible. However, in 2009, the leaders of K-C ascertained that something needed to be done. The *Kleercut* campaign was a distraction that made it discordant for K-C to discuss its positive sustainability record. The company recognized that its sourcing methods reflected on the company's image, just as much as their innovative, high-quality products and processes, and they could also provide an advantage. K-C reached out to Greenpeace, and despite years of negativity, they began to work together. This is a testament to an open perspective. Note that there was one major difference in the approach on negotiating teams: during the first stage, the parties had relatively large delegations (six to eight people), which led to posturing and excessive process. In the second round, one person led the negotiations from each organization; thus they could and did build a relationship of trust.

Before long, K-C further toughened its procurement guidelines based on Greenpeace's recommendations, a shift the two sides announced at a joint news conference in August 2009. At the press briefing they announced the company's new fiber buying policy and the end of the *Kleercut* campaign. Conflict and confrontation turned into collaboration that continues to this day. The enemies had become friends.

Organizations and businesses need to ensure there are processes and systems in place for collaboration so they are not people dependent. That's what has transpired in this relationship. The original members of the negotiating team have moved on, and Lisa Morden Sr. (director of sustainability at K-C) and Rolf Skar (U.S. Forest Campaign leader for Greenpeace) have taken over the role. They continue the process of engaging individually and as a team on a periodic basis. Rolf sums up well what happens in these meetings: "I don't think either side has ever blindly accepted what the other side has said. But we both now know that anything but transparency, clear communication and acting in good faith will end up back-firing."

After Five Years of Positive Collaboration

Both sides currently feel there are valuable lessons to be shared and that there are many benefits to be reaped by resolving the conflict and forming a collaborative relationship. Businesses can apply these lessons in collaborations with NGOs and thus advance both the cause of sustainability and their own success. Both Lisa Morden and Rolf Skar shared with us the following lessons.

Kimberly-Clark's Five Valuable Lessons Learned

1. *Common ground is within reach*: K-C and Greenpeace learned that we both want forest management practices to improve around the world, but we had to work on being open-minded with each other. At first, it was hard to truly listen.
2. *Transparency and trust are keys*: Both parties must be transparent regarding their objectives, plans, and processes. It began with a discussion of setting specific and measurable targets and the importance of meeting or exceeding those promised levels of performance as the way to build trust by delivering results. Getting past words to deeds is the key to a strong relationship. We had to push past our hesitancy to share internal information, which was critical to building trust.
3. *Both parties' reputations are on the line*: We learned that Greenpeace has just as much at stake as K-C does. Both teams highly value their reputation with their stakeholders and want to be respectful to all as they work together.
4. *Know the customer*: Understand the value drivers, priorities, and processes of your customer. This is critical to finding the middle ground and a principle that applies equally to NGOs.
5. *Set the pace of change*: NGOs want to see change happen faster than a company may be prepared to realize. Thus, expectations may be seen as unrealistic or not financially viable. By striking an ambitious timeline for change, there is an opportunity to demonstrate leadership ahead of the curve and, perhaps, realize value you never anticipated you could.

Greenpeace's Five Valuable Lessons Learned

1. *Dare to trust*: When asked what it was that turned years of conflict to collaboration, it is hard to pretend there weren't a mix of issues at play. That said, things began to change when lead negotiators from both sides started to trust each other. That's not an easy thing to do. Campaigners have, for good reason, a healthy suspicion of companies and their spokespersons. Too

often companies are greenwashing (a term used for using a green curtain to conceal dark motives) versus making a real change. And it's not hard to understand why it may be difficult for those within companies to be comfortable trusting someone who beat up their brands for years. But trust building has a natural momentum to it. At first, it is risky. Then, when it turns out trusting was the right decision, it gets easier to do it again. That is why trust building has continued between K-C and Greenpeace over the last five years.

2. *Don't limit potential benefits*: The Greenpeace *Kleercut* campaign stemmed from concerns about the Canadian boreal forest. And, while K-C has had a positive effect on boreal forest conservation since 2009, K-C and Greenpeace collaborate on issues of common interest. At the recent Forest Stewardship Council General Assembly, K-C helped Greenpeace craft and get approved a motion to conserve intact forest landscapes. This improves the world's most respected forest certification system and will have positive effects on forests far beyond the K-C supply chain.

3. *Let the haters hate*: The announcement of the new Kimberly-Clark fiber buying policy in 2009 was not without any controversy. Some environmentalists said Kimberly-Clark's plan wasn't good enough. Anti-conservation hacks said K-C had made a big mistake. We even saw a company lash out against Greenpeace and K-C, cynically seeking to boost its own sales on the back of the media attention our collaboration was garnering. Over time, the haters fell silent as benefits to forests and the bottom line proved them wrong. You can't make everyone happy, but you can do what's right and wait out the hate.

4. *Waiting can be worth it*: The *Kleercut* campaign was a long one, spanning almost five years. At times, some thought there might never be resolution to the campaign. After all, we were asking the company to make new global procurement standards for the main ingredient to its core products. New pulp buying standards could mean an increase in price, something competitive companies try to avoid at all cost (pun intended). When K-C and

Greenpeace finally did reach agreement, the company's commitment to its new procurement policy may have been stronger than it may have otherwise been. There was a lot at stake for the company to make it work. Backtracking or pursuing the new commitments with something less than real ambition would doubtless backfire. We learned that lasting change sometimes requires a bigger investment up front, and though Greenpeace did not plan it this way, we are glad about the results.

5. *The "end" is the beginning of real work*: Unlike the haters, a lot of people are ready for good news. So when conflict ends and collaboration begins, it is easy for people to applaud and assume the problem (whatever it was) has been fixed. Not so. Many corporate commitments have faltered, some famously so. And NGOs like Greenpeace often find it easier to run advocacy campaigns than to resource long-term implementation work that creates real results on the ground. While Greenpeace has invested in following through with K-C, there are plenty of things we can do better. For example, it shouldn't take five years for us to take a step back, celebrate what's been accomplished, and communicate that to the world!

KEY TAKEAWAYS

- The right NGO-corporate partnership can improve a company's image relative to societal issues, including nature conservation and community development and welfare.
- NGOs can play several useful roles for companies, including as trusted advisors that help expand existing businesses or help innovate and build new businesses.
- Companies and NGOs should develop an open, flexible attitude toward partnerships while shedding the inflexible, legacy way of thinking.
- NGO relationships can be nurtured by managing expectations, setting clear and attainable goals, and maintaining open communication channels.

To effectively *drive the top-line growth with triple-bottom-line thinking* **with NGOs, a company should:**

1. Vet and select the right partner NGOs.
2. Seek advice from partner NGOs when considering expansion or entry into new markets.
3. Nurture NGO relationships, just as it would with any other business partner.
4. Proactively manage business continuity risks, working closely with trusted NGO partners.

11 Stakeholder Sustainability Audit (SSA) Tool

Self-Survey: The intent of this sustainability audit is to capture your perception of where the company in question is vis-à-vis their sustainability journey. This will be developed and administered as a web-based survey.

- The top-line results are emailed back to you.
- The anonymous ratings are mailed back to the company for whom you are taking this audit survey.

Personal – Demographic Questions

- Name:
- Company you are doing this audit for:
- Email address (This is so that we can send you results. We will also notify you of any updates to the audit tool and book.):
- Relation to the company:
  - Stakeholder
  - Internal team member
- If stakeholder, please identify which classification of stakeholder:
  - Consumer
  - Customer (B2B)
  - Employee
  - Supplier
  - Investor

- Community
- Government
- Media
- Nongovernmental organization

Based upon your response about your relationship with the company, a customized survey is presented to you consisting of 10 questions tailored for each classification of stakeholder. A comprehensive list of 60 questions is presented for the internal team.

Survey for Consumers (Engage, Act, Measure, Report)

Rate how well each of the 10 statements reflects your perceptions of the assessed company's practices.

Scale will show STRONGLY AGREE, AGREE, NEITHER AGREE NOR DISAGREE, DISAGREE, STRONGLY DISAGREE, and N/A or NO RESPONSE (if it's irrelevant or the respondent doesn't want to answer).

Questions
1. You are aware that the company has a Comprehensive Code of Ethics Policy in place.
2. The company regularly asks you to identify the issues that are most important to you.
3. You believe the company's long-term (5+ years) sustainability goals and metrics are balanced across all three pillars – environmental, social, and economic.
4. You believe the company regularly improves the methods they use to create their products and services to address environmental and social issues.
5. The company makes it clear to which sustainability-focused industry groups and forums they belong and contribute.
6. The company's brands articulate their "Purpose," which connects with your personal values.
7. The company's brands educate you on sustainable behaviors across the value chain.

8. The company's brands embrace a cradle-to-cradle consumption mindset, helping you to understand what to do when your use of their product finishes.

9. The company's brands undertake specific research and activities to understand your attitudes toward sustainable products and services.

10. The company's brands provide you with the ability to easily determine the most sustainable product/service choice offering in the category.

Survey for Customers (B2B) (Engage, Act, Measure, Report)

Rate how well each of the 10 statements reflects your perceptions of the assessed company's practices.

Scale will show STRONGLY AGREE, AGREE, NEITHER AGREE NOR DISAGREE, DISAGREE, STRONGLY DISAGREE, and N/A or NO RESPONSE (if it's irrelevant or the respondent doesn't want to answer).

Questions

1. You are aware that the company has a Comprehensive Code of Ethics Policy in place.

2. The company regularly asks you to identify the issues that are most important to you.

3. You are aware of the company's long-term (5+ years) sustainability goals and metrics.

4. You believe the company's sustainability goals are balanced across all three pillars – environmental, social, and economic.

5. The company makes it clear to which sustainability-focused industry groups and forums they belong and contribute.

6. The company communicates to you how their products or services can enhance your sustainability positions, image, and profitability.

7. The company collaborates with you to educate end consumers on sustainable practices.

8. The company works with you to eliminate waste across the value chain.
9. The company provides products or services that meet your defined or preferred certification and sourcing standards.
10. The company participates with you on community-benefit programs – further enhancing your collective image.

Survey for Employees (Engage, Act, Measure, Report)

Rate how well each of the 10 statements reflects your perceptions of the assessed company's practices.

Scale will show STRONGLY AGREE, AGREE, NEITHER AGREE NOR DISAGREE, DISAGREE, STRONGLY DISAGREE, and N/A or NO RESPONSE (if it's irrelevant or the respondent doesn't want to answer).

Questions
1. You are aware that the company has a Comprehensive Code of Ethics Policy in place.
2. The company regularly asks you to identify the issues that are most important to you.
3. You are aware of the company's long-term (5+ years) sustainability goals and metrics.
4. You believe the company's sustainability goals are balanced across all three pillars – environmental, social, and economic.
5. The company makes it clear to which sustainability-focused industry groups and forums they belong and contribute.
6. The company involves you in the creation and implementation of sustainability-related employee engagement and social programs.
7. You can clearly see how the employee engagement programs you participate in are linked to the company's sustainability strategy and goals.
8. The company leaders are committed to engage and provide financial resources for employee-led sustainability engagement programs.

9. The company measures and reports progress of the employee engagement programs to you periodically.
10. The company's employee engagement programs help you feel more connected to your fellow employees and the company as a whole.

Survey for Suppliers (Engage, Act, Measure, Report)

Rate how well each of the 10 statements reflects your perceptions of the assessed company's practices.

Scale will show STRONGLY AGREE, AGREE, NEITHER AGREE NOR DISAGREE, DISAGREE, STRONGLY DISAGREE, and N/A or NO RESPONSE (if it's irrelevant or the respondent doesn't want to answer).

Questions
1. You are aware that the company has a Comprehensive Code of Ethics Policy in place.
2. The company regularly asks you to identify the issues that are most important to you.
3. You are aware of the company's long-term (5+ years) sustainability goals and metrics.
4. You believe the company's sustainability goals are balanced across all three pillars – environmental, social, and economic.
5. The company makes it clear to which sustainability-focused industry groups and forums they belong and contribute.
6. The company partners with you in developing sustainable solutions.
7. The company shares information with you about sustainable options to increase overall value-chain sustainability.
8. The company shares with you its Supplier Code of Conduct and helps you to implement and maintain the standard.
9. The company continually assesses progress on supplier sustainability objectives based on ESG (environmental, social, and governance) to drive supplier selection and retention.

10. The company measures, communicates, and reports supplier-related KPIs (e.g., percent of suppliers audited, percent of purchase from preferred suppliers, Scope 3 greenhouse gas emissions), and specifics on supplier corrective action plans.

Survey for Investors (Engage, Act, Measure, Report)

Rate how well each of the 10 statements reflects your perceptions of the assessed company's practices.

Scale will show STRONGLY AGREE, AGREE, NEITHER AGREE NOR DISAGREE, DISAGREE, STRONGLY DISAGREE, and N/A or NO RESPONSE (if it's irrelevant or the respondent doesn't want to answer).

Questions:
1. You are aware that the company has a Comprehensive Code of Ethics Policy in place.
2. The company regularly asks you to identify the issues that are most important to you.
3. You are aware of the company's long-term (5+ years) sustainability goals and metrics.
4. You believe the company's sustainability goals are balanced across all three pillars – environmental, social, and economic.
5. The company makes it clear to which sustainability-focused industry groups and forums they belong and contribute.
6. The company routinely communicates to you their sustainability credentials when it comes to water, carbon, governance, and supply chain issues.
7. The company shows commitment by supporting public policy declarations, e.g., signing CDP and Ceres (Coalition for Environmentally Responsible Economies) declarations and joining the Global Compact.
8. The company participates in sustainability surveys – e.g., DJSI (Dow Jones Sustainability Index), CDP – to benchmark progress.

9. The company measures and tracks the impacts of sustainability activities on core metrics – revenue growth, cost reduction, risk management, and reputation.
10. The company publishes the core metrics impact using the GRI (Global Reporting Initiative) G4 format and integrated reports.

Survey for Communities (Engage, Act, Measure, Report)

Rate how well each of the 10 statements reflects your perceptions of the assessed company's practices.

Scale will show STRONGLY AGREE, AGREE, NEITHER AGREE NOR DISAGREE, DISAGREE, STRONGLY DISAGREE, and N/A or NO RESPONSE (if it's irrelevant or the respondent doesn't want to answer).

Questions
1. You are aware that the company has a Comprehensive Code of Ethics Policy in place.
2. The company regularly asks you to identify the issues that are most important to you.
3. You are aware of the company's long-term (5+ years) sustainability goals and metrics.
4. You believe the company's sustainability goals are balanced across all three pillars – environmental, social, and economic.
5. The company makes it clear to which sustainability-focused industry groups and forums they belong and contribute.
6. The company implements social programs that help address global issues while engaging and involving the community.
7. The company provides matching grants or donations that support volunteerism and local community programs and charities.
8. The company partners with local organizations to enhance the long-term sustainability of the community.
9. The company tracks progress made by the social programs in the community.

10. The company periodically communicates the impact of their social program on the community.

Survey for Governments (Engage, Act, Measure, Report)

Rate how well each of the 10 statements reflects your perceptions of the assessed company's practices.

Scale will show STRONGLY AGREE, AGREE, NEITHER AGREE NOR DISAGREE, DISAGREE, STRONGLY DISAGREE, and N/A or NO RESPONSE (if it's irrelevant or the respondent doesn't want to answer).

Questions
1. You are aware that the company has a Comprehensive Code of Ethics Policy in place.
2. The company regularly asks you to identify the issues that are most important to you.
3. You are aware of the company's long-term (5+ years) sustainability goals and metrics.
4. You believe the company's sustainability goals are balanced across all three pillars – environmental, social, and economic.
5. The company makes it clear to which sustainability-focused industry groups and forums they belong and contribute.
6. The company strategically engages with government offices to promote development of common standards on sustainability issues.
7. The company takes advantage of government engagement incentives such as long-term research tax credits to invest in the long-term technology solutions to address societal problems.
8. The company participates with industrial groups in collaboration with government(s) to address global challenges.
9. The company measures the impact of government collaboration on both the company core metrics and the core goals of the government.

10. The company publishes contributions made to the political and industry associations in a transparent and timely way.

Survey for Media (Engage, Act, Measure, Report)

Rate how well each of the 10 statements reflects your perceptions of the assessed company's practices.

Scale will show STRONGLY AGREE, AGREE, NEITHER AGREE NOR DISAGREE, DISAGREE, STRONGLY DISAGREE, and N/A or NO RESPONSE (if it's irrelevant or the respondent doesn't want to answer).

Questions
1. You are aware that the company has a Comprehensive Code of Ethics Policy in place.
2. The company regularly asks you to identify the issues that are most important to you.
3. You are aware of the company's long-term (5+ years) sustainability goals and metrics.
4. You believe the company's sustainability goals are balanced across all three pillars – environmental, social, and economic.
5. The company makes it clear to which sustainability-focused industry groups and forums they belong and contribute.
6. The company shares compelling stories in press releases, reports, and social media to showcase sustainability initiatives and progress for all relevant stakeholders.
7. The company communicates its core values with its media partners.
8. The company works with media partners to evaluate effective media options to communicate sustainability.
9. The company works with media partners for effectively and efficiently monitoring, managing, and communicating on social media.

10. The company leverages media partners to develop innovative ways to communicate sustainability on new and emerging media platforms.

Survey for NGOs (Engage, Act, Measure, Report)

Rate how well each of the 10 statements reflects your perceptions of the assessed company's practices.

Scale will show STRONGLY AGREE, AGREE, NEITHER AGREE NOR DISAGREE, DISAGREE, STRONGLY DISAGREE, and N/A or NO RESPONSE (if it's irrelevant or the respondent doesn't want to answer).

Questions
1. You are aware that the company has a Comprehensive Code of Ethics Policy in place.
2. The company regularly asks you to identify the issues that are most important to you.
3. You are aware of the company's long-term (5+ years) sustainability goals and metrics.
4. You believe the company's sustainability goals are balanced across all three pillars – environmental, social, and economic.
5. The company makes it clear to which sustainability-focused industry groups and forums they belong and contribute.
6. The company applies a strategic process to vet, select, and partner with the right NGOs.
7. The company articulates how partnering with you would add strategic value to both organizations.
8. The company applies the following principles with their NGO partners to build trust: start small, over-communicate, be open, and be willing to compromise to develop a win-win outcome.
9. The company works with you to develop and track mutual SMART (specific, measurable, attainable, relevant, and time-based) goals.
10. The company clearly communicates progress on NGO-partner projects in a timely and transparent manner.

Survey for Internal Teams (Engage, Act, Measure, Report)

Rate how well each of the 60 statements reflects your perceptions of the assessed company's practices.

Scale will show STRONGLY AGREE, AGREE, NEITHER AGREE NOR DISAGREE, DISAGREE, STRONGLY DISAGREE, and N/A or NO RESPONSE (if it's irrelevant or the respondent doesn't want to answer).

General Questions
1. Board of directors is diverse (female and/or minority) (minimum of 25 percent).
2. Board of directors is independent (minimum 50 percent).
3. Board of directors reviews sustainability position and progress quarterly.
4. You are aware that the company has a Comprehensive Code of Ethics Policy in place and it is administered annually to all stakeholders.
5. Chief sustainability officer reports to senior management and/or the CEO.
6. The company regularly asks you for issues that are most important to you.
7. Company strategies address high-impact sustainability issues related to business growth, productivity, and risks.
8. You are aware of the company's long-term (5+ years) sustainability goals and metrics.
9. Sustainability goals are balanced across all three pillars – environmental, social, and economic.
10. Senior management's compensation is tied to progressing and achieving sustainability.
11. An external Sustainability Advisory Board is in place to guide and push the company to become a best-in-class sustainable company.
12. Compliance with Code of Ethics is audited/verified by an independent third party.
13. Compliance with sustainability reporting is audited/verified by an independent third party.

14. The company routinely examines the supply chains and assesses risks against established sustainability criteria.
15. The company actively participates in sustainability-focused industry forums and surveys, such as Dow Jones Sustainability Index, CDP, and Ethisphere.

Consumer Questions
1. The company's brands articulate their "Purpose," which connects with the consumer's personal values.
2. The company's brands educate consumers on sustainable behaviors across the value chain.
3. The company's brands embrace a cradle-to-cradle consumption mindset.
4. The company's brands undertake specific research and activities to understand the consumer's attitudes toward sustainable products and services.
5. The company's brands provide consumers with the ability to easily determine the most sustainable product/service choice offering in the category.

Customer (B2B) Questions
1. The company communicates to customers how their products or services can enhance their sustainability positions, image, and profitability.
2. The company collaborates with customers to educate end consumers on sustainable practices.
3. The company works with customers to eliminate waste across the value chain.
4. The company provides products or services that meet the customer's defined or preferred certification and sourcing standards.
5. The company participates with customers on community-benefit programs – further enhancing your collective image.

Employee Questions

1. The company involves employees in the creation and implementation of sustainability-related employee engagement and social programs.
2. Employees can clearly see how the employee engagement programs they participate in are linked to the company's sustainability strategy and goals.
3. The company's leaders are committed to engage and provide financial resources for employee-led sustainability engagement programs.
4. The company measures and reports progress of the employee engagement programs to employees periodically.
5. The company's employee engagement programs help employees feel more connected to the rest of their fellow employees and the company overall.

Supplier Questions

1. The company partners with suppliers in developing sustainable solutions.
2. The company shares information with suppliers about sustainable options to increase overall value-chain sustainability.
3. The company shares with suppliers its Supplier Code of Conduct and helps them to implement and maintain the standard.
4. The company continually assesses progress on supplier sustainability objectives based on ESG (environmental, social, and governance) to drive the supplier selection and retention process.
5. The company measures, communicates, and reports supplier/supply chain–related KPIs (e.g., percent of suppliers audited, percent of purchase from preferred suppliers, Scope 3 greenhouse gas emissions, and specifics on supplier corrective action plans).

Investor Questions
1. The company routinely communicates to investors their sustainability credentials when it comes to water, carbon, governance, and supply chain issues.
2. The company shows commitment by supporting public policy declarations, e.g., signing CDP and Ceres (Coalition for Environmentally Responsible Economies) declarations and joining the Global Compact.
3. The company participates in sustainability surveys – e.g., DJSI (Dow Jones Sustainability Index), CDP – to benchmark progress.
4. The company measures and tracks the impacts of sustainability activities on core metrics – revenue growth, cost reduction, risk management, and reputation.
5. The company publishes the core metrics impact using the GRI (Global Reporting Initiative) G4 format and integrated reports.

Community Questions
1. The company implements social programs that help address global issues while engaging and involving the community.
2. The company provides matching grants or donations that support volunteerism and local community programs and charities.
3. The company partners with local organizations to enhance the long-term sustainability of the community.
4. The company tracks progress made by the social programs in the community.
5. The company periodically communicates the impact of their social programs on the community.

Government Questions
1. The company strategically engages with government offices to promote development of common standards on sustainability issues.
2. The company takes advantage of government engagement incentives such as long-term research tax credits to invest in the long-term technology solutions to address societal problems.

3. The company participates with industrial groups in collaboration with government(s) to address global challenges.
4. The company measures the impact of government collaboration on both the company core metrics and the core goals of the government.
5. The company publishes contributions made to the political and industry associations in a transparent and timely way.

Media Questions
1. The company shares compelling stories in press releases, reports, and social media to showcase sustainability initiatives and progress for all relevant stakeholders.
2. The company communicates its core values with media partners.
3. The company works with media partners to evaluate effective media options to communicate sustainability.
4. The company works with media partners for effectively and efficiently monitoring, managing, and communicating on social media.
5. The company leverages media partners to develop innovative ways to communicate sustainability on new and emerging media platforms.

NGO Questions
1. The company applies a strategic process to vet, select, and partner with the right NGOs.
2. The company articulates how partnering with a particular NGO would add strategic value to both organizations.
3. The company applies the following principles with their NGO partners to build trust: start small, over-communicate, be open, and be willing to compromise to develop a win-win outcome.
4. The company works with NGOs to develop and track mutual SMART (specific, measurable, attainable, relevant, and time-based) goals.
5. The company clearly communicates progress on NGO-partner projects in a timely and transparent manner.

Notes

Chapter 1: Introduction

1 Rice, Doyle. (April 22, 2016). 175 Nations Sign Historic Paris Climate Deal on Earth Day. http://www.usatoday.com/story/news/world/2016/04/22/paris-climate-agreement-signing-united-nations-new-york/83381218/.

2 Nevius, John, and Horkovich, Robert. (February 3, 2015). Climate Change and Its Impact on the Insurance Industry. *Risk Management*. http://www.rmmagazine.com/2015/02/03/climate-change-and-its-impact-on-the-insurance-industry/.

3 Pope Francis. (June 15, 2013). Letter of Holy Father Francis to H.E. Mr. David Cameron, British Prime Minister on the Occasion of the G8 meeting. http://w2.vatican.va/content/francesco/en/letters/2013/documents/papa-francesco_20130615_lettera-cameron-g8.html.

4 Nielsen. (June 23, 2014). Investing in the Future: Millennials Are Willing to Pay Extra for a Good Cause. http://www.nielsen.com/us/en/insights/news/2014/investing-in-the-future-millennials-are-willing-to-pay-extra-for-a-good-cause.html.

5 Matthews, Chris. The Myth of the 1% and the 99%. *Fortune*. http://fortune.com/2015/03/02/economic-inequality-myth-1-percent-wealth/.

6 Edelman. (2014). *Trust in Business*. www.edelman.com/insights/intellectual-property/2014-edelman-trust-barometer/trust-in-business.

7 Coyne, Kevin P. (January–February 1986). Sustainable Competitive Advantage – What It Is, What It Isn't. *Business Horizons*, pp. 54–61.

http://dirkjanswagerman.nl/static/files/MBI/Module%203/3%20
Coyne%201986.pdf.

8 Ray Anderson Reflects and Provides Vision for the Future. (August 31,
   2009). YouTube, uploaded by "trigflor." https://www.youtube.com/
   watch?v=NskixbVn0BE&feature=share.

9 Interface. (May 28, 2016). Sustainability. http://www.interfaceglobal.
   com/Sustainability/Our-Progress/AllMetrics.aspx; Interface. (May 2016).
   Investor Relations Presentation. http://www.interfaceglobal.com/
   investor-relations.aspx.

10 Davidson, Alex. (January 11, 2016). "Sustainable Investing" Goes
   Mainstream. *Wall Street Journal*, p. R5. http://www.wsj.com/articles/
   sustainable-investing-goes-mainstream-1452482737.

11 CDP. *Climate Action & Profitability*. https://www.cdp.net/CDPResults/
   CDP-SP500-leaders-report-2014.pdf, accessed August 18, 2015.

12 DB Climate Change Advisors. (June 2012). *Sustainable Investing*. https://
   institutional.deutscheawm.com/content/_media/Sustainable_
   Investing_2012.pdf.

13 Dill, Kathryn. (January 21, 2015). The World's Most Sustainable
   Companies 2015. *Forbes*. http://www.forbes.com/sites/kathryndill/
   2015/01/21/the-worlds-most-sustainable-companies-2015/
   #5e6d3b006f24.

14 Sisodia, R.S., Wolfe, D.B., and Sheth, J.N. (2007). *Firms of Endearment:
   How World-Class Companies Profit from Passion and Purpose*. Upper
   Saddle River, NJ: Pearson–Prentice Hall.

15 SCA. *Sustainability Report 2014*. http://www.sca.com/Documents/
   en/Env_Reports/2014/SCA-sustainability-report-2014.
   PDF?epslanguage=en. August 20, 2015.

Chapter 2: Motivating Consumers

1 Brown, Ashley. *Every Day Is Election Day*. http://www.coca-colacompa
   ny.com/coca-cola-unbottled/every-day-is-election-day, March 24,
   2015.

2 WBCSD. Vision 2050: The New Agenda for Business. http://www
   .wbcsd.org/pages/edocument/edocumentdetails.aspx?id=219&nosea
   rchcontextkey=true, March 23, 2015.

3 Sheth, Jagdish, Sethia, Nirmal, and Srinivas, Shanthi. (February 2011). Mindful Consumption: A Customer-Centric Approach to Sustainability. *Journal of the Academy of Marketing Sciences* 39 (1): 21–39. http://link .springer.com/article/10.1007/s11747-010-0216-3.

4 The Sustainability Imperative. (October 2015). Nielsen Global Sustainability Report. http://www.nielsen.com/us/en/insights/ reports/2015/the-sustainability-imperative.html.

5 National Geographic. *Greendex 2012: Consumer Choice and the Environment.* http://environment.nationalgeographic.com/ environment/greendex/, March 23, 2015.

6 Franklin Goose. (August 28, 2013). Seventh Generation Disposable Diapers. http://franklingoose.typepad.com/my-blog/2013/08/ seventh-generation-disposable-diapers.html.

7 Gould, Hannah. (January 31, 2013). Engaging Consumers in Sustainable Behavior – Discussion Round Up. *Guardian.* http://www.theguardian .com/sustainable-business/engaging-consumers-sustainable-behaviour- round-up.

8 Business Wire. (March 11, 2010). GE GeoSpring Cruises into Spring with Marketing Momentum. http://www.businesswire.com/news/ home/20100311006258/en/GE-GeoSpring%E2%84%A2-Cruises- Spring-Marketing-Momentum.

9 Cone Communications. (March 27, 2012). Consumers Still Purchasing, But May Not Be "Buying" Companies' Environmental Claims. http:// www.prnewswire.com/news-releases/consumers-still-purchasing- but-may-not-be-buying-companies-environmental-claims-144368945 .html, March 24, 2015.

10 Dhar, Ravi, et al. (May 8, 2010). Does Sustainability Matter to Consumers? *Yale Insights.* http://insights.som.yale.edu/insights/ does-sustainability-matter-consumers.

11 Institute for Health Metrics and Evaluation. Deaths from Cardio- vascular Disease Increasing Globally While Mortality Rates Decrease. http://www.healthdata.org/news-release/deaths-cardiovascular- disease-increase-globally-while-mortality-rates-decrease, accessed September 22, 2015.

12 Boseley, Sarah. (February 3, 2014). Worldwide Cancer Cases Expected to Soar by 70% over Next 20 Years. *Guardian.* http://www

.theguardian.com/society/2014/feb/03/worldwide-cancer-cases-soar-next-20-years.

13 World Health Organization. (January 2015). *Obesity and Overweight Fact Sheet*. http://www.who.int/mediacentre/factsheets/fs311/en/.

14 Rattue, Grace. (June 22, 2012). Autoimmune Disease Rates Increasing. *Medical News Today*. http://www.medicalnewstoday.com/articles/246960.php.

15 Ingraham, Christopher. (October 29, 2014). Child Poverty in the US Is among the Worst in the Developed World. *Washington Post*. https://www.washingtonpost.com/news/wonkblog/wp/2014/10/29/child-poverty-in-the-u-s-is-among-the-worst-in-the-developed-world/.

16 Helliwell, John F., Layard, Richard, and Sachs, Jeffrey. (April 29, 2015). *The World Happiness Report 2015*. http://worldhappiness.report/wp-content/uploads/sites/2/2015/04/WHR15-Apr29-update.pdf.

17 Riffkin, Rebecca. (January 14, 2016). Government, Economy Return as Most Important U.S. Problems. Gallup. http://www.gallup.com/poll/188159/government-economy-return-important-problems.aspx?g_source=Politics&g_medium=lead&g_campaign=tiles.

18 Ariaratnam, Suresh. (January 15, 2013). Businesses Are Not Just Agents of Consumerism but Also of Society. *Guardian*. http://www.theguardian.com/sustainable-business/blog/business-agents-consumerism-society-customers?INTCMP=SRCH.

19 Wohl, Jessica. (May 24, 2007). Clorox Gives Brita One to Two Years to Improve. Reuters. http://www.reuters.com/article/2007/05/24/us-clorox-meeting-brita-idUSN2445807120070524.

20 Gallea, Bonnie. (February 22, 2013). Brita Filtered Water Bottle Marketing Plan. Concordia University, St. Paul, MN. http://www.slideshare.net/BonnieGallea/marketing-plan-16701441.

21 Hartman, E. (July 15, 2007). Know Your Drinking Water: Bottled vs. Brita. *Washington Post*. http://www.washingtonpost.com/wp-dyn/content/article/2007/07/12/AR2007071201862.html.

22 Neff, Jack. (November 16, 2009). Brita's Marketing Flows from Grassroots Effort. *Advertising Age*. http://adage.com/article/cmo-interviews/brita-s-marketing-flows-grassroots-effort/140519/.

Chapter 3: Collaborating with Customers

1 AT&T Corporation. (2014). Sustainability Reporting. http://about.att
.com/content/dam/csr/sustainability-report/2014/ATT-RLS-Letter.pdf.

2 Murray, James. (February 2, 2015). IKEA Sustainability Chief on
"Radical Change" and the Bottom Line. *GreenBiz*. https://www.
greenbiz.com/article/ikea-Steve-Howard-renewable-energy-business-
incrementalism-sustainability.

3 Target Corporation. (May 29, 2014). Jessica Alba's The Honest Company
to Launch at Target. https://corporate.target.com/discover/article/
Jessica-Alba-s-The-Honest-Company-to-launch-at-Tar.

4 United Natural Foods, Inc. Retail Services. https://www.unfi.com/
ProductsAndServices/Pages/RetailServices.aspx. March 23, 2015.

5 Mui, Ylan Q. (February 26, 2010). Wal-Mart Promises to Lower Greenhouse Gas Emissions by 2015. *Washington Post*. http://www.washington
post.com/wp-dyn/content/article/2010/02/25/AR2010022505453.
html.

6 All about Retail in Thailand. (June 30, 2011). Tesco & Unilever Go Go
Green. http://thairetail.blogspot.com/2011/06/tesco-unilever-go-go-
green.html.

7 WBCSD. (February 9, 2015). WBCSD Releases Updated Global Water
Tool for Sustainable Water Management. http://www.wbcsd.org/
Pages/eNews/eNewsDetails.aspx?ID=16464&NoSearchContextKey=
true.

8 Forum for the Future. (August 11, 2015). *Tea 2030: Multi-stakeholder
Project Exploring the Challenges Facing the Tea Sector's Future – and How
to Overcome Them*. https://www.forumforthefuture.org/project/tea-
2030/overview.

9 World Wildlife Fund. Forests. https://www.worldwildlife.org/initia-
tives/forests, accessed August 11, 2015.

10 AT&T Corporation. (2014). Sustainability Reporting. http://about.att
.com/content/csr/home/sustainability-reporting.html.

11 Duffy, Gary. (December 19, 2013). AT&T Consumer Blog. http://www
.about.att.com/content/csr/home/blog/2014/01/start_the_year_offf
.html.

12 Berst, Jesse. (July 2014). Patching up the Pipes: How Smart Techno-logies Help Cities Prevent Leaks and Save Money. *WaterWorld* 30 (7). http://www.waterworld.com/articles/print/volume-30/issue-7/editorial-features/patching-up-the-pipes-how-smart-technologies-help-cities-prevent-leaks-and-save-money.html.

13 Bernier, Paula. (August 10, 2015). Pipe Dream: AT&T, Partners Help Conserve Water via Leak Prevention Solution. *IoT Evolution.* http://www.iotevolutionmagazine.com/features/articles/408092-pipe-dream-att-partners-help-conserve-water-via.htm, accessed October 5, 2015 [free subscription required for access].

14 Bangor Water. *Aging Infrastructure Renewal Plan.* http://www.bangor-water.org/customer%20service%20home/Pipe%20renewal%20plan.pdf, accessed October 7, 2015.

15 PR Newswire. AT&T Leads the Industry in the Internet of Things: Connecting the Connected: More Than 136 New IoT Agreements Signed in 2015 (June 15, 2015). http://www.prnewswire.com/news-releases/att-leads-the-industry-in-the-internet-of-things-300099193.html, accessed October 7, 2015.

16 HydroPoint Data Systems Inc. (January 8, 2015). HydroPoint Shuts Down Water Waste with an Internet of Things Solution. https://www.business.att.com/content/customertestimonial/hydropoint-internet-of-things-case-study.pdf.

17 Bernier, Pipe Dream: AT&T, Partners Help Conserve Water via Leak Prevention Solution.

Chapter 4: Inspiring Employees

1 Esty, Daniel C., and Winston, Andrew S. (2006). *Green to Gold: How Smart Companies Use Environmental Strategy to Innovate, Create Value, and Build Competitive Advantage.* New Haven, CT: Yale University Press, p. 32.

2 Achor, Shawn. (2010). *The Happiness Advantage: The Seven Principles of Positive Psychology That Fuel Success and Performance at Work.* New York: Crown Business.

3 Sorenson, Susan. (June 20, 2013). How Employee Engagement Drives Growth. *Gallup Business Journal.* http://www.gallup.com/business-journal/163130/employee-engagement-drives-growth.aspx.

4 Lovins, Hunter. (July 5, 2012). Employee Engagement Is Key to Sustainable Success. Sustainable Brands. http://www.sustainable brands.com/news_and_views/jul2012/employee-engagement-key-sustainable-success.

5 Serafeim, George, Eccles, Robert G., and Clay, Tiffany A. (March 2011). Caesars Entertainment: CodeGreen. Harvard Business School Case 111-115.

6 Ernst & Young. *Six Growing Trends in Corporate Sustainability*. http://www.ey.com/US/en/Services/Specialty-Services/Climate-Change-and-Sustainability-Services/Six-growing-trends-in-corporate-sustainability_Trend-3, accessed February 19, 2015.

7 Intel. *2012 Corporate Responsibility Report*. http://csrreportbuilder.intel.com/PDFFiles/CSR_2012_Full-Report.pdf.

8 C-Suite Network. http://c-suitenetwork.com/, accessed July 27, 2015.

9 Hewlett-Packard. *Social Investment – HP 2014 Living Progress Report – English*. Page 46. http://www8.hp.com/h20195/v2/GetDocument. aspx?docname=c04152740, accessed May 19, 2016.

10 Bemporad, Raphael. (February 28, 2012). Employee Engagement: Five Companies That Get It. Triple Pundit. http://www.triplepundit. com/2012/02/employee-engagement-five-companies/.

11 Google. https://www.google.com/green/efficiency/oncampus/ #commuting, accessed July 27, 2015.

12 CLIF Bar Company. http://www.clifbar.com/article/clif_bar_ company_story. July 27, 2015.

13 Maw, Liz. (October 18, 2013). To Advance Sustainability, Go Beyond Traditional Employee Engagement Efforts. Sustainable Brands. http://www.sustainablebrands.com/news_and_views/employee_ engagement/liz-maw/advance-sustainability-go-beyond-traditional-employee-eng.

14 Ibid.

15 WeSpire. http://www.wespire.com/, accessed February 19, 2015.

16 GreenNexxus. http://www.greennexxus.com/, accessed February 19, 2015.

17 CloudApps, http://www.cloudapps.com/.

18 Ryan, Timothy. (December 30, 2011). Game Uses Employees' Carbon Footprints to Determine End of Year Bonuses [Future of Gaming]. PSFK. http://www.psfk.com/2011/12/

game-uses-employees-carbon-footprints-to-determine-end-of-year-bonuses-future-of-gaming.html.

19 GE Sustainability. Energy and Climate: Employee Engagement. http://www.gesustainability.com/building-things-that-matter/energy-and-climate/employee-engagement/, accessed September 22, 2015.

20 Kimberly-Clark. *Kimberly-Clark 2011 Corporate Sustainability Report.* http://www.sustainabilityreport2011.kimberly-clark.com/people/employees/employee-engagement/crystal-tree-award.aspx, accessed February 19, 2015.

21 Stevens, Susan Hunt. Employee Engagement: A Sustainability Super-Strategy? *Guardian.* (November 12, 2013). http://www.theguardian.com/sustainable-business/employee-engagement-sustainability-strategy.

22 BBMG. Walmart Engaging Employees across 28 Countries. http://bbmg.com/work/walmart/, accessed August 25, 2015.

Chapter 5: Nurturing Suppliers

1 IKEA. IKEA Group Sustainability Report FY14. http://www.ikea.com/ms/en_US/pdf/sustainability_report/sustainability_report_2014.pdf, accessed July 27, 2015.

2 Copeland, Ella. (October 9, 2012). Sustainable Procurement Makes Good Business Sense. Supply Chain Digital. http://www.supplychaindigital.com/procurement/2135/Sustainable-procurement-makes-good-business-sense.

3 Prokesch, Steven. (October 2010). The Sustainable Supply Chain: An Interview with Peter Senge. *Harvard Business Review.* https://hbr.org/2010/10/the-sustainable-supply-chain/ar/1.

4 McGill Murphy, Richard. (February 2, 2010). Why Doing Good Is Good for Business. *Fortune.* http://archive.fortune.com/2010/02/01/news/companies/dov_seidman_lrn.fortune/index.htm.

5 CERES. Shareholder Resolutions. http://www.ceres.org/investor-network/resolutions, accessed March 5, 2015.

6 Nisen, Max. (May 9, 2013). How Nike Solved Its Sweatshop Problem. http://www.businessinsider.com/how-nike-solved-its-sweatshop-problem-2013-5.

7 Ibid.

8 Sustainable Business News. (August 14, 2013). Green Investors Push Firms on GHG Emissions, Supply Chain. GreenBiz. https://www .greenbiz.com/blog/2013/08/14/green-investors-push-firms-ghg-emissions-supply-chain.

9 Guthrie, Doug. (March 9, 2012). Building Sustainable and Ethical Supply Chains. *Forbes*. http://www.forbes.com/sites/ dougguthrie/2012/03/09/building-sustainable-and-ethical-supply-chains/.

10 Herrera, Tilde. (October 11, 2010). 10 Things to Know About Engaging Suppliers for Green Programs. GreenBiz. https://www.greenbiz.com/ blog/2010/10/11/10-things-know-about-engaging-suppliers-green-programs.

11 Heinz Corporation. Heinz Tomatoes: Cultivating a Sustainable Commitment. http://www.heinz.com/data/pdf_files/Tomato_ Sustainability_Report.pdf, accessed March 5, 2015.

12 Siemens Corporation. (2012). Sustainable Automation Solutions to Our Most Important Resource, p. 34. http://w3.siemens.com/mcms/ water-industry/en/documents/e20001-a90-t122-x-7600_ws_ reference-booklet-water_us.pdf.

13 Prokesch, Sustainable Supply Chain.

14 Zero Discharge of Hazardous Chemicals. Roadmap to Zero Discharge of Hazardous Chemicals. http://www.roadmaptozero.com/, accessed March 5, 2015.

15 Copeland, Ella. (October 9, 2012). Sustainable Procurement Makes Good Business Sense. Supply Chain Digital. http://www.supplychaindigital. com/procurement/2135/Sustainable-procurement-makes-good-business-sense.

16 Herrera, 10 Things to Know About Engaging Suppliers for Green Programs.

17 UN Global Compact and BSR. (2010). Supply Chain Sustainability: A Practical Guide for Continuous Improvement. http://www.bsr.org/ reports/BSR_UNGC_SupplyChainReport.pdf.

18 Herrera, 10 Things to Know About Engaging Suppliers for Green Programs.

Chapter 6: Investing in Communities

1 The Quotable Jamesetji Tata. (March 2008). http://www.tata.com/aboutus/articlesinside/The-quotable-Jamsetji-Tata.

2 *Economist*. (March 21, 2015). The Business of Business. Schumpeter, p. 62. http://www.economist.com/news/business/21646742-old-debate-about-what-companies-are-has-been-revived-business-business.

3 Nadkarni, Anant G., and Branzai, Oana. (March/April 2008). The Tata Way: Evolving and Executing Sustainable Business Strategies. *Ivey Business Journal*. http://iveybusinessjournal.com/publication/the-tata-way-evolving-and-executing-sustainable-business-strategies.

4 Sheth, Jagdish N., and Sinha, Mona. (October 2015). B2B branding in Emerging Markets: A Sustainability Perspective. *Industrial Marketing Management* 51: 79–88.

5 Mead, J., Hartman, L.P., and Werhane, P. (March 24, 2008). *BHP Billiton and Mozal A & B Case Study*. Darden Business School, University of Virginia.

6 Sheth and Sinha, B2B branding in Emerging Markets: A Sustainability Perspective.

7 Newenham-Kahindi, A., and Beamish, P.W. (October 20, 2010). *Barrick Gold Corporation – Tanzania Case Study*. Richard Ivey School of Business, University of Western Toronto.

8 Chakraborty, Saheli. (August 10, 2010). Corporate Social Responsibility and the Society. Business That Cares. http://businessthatcares.blogspot.ca/2010/08/corporate-social-responsibility-and.html.

9 International Institute for Sustainable Development. *Corporate Social Responsibility (CSR)*. http://www.iisd.org/business/issues/sr.aspx, accessed March 24, 2015.

10 International Institute for Sustainable Development. *Corporate Social Responsibility Monitor*. https://www.iisd.org/business/issues/sr_csrm.aspx, accessed March 25, 2015.

11 International Institute for Sustainable Development, *Corporate Social Responsibility (CSR)*.

12 Thorpe, Devin. (May 18, 2013). Why CSR? The Benefits of Corporate Social Responsibility Will Move You to Act. *Forbes*. http://www.

forbes.com/sites/devinthorpe/2013/05/18/why-csr-the-benefits-of-corporate-social-responsibility-will-move-you-to-act/.

13 *Lansing Business News*. Downtown Lansing Revitalization Fostered by Historic Preservation. http://lansingbusinessnews.com/OLD/index.php?option=com_content&view=article&id=2290:downtown-lansing-revitalization-fostered-by-historic-preservation&catid=13&Itemid=167, accessed October 7, 2015.

14 JPMorgan Chase. Chase Community Development Banking. https://www.chase.com/commercial-bank/finance/community-development, accessed June 16, 2015.

15 AkzoNobel. Community Program: How Can a Big, Global Organization Make a Difference to a Small, Local Community? https://www.akzonobel.com/powder/_sustainability/community_program/, accessed March 24, 2015.

16 Thorpe, Why CSR?

17 AkzoNobel, Community Program. https://www.akzonobel.com/sustainability/stories/community_program/, accessed April 15, 2015.

18 Grameen Creative Lab. Live Examples: Grameen Danone Foods Ltd. http://www.grameencreativelab.com/live-examples/grameen-danonee-foods-ltd.html, accessed April 15, 2015.

19 Gittleson, Kim. (January 19, 2012). Can a Company Live Forever? BBC News. http://www.bbc.com/news/business-16611040.

20 Tata Values and Purpose. http://www.tata.com/aboutus/articlesinside/Values-and-purpose.

Chapter 7: Attracting Investors

1 Cook, Jackie. (July 2013). Research Proxy Season Roundup Shareholder Resolutions. CookESG Research. http://www.fund-votes.com/downloads/2013%20Proxy%20Season%20Roundup_Shareholder%20Resos_CookESG.pdf.

2 USSIF. (2014). Report on US Sustainable, Responsible and Impact Investing Trends 2014, p. 12. http://www.ussif.org/Files/Publications/SIF_Trends_14.F.ES.pdf.

3 Schmid, Daniel. (December 2, 2014). Sustainability Indices Benchmarks of Listed Companies Future Viability. CSRWire. http://www.csrwire.com/blog/posts/1475-sustainability-indices-benchmarks-of-listed-companies-future-viability.

4 Davidson, Alex. (January 11, 2016). "Do Good" Investing Turns Corner. *Wall Street Journal*, 5R. http://www.wsj.com/articles/sustainable-investing-goes-mainstream-1452482737.

5 Climate Action & Profitability (CDP S&P 500 Climate Change Report), p. 4. https://www.cdp.net/CDPResults/CDP-SP500-leaders-report-2014.pdf.

6 Ibid.

7 Thomson Reuters Accelus. Supply Chain Management Challenges. http://financial.thomsonreuters.com/content/dam/openweb/documents/pdf/financial/supply-chain-management-challenges.pdf, accessed September 22, 2015.

8 Eccles, Robert G., Krzus, Michael P., and Serafeim, George. (September 22, 2011). *Market Interest in Nonfinancial Information*. Harvard Business School Working Paper 12-018.

9 World Business Council for Sustainable Development. *Vision 2050*. http://www.wbcsd.org/vision2050.aspx, accessed April 27, 2015.

10 Grady, Barbara. (August 19, 2015). Institutional Investors to Big Food: Come Clean on Water Risks. GreenBiz. https://www.greenbiz.com/article/institutional-investors-big-food-come-clean-water-risks.

11 Davidson, "Do Good" Investing Turns Corner.

12 Morgan Stanley. *Institute for Sustainable Investing*. http://www.morganstanley.com/what-we-do/institute-for-sustainable-investing/, accessed April 27, 2015.

13 King, Bart. (September 10, 2013). Materiality Assessments: The Missing Link for Sustainability Strategy. GreenBiz. https://www.greenbiz.com/blog/2013/09/10/materiality-assessments-missing-link-sustainability-strategy.

14 Nestlé Corporation. Materiality. http://www.nestle.com/csv/what-is-csv/materiality, accessed April 27, 2015.

15 AT&T Corporation. Materiality Assessment. http://about.att.com/content/csr/home/sustainability-reporting/materiality-assessment.html, accessed April 27, 2015.

16 Mitsubishi Chemical Company. Message from the President. http://
    www.mitsubishichem-hd.co.jp/english/kaiteki_management/
    message/, accessed April 27, 2015.
17 Bonini, Sheila, and Görner, Stephan. (2011). The Business of
    Sustainability: Putting It into Practice. McKinsey & Company. p. 4.
18 Lubin, David A., and Esty, Daniel C. (Summer 2014). Bridging the
    Sustainability Gap, MIT Sloan Management Review. https://www.eli
    .org/sites/default/files/media/14-10-21-DC/esty-bridging-sustain
    ability-gap.pdf.
19 DuPont. (2014). Global Reporting Initiative Report. http://www
    .dupont.com/content/dam/assets/corporate-functions/our-
    approach/sustainability/documents/DuPont2014GRIReport.pdf.
20 Lubin and Esty, Bridging the Sustainability Gap.

Chapter 8: Leveraging Media

 1 Boykoff, Maxwell, and Boykoff, Jules. (2004). Balance as Bias: Global
    Warming and the US Prestige Press. *Global Environmental Change*
    14: 125–36. http://sciencepolicy.colorado.edu/admin/publication_
    files/2004.33.pdf.
 2 Vaidyanathan, Gayathri. (January 30, 2015). Big Gap between What
    Scientists Say and Americans Think about Climate Change. *Scientific
    American*. http://www.scientificamerican.com/article/big-gap-
    between-what-scientists-say-and-americans-think-about-climate-
    change/.
 3 Toennesen, Christian. (November 24, 2009). Media's Role in the Journey
    from Consumer to Citizen. *Guardian*. http://www.theguardian.com/
    sustainability/blog/csr-media-literacy-education-media-responsibilities.
 4 McGoey, Linsey. (September 2012). The Logic of Strategic Ignorance.
    British Journal of Sociology 63 (3): 533–76.
 5 Livingstone, Sonia. (2003). *The Changing Nature and Uses of Media
    Literacy*. Media@LSE electronic working papers, 4. London School
    of Economics and Political Science, London, UK. http://eprints.lse
    .ac.uk/13476/.
 6 Parsai, Gargi. (October 25, 2014). Modi Lauds Media Role in Swachh
    Bharat Campaign. *The Hindu*. http://www.thehindu.com/news/

national/clean-india-campaign-modi-praises-media-for-coverage/article6532872.ece.

7 WPP. (August 16, 2015). WPP Sustainability Report 2012, p. 78. http://www.wpp.com/sustainabilityreports/2012/pdfs/wpp-sr12-sustainability-report-2012-2013.pdf.

8 McPherson, Susan. (May 27, 2014). Empowering Women and Girls One Hashtag at a Time. *Forbes.* http://www.forbes.com/sites/susanmcpherson/2014/05/27/empowering-women-and-girls-one-hashtag-at-a-time/2/.

9 Mahmud, Shahnaz. (June 16, 2008). Media Plan of the Year. http://www.adweek.com/news/advertising-branding/media-plan-year-08-96433?page=4.

10 Meaningful Brands. Havas Media. http://www.meaningful-brands.com/, accessed March 11, 2015.

11 Stock, Kyle. (November 25, 2013). Patagonia's Confusing and Effective Campaign to Grudgingly Sell Stuff. *Bloomberg Business.* http://www.bloomberg.com/news/articles/2013-11-25/patagonias-confusing-and-effective-campaign-to-grudgingly-sell-stuff.

12 Yeomans, Matthew. (September 2013). The SMI-Wizness Social Media Sustainability Index. Social Media Influence. http://publisher.wizness.com/reports/the-smi-wizness-social-media-sustainability-index-2012.

13 Smarter Planet. What's New on a Smarter Planet? IBM. http://www.ibm.com/smarterplanet/us/en/?ca=v_smarterplanet, accessed August 16, 2015.

14 General Electric. GE Imagination at Work. http://www.ge.com/about-us/ecomagination, accessed August 16, 2015.

15 BetaCup Challenge. https://betacup.jovoto.com/, accessed August 16, 2015.

16 Causes. Campaign to Make a Difference. https://www.causes.com/, accessed August 16, 2015.

17 Magnet Media Corporate. *Adobe: Micro-Documentary Video Production.* http://www.magnetmediafilms.com/case-study/adobe-micro-documentary-video-production, accessed June 4, 2015.

18 Wilson, Kimberly. (April 13, 2012). Social Media: A New Tactic for Corporate Sustainability? Triple Pundit. http://www.triplepundit.com/2012/04/social-media-new-tactic-corporate-sustainability/.

19 Smith, Aaron. (February 3, 2014). 6 New Facts about Facebook. Pew Research Center. http://www.pewresearch.org/fact-tank/2014/02/03/6-new-facts-about-facebook/.

20 Westervelt, Amy. (October 5, 2012). 5 Lessons on How to Tackle Toxics from DuPont, 3M and H&M. GreenBiz. https://www.greenbiz.com/news/2012/10/05/5-lessons-toxics-dupont-3M-HM.

21 P&G. Partners and Suppliers. http://www.pgconnectdevelop.com/home/frequently_asked_questions/about-partnering-with-pg.html, accessed March 11, 2015.

22 Oliver Russell. Forging a Sustainable Partnership with HP. http://www.oliverrussell.com/marketing-agency-hewlett-packard-direct-mail, accessed March 11, 2015.

Chapter 9: Engaging Government

1 Hawken, Paul. (May 6, 2015). Sustainable Solutions: Government. Learning Sustainability. http://www.learningsustainability.com/government.html.

2 Ibid.

3 Cohen, Stephen. (October 2, 2014). The Role of Government in the Transition to a Sustainable Economy. *Huffington Post: Green*. http://www.huffingtonpost.com/steven-cohen/the-role-of-government-in_b_4759621.html.

4 World Vision International. (January 20, 2015). At Davos, World Vision Says "Business as Usual" Will Not Deliver an End to Extreme Poverty. http://www.wvi.org/united-nations-and-global-engage-ment/pressrelease/davos-world-vision-says-%E2%80%98business-usual%E2%80%99-will-not.

5 U.S. EPA. Combined Heat and Power Partnership. https://www.epa.gov/sites/production/files/2015-07/documents/utility_incentives_for_combined_heat_and_power.pdf, accessed August 4, 2015.

6 Knittel, Christopher. (February 14, 2014). California's Auto Emissions Policy Hits a Tesla Pothole. http://www.wsj.com/articles/SB100014240527023036502045793768011032008 52.

7 Posson, Mark. (May 19, 2011). Promoting Sustainability through Unconventional Government. The Green Tie. http://www

.thegreentie.org/voices/promoting-sustainability-through-unconventional-government.

8 National Science Foundation. Floating Wind Turbines Bring Electricity Where It's Needed. http://www.nsf.gov/discoveries/disc_summ .jsp?cntn_id=134023&org=NSF, accessed August 4, 2015.

9 Global Reporting Initiative. (December 14, 2011). *The Role of Governments in Mainstreaming Sustainability Reporting.* https://www .globalreporting.org/information/news-and-press-center/Pages/The-role-of-governments-in-mainstreaming-sustainability-reporting.aspx.

10 Ibid.

11 Ackerman, Frank, and Stanton, Elizabeth A. (May 2008). What We'll Pay if Global Warming Continues Unchecked. Natural Resources Defense Council. https://www.nrdc.org/globalWarming/cost/fcost .pdf.

12 Wipro Education. *Wipro Applying Thought in Schools Annual Update 2013–2014.* http://wiproeducation.com/sites/default/files/WATIS%20 Annual%20Updates_2013-14_0.pdf, accessed August 10, 2014.

13 UN Women. (June 2, 2014). UN Women Launches Private Sector Leadership Advisory Council. http://www.unwomen.org/en/ news/stories/2014/6/private-sector-leadership-advisory-council-launched#sthash.OncFlPyv.dpuf.

14 Watson, Elaine. (April 15, 2014). Quirky, Cult-like, Aspirational, but Affordable: The Rise and Rise of Trader Joe's. Food Navigator-USA. http://www.foodnavigator-usa.com/Markets/Quirky-cult-like-aspirational-but-affordable-The-rise-and-rise-of-Trader-Joe-s.

15 Korosec, Kirsten. (June 11, 2015). Walmart Sustainable Products Director Leaves for Company-Backed Recycling Fund. *Environmental Leader.* http://www.environmentalleader.com/2015/06/11/walmart-sustainable-products-director-leaves-for-company-backed-recycling-fund/#ixzz3iR3naXio.

Chapter 10: Partnering with NGOs

1 Blake, John. (March 9, 2013). Two Enemies Discover a "Higher Call" in Battle. *CNN.* http://www.cnn.com/2013/03/09/living/ higher-call-military-chivalry/.

2 Knoll, Maureen. (November 13, 2013). An Insider's Story: How Burt's Bees® and Greenworks® Helped Change Clorox's Image. San Francisco Public Relations Round Table. http://sfprrt.org/an-insiders-story-how-burts-bees-and-greenworks-helped-change-cloroxs-image/.

3 NGO Global Network. Definition of NGOs. http://www.ngo.org/ngoinfo/define.html, accessed June 10, 2015.

4 International Relations ONLINE. Environmental NGOs. https://internationalrelationsonline.com/ngo-careers/environmental-ngos/, accessed June 10, 2015.

5 C&E Advisory. Corporate-NGO Partnerships Barometer 2014. http://www.candeadvisory.com/barometer, accessed June 10, 2015.

6 United Nations. Millennium Goals. http://www.un.org/millennium goals/, accessed June 10, 2015.

7 Kanal, Vijay. (December 21, 2009). NGOs: Friend or Foe to Business & Sustainability? Triple Pundit. http://www.triplepundit.com/2009/12/ngos-business-sustainability/.

Index

Accenture, 141
Achor, Shawn: *The Happiness Advantage*, 70
Action Sustainability, 92, 101; Ian Heptonshall, 101
Adobe, 157; Adobe Youth Voices, 157; Linda McNair, 157
Ahmad Teas, 62
AkzoNobel, 121, 122; Community Program, 121; Decorative Paints, Functional Chemicals and Powder Coatings, 122; Shepherd's Field Children's Village, 122
Alibaba, 61
AliveCor: Kardia (smartphone app), 61
Altaeros, 169; Buoyant Airborne Turbine (BAT), 169
Amazon, 61
American Association for the Advancement of Science, 149
American Idol (TV show), 82
American Water Works Association, 66
Angie's List, 51
Anti-Slavery Society, 181
Apple, 97, 133; Tim Cook, 97
Arthur Andersen, 111

AT&T Inc., 63–9, 141, 157; Cargo View, 67; Connected Jukebox, 67; Gary Duffy, 65; Mobeen Khan, 67, 68; Smart Bin, 67

B2B relationships, 50, 56, 61, 69, 205, 214
baby boomers, 7
Bank of America/Merrill Lynch, 135
Barrick Gold Corp., 114
BBMG, 86
Bertelsmann, 112
Better Cotton Initiative, 91
BHP Billiton, 113
Biggest Loser, The (TV show), 46
Black, John, 178
BlackRock Inc., 134; BlackRock U.S. Equity Fund (BIRAX), 134
Bloomberg, 136; ESG Valuation Tool, 136
BMW, 135
Bono (U2), 45
Bosch, 112
Boykoff, Jules M., 148
Boykoff, Maxwell T., 148
BP: Boycott BP Facebook group, 158; oil spill, 158
Brand Finance (UK), 13

Brita, 26, 43–7; AquaView, 44; Better
Water, Less Waste message, 46;
Filter for Good program, 45–6;
On-the-Go bottles, 46–7. *See also*
Clorox Co.
British Heart Foundation (BHF), 152
Burt's Bees, 26
Business for Social Responsibility
(BSR), 102

C-Suite Network, 76
C&E Advisory consultants, 183–4;
Corporate-NGO Partnerships
Barometer, 183–4
Caesars Entertainment, 73;
CodeGreen, 73; Gwen Migita, 73
CalPERS, 116
Calvert Investments Inc., 11; John
Streur, 11
Cameron, David (UK prime
minister), 6
Campbell's Soup: Let's Can Hunger
campaign, 121
capstone research, 13
Carbon Disclosure Project (CDP), 11,
104, 134–6, 208, 216
CARE International, 188
Carlsberg, 112
Carnegie, Dale, 80–1; *How to Win
Friends and Influence People*, 80
Centers for Disease Control and
Prevention (CDC), 139, 214
Ceres, 95, 131–2, 137, 139, 208,
216; Blueprint for Sustainable
Investing, 139; Mindy Lubber,
131–2
Cerulli Associates, 134
Chipotle, 32
CISCO Systems, 56
Clean Technology and Renewable
Energy Job Training program, 168

Clif Bar, 80
Climate Disclosure Leadership
Indices (CDLI), 135
Clinton Global Initiative, 88
Clorox Co., 26, 43–7, 55, 180–1; Bill
Morrissey, 26, 44; Don Knauss, 44;
Eco-office, 26; Greenworks, 26;
Kathryn Caulfield, 181. *See also*
Brita
Closed Loop Fund, 176
closed-loop/circular economy, 38,
66, 160, 163–4, 176, 191
CloudApps, 82–3; Sustainability
Momentum (SuMo), 83–4, 83f
Coca-Cola, 27, 100, 120, 133, 174, 176,
189; Ashley Brown, 27; Muhtar
Kent, 174
combined heat and power (CHP),
165
Cone Communications, 75
Consumer Goods Forum, 23, 59
Corporate Knights (Canada), 13, 14,
139; Global 100 Index, 14, 15f
corporate social responsibility (CSR),
11, 13, 66, 77, 115, 118, 122, 157
Costco, 51, 57
Coyne, Kevin P., 8
CSRHub, 12, 13; Cynthia Figge, 12,
13
customer relationship management
(CRM), 4, 15
CVS Pharmacy, 55

Danone Foods, 123, 191; Grameen
Danone Foods project, 123, 191
Dean Foods, 138
Department of Transportation (U.S.),
164–5
Deutsche Bank Advisors: *Sustainable
Investing* (2012), 11
Dow Chemical Company, 142, 188

Dow Jones Sustainability Index
(DJSI), 136, 139, 208, 214, 216
Drucker, Peter, 84, 170
Dupont, 143–4, 158–9; Ellen
Kullman, 143; Teflon crisis, 158–9
Dyer, Jeffrey H., 93

Earth Day, 5–6, 76–7, 81
EBIT (earnings before interest and
tax), 136
EBITDA (earnings before interest,
taxes, depreciation, and
amortization), 13
Edelman Trust barometer, 7
Energy Star, 167
Enron, 111
Environics International, 116
environmental nongovernmental
organization (ENGO), 179, 182,
189
Environmental Protection Agency
(EPA), 54, 65, 66, 164–5, 167;
*Guidance on the Acquisition of
Environmentally Preferable Products
and Services*, 167
environmental, social, and gover-
nance (ESG) responsibility, 12, 22,
134, 136, 138, 140, 207, 215
Eosta: Michael Wilde, 33
Ernst & Young, 73–4
Esprit, 100
Esty, Daniel, 142
Ethical Tea Partnership, 62
Ethisphere, 214

Facebook, Inc., 133
Fairtrade International, 62
fast-moving consumer goods
(FMCGs), 96
Federal Trade Commission (FTC),
166; Green Guides, 166

Financial Accounting Standards
Board (FASB), 170
Finland, Government of, 170–1
Firms of Endearment (Sisodia, Wolfe,
and Sheth), 16
Food and Drug Administration,
164
Forest Dialogue, 194
Forest Stewardship Council (FSC),
22, 23, 54, 57, 63, 91, 117, 120, 190,
194, 200
Forum for the Future (FFTF), 53, 62;
Sally Uren, 53
Foster, Richard, 125
Foxconn, 97
Fresh Del Monte, 138
Fund Votes: Jackie Cook, 133

G-Star Raw, 100
Gallup polling agency, 41, 70–1;
Jim Harter, 70–1
Gap Inc., 97, 100
GE (General Electric), 33, 35, 42, 84,
156; Ecomagination Challenge,
156; Ecomagination Nation, 84;
Ecomagination program, 84;
Ecomagination-certified products,
35; Power and Water business,
84
General Motors, 119; General Motors
Foundation, 119; teamGM Cares,
119
Generation X, 7, 46, 82, 116
Generation Y (millennials), 6, 7,
35–6, 40, 42, 46, 75, 82, 116, 129
Georgia Pacific: e-Motion towel
dispenser, 56
Gifford, Kathie Lee, 96
Global City Teams Challenge, 67
Global Reporting Initiative (GRI),
125, 136, 143, 170, 209, 216

Goldman Sachs, 134, 176; Goldman Sachs Imprint Capital Advisors Fund, 134
Google, 5, 42, 78–9, 133; Nest, 42
Government Accountability Office (U.S.), 66
Grameen Bank, 123; Grameen Danone Foods project, 123, 191; Grameen Foundation USA (GFUSA), 123
Green Building Council, 167
greenhouse gas (GHG) emissions, 5, 9, 65, 74–5, 74f, 78, 84, 97, 98, 136, 143–4
GreenNexxus, 82–3; Acts of Good calculator, 83
Greenpeace, 179–81, 185, 186, 190–1, 194, 196–201; *Kleercut* campaign, 180, 197–8, 200; Rolf Skar, 198–9; Scott Paul, 178
Grey Advertising, 152

Habitat for Humanity Lansing, 119
Happiness Advantage, The (Achor), 70
Havas Media Group, 154
Healthy Child Healthy World: Christopher Gavigan, 56
Heinz Corp., 98, 138
Hewlett-Packard (HP), 76–7, 160; Eco Advocates program, 77; Sustainability Network, 76
Honest Company, 56–7; Jessica Alba, 56
How Good We Can Be (Hutton), 112
How to Win Friends and Influence People (Carnegie), 80
How: Why How We Do Anything Means Everything (Seidman), 93
Hutton, Will, 111–12; *How Good We Can Be*, 112

Hyatt Hotels & Resorts, 78; Green Teams, 78; Hyatt Thrive, 78
HydroPoint, 67–8; WeatherTRAK, 67

IBM, 61, 156; Smarter Planet website, 156
IDH – the Sustainable Trade Initiative, 62
IKEA, 51, 54, 56, 91–2, 94, 106–10, 132; Steve Howard, 91; IWAY (code of conduct), 91, 106–7, 109; IWAY MUST standards, 107; Supplier Energy & Efficiency Project (SEEP), 107–8; Sustainable Product scorecard, 108; Thomas Schaefer, 91, 109–10
Inditex, 100
Intel, 74–5, 74f, 132; Corporate Sustainability Report (2012), 74–5
Interbrand and Reputation Institute, 13
Interface Carpet, Inc., 8–10; Jim Hartzfeld, 8; Mission Zero, 9, 10; Ray Anderson, 8–9
Internet of things (IoT), 67–8, 68f
Investis IQ, 13
ISO 26000, 115

J.B. Hunt, 89
Jack Wolfskin, 100
James Finlay, 62
JetBlue, 71–2; Steven Slater, 71–2
Johnson & Johnson, 158, 176; Tylenol crisis, 158
Johnson Controls, 75
Joint Roadmap, 100
Jones, Vinnie, 152
Jovoto online community, 156–7
JPMorgan Chase, 119

Kanal Consulting, 187
key performance indicators (KPIs),
    13, 141, 208, 215
Kimberly-Clark Corp. (K-C), 4, 34,
    37–8, 54, 57–9, 118–20, 166, 180,
    184, 186, 191, 194, 196–201; Crystal
    Tree Award, 84–5; Every Little
    Bottom Counts campaign, 121;
    Kleenex brand, 180; Lisa Morden,
    184, 191, 198–9; Mark Buthman,
    135; Robert Abernathy, 180; Scott
    Naturals, 34; Small Steps pro-
    gram, 58; Smart Flush campaign,
    37; Thomas Falk, 197; Water for
    Life program, 118–19
Kingfisher, 51
Kohl's, 97

Lacey Act (2008), 166
Leadership in Energy and
    Environmental Design (LEED),
    167
Lederhausen, Mats, 70, 72–3
Lehman Brothers, 111
Levi Strauss & Co., 100
life cycle assessments (LCAs), 22f,
    37, 108
Limited Brands, 100
Liu, John, 97
Livingstone, Sonia, 150
Lowes, 51
Lubin, David, 142

Mack, Michael, 27
Magnet Media Company, 146–7,
    157–8; Megan Cunningham,
    146–7, 158
Maisa (Chile), 113–14
Marine Stewardship Council (MSC),
    54

Marks & Spencer (M&S), 42, 100,
    132; "love food, hate waste"
    campaign, 42
McGoey, Linsey, 150
McPherson, Susan, 152
Meaningful Brands, 154; Meaningful
    Brand index, 154
media literacy, 150–1
MedShare, 194
Metavu: Mark A. Serwinowski,
    140
Meyer, Colin, 112
Microsoft, 61, 62
millennials. See Generation Y
mindful consumption (MC), 28, 38,
    48
Mitsubishi Chemical Holdings
    (MCHC) Group, 141–2
Modi, Narendra (Indian prime min-
    ister), 151; Clean India campaign,
    151
Monster Beverage, 138
Morgan Stanley, 14, 134, 139; All
    Country World Index (ACWI),
    14; ESG Impact Monitor, 136;
    Institute for Sustainable Investing,
    139; Morgan Stanley Corporate
    Indexes (MSCI), 14, 15f, 136
Morning Star, 11
Mueller Water Products, 66–7
Mullen: Mediahub, 153
Munich Re (insurance company), 6

Nalgene Outdoor Products, 45–6;
    Filter for Good program, 45–6
National Australian Bank, 135
National Chamber of Commerce
    (India), 174
National Geographic Society:
    Greendex study (2014), 30

National Institute of Standards
and Technology (NIST): 2015
Challenge, 66–7
National Science Foundation (NSF),
169; Small Business Innovation
Research grants, 169
Natural Resources Defense Council
(NRDC), 171, 190, 197
Nature Conservancy, the (TNC),
188
Nestlé Corp., 132, 140–1; Creating
Shared Value commitments, 141
Net Impact Conference, 79
New Balance Athletic Shoe Inc.,
100
Nielsen, 6, 29–30; Dark Green con-
sumers, 29; Global Responsibility
Report (2015), 31f; global sus-
tainability survey (2014), 6;
Light Green consumers, 29–30;
Non-green consumers, 29–30;
Sustainability Imperative report
(2015), 30
Nike Company, 96–7; Fair Labor
Association (FLA), 96–7
Nissan car manufacturer, 167

Oliver Russell agency, 160
Oxfam, 190

Paris summit (2015), 5–6
Patagonia, 32, 35, 38–9, 81, 154–5;
Footprint Chronicles, 35; Yuon
Chouinard, 38
Pepsi, 120, 132, 176
PetSmart, 117–18; PetSmart
Charities, 117–18
Pew Research, 158
Piotroski F-Score, 13
Pope Francis, 6
Practically Green. See WeSpire

Practice Greenhealth, 60; CleanMed
Conference, 60; Health Care
Without Harm campaign, 60
Preserve: Gimme 5 programs, 46
Principles for Responsible
Investment (PRI), 134; Fiona
Reynolds, 134
Procter & Gamble (P&G), 4, 37–8, 50,
103, 159, 176; Larry Loftus, 103;
Tide Coldwater Clean detergent, 38
PSFK: Future of Gaming report, 84;
Timothy Ryan, 84
PUR, 43
PVH Corp., 100

QuEST Forum, 65–6

Rainforest Alliance, 62
Red Cross, 181
RepRisk, 13
Russell 1000 Index companies, 139

S&D Coffee and Tea, 62
S&P 500, 11, 125, 134; Climate Change
2014, 11
Save the Children, 92
SCA (Svenska Cellulosa
Aktiebolaget), 21–4; Kersti
Strandqvist, 21; Sustainability
Report (2015), 21, 22t
Schmid, Daniel, 134
Schwab, Charles, 80–1
Securities and Exchange
Commission (SEC), 137, 166
Seidman, Dov: How: Why How We
Do Anything Means Everything, 93
Senge, Peter, 93
Seventh Generation, 32
sharing culture, 42, 60–1; Airbnb, 42,
61; Uber, 42, 60; Zipcar, 42, 61
Shark Tank (TV show), 82

Sheth, Jagdish, 28; "B2B Branding in Emerging Markets," 113; *Firms of Endearment*, 16
short-termism, 51, 77, 129, 131, 162, 164
Siemens Corp., 99
Sierra Club, 26
Singapore Airlines, 130
Sinha, Mona: "B2B Branding in Emerging Markets," 113
Sisodia, R.S.: *Firms of Endearment*, 16
60 Minutes (TV show), 97
smart cities/communities, 5, 66–7
SMI-Wizness, 156; Social Media Sustainability Annual Index, 156
social media, 6, 25f, 27, 36, 48, 72, 95, 116, 147–8, 147f, 152, 155–61, 190–1, 211, 217; Facebook, 78, 146, 156, 158; Instagram, 156; Pinterest, 146, 156; Snapchat, 156; Tumblr, 146; Twitter, 146, 152, 156, 158; YouTube, 146, 156, 158
social NGO, 182
social responsibility, definition of, 115
socially responsible investment (SRI), 12f, 118, 133–4, 137
Sony Electronics, 85; Eric Johnson, 85; Road to Zero, 85; Sony Bucks, 85
Stakeholder Sustainability Audit (SSA), 23, 203; SSA tool, 203–17
stakeholders, 19f; direct impact stakeholders, 18, 25f, 49f, 71f; enabler impact stakeholders, 18, 92f, 112f, 132f; indirect impact stakeholders, 18, 147f, 163f, 179f
Starbucks, 62, 156–7; BetaCup Challenge, 156; Karma cup, 157
Stevens, Susan Hunt, 85
Sundance Film Festival, 45–6
supplier diversity policies, 102–3

supplier sustainability code of conduct, 102
Surya Lumen (publisher): Suresh Ariaratnam, 42–3
Sustainability Consortium, the (TSC), 35, 60, 104, 193; category sustainability profiles (CSPs), 60
Sustainability Index, 35
sustainability sacrifice, 30–1
Sustainable Investment Research Analyst Network (SIRAN), 135

Target, 51, 57, 97; better-for-you brands, 57
Tata group, 112–13, 123–30; Dorab Tata, 124; Index for Sustainable Human Development, 112, 126; Indian Institute of Science, 124; Jamsetji N. Tata, 111, 124; JN Tata Endowment, 124; Mukund Rajan, 123–5, 129–30; Ratan Tata, 124, 126; Tata Business Excellence Model (TBEM), 126–8, 128f; Tata Council for Community Initiatives (TCCI), 125–6; Tata Global Beverages, 62; Tata Global Sustainability Council, 123, 125, 129; Tata Index for Sustainable Human Development, 112, 123, 124, 126, 127f; Tata Sons Ltd., 123–5; Tata Sustainability Framework, 128–9; Tata Sustainability Group (TSG), 125; Tata Trusts, 124
Tea 2030, 62–3
Tesco Group, 51, 54, 59
Tesco Lotus (Thailand), 59; Preventing Global Warming and Let's Go Green campaign, 59
Tesla car manufacturer, 167–8
Thomson Reuters, 135–6; Accelus, 135
thredUP, 60

3M, 82; Heather Phansey, 82;
    Sustainability Power Pitch, 82
Timberland, 153–4; Earthkeeper
    brand, 153
total quality management (TQM),
    4, 15
Trader Joe's, 55, 175
Tyson Foods, 138

Unilever, 36, 50, 62, 89, 132, 174, 176;
    Paul Polman, 174; Real Beauty
    campaign, 36; Sustainable Living
    program, 81–2
Unilever Thai Holding, 59
United Colors of Benetton, 100
United Healthcare, 89
United Nations (UN):
    #WomenShould campaign,
    152; Agenda for Sustainable
    Development, 183–4; Ban Ki-moon
    (secretary general), 6; definition
    of NGO, 182; Millennium
    Development Goals (MDGs), 173,
    183; Sustainable Development
    Goals (SDGs), 164, 173–4, 183–4;
    UN Development Programme
    (UNDP), 125; UN Global Compact
    (UNGC), 102, 125, 174, 192;
    UNICEF, 92; Women Private Sector
    Leadership Advisory Council, 174
United Natural Foods Inc. (UNFI),
    51, 55, 57
United Way, 121
UniversalGiving Corporate, 193
UPS, 89

Vistara airline, 130

Walmart, 35, 50–1, 58–60, 85–9,
    97–8, 101, 167, 176, 190; Global

Customer Insights and Analytics,
    85; Lea Jepson, 98; Lee Scott,
    85; Matt Kistler, 85, 88, 89; My
    Sustainability Plan (MSP),
    35, 58, 78, 85–9, 87f; Personal
    Sustainability Plan (PSP),
    85–6; Sustainability Index,
    60; Sustainable Product Expo
    (2014), 176
waste-based economy, 164
WeSpire, 82–3
West Monroe Partners, 122; 1+1+1
    Program, 122; Gary Beu, 122
Westervelt, Amy, 159
Whole Foods Market, 32, 54–5
Wipro Foundation, 8, 172; Anurag
    Behar, 8; Wipro Applying
    Thought in Schools initiative, 172
Wolfe, D.B.: *Firms of Endearment*, 16
World Bank, 66
World Business Council for
    Sustainable Development
    (WBCSD), 23, 62, 137; Global
    Water Tool (GWT), 62; Vision
    2050, 137
World Economic Forum, 164
World Vision International, 164
World Wildlife Fund (WWF), 63,
    92, 100, 185, 189, 190, 194; Global
    Forest Trade Network (GFTN), 63
WorldCom, 111
WPP Company, 151–2
Wujin Chu, 93

Yellow Pages, 51
Yorkshire Tea, 62

zero discharge of hazardous
    chemicals (ZDHC), 100
zero-tolerance list, 102